Managing Marketing

CIM Coursebook: Managing Marketing

Edited by: Andrew Sherratt

and

Authored by: Francis Nicholson
Richard Meek

AMSTERDAM • BOSTON • HEIDELBERG • LONDON • NEW YORK • OXFORD
PARIS • SAN DIEGO • SAN FRANCISCO • SINGAPORE • SYDNEY • TOKYO
Butterworth-Heinemann is an imprint of Elsevier

Butterworth-Heinemann is an imprint of Elsevier
Linacre House, Jordan Hill, Oxford, OX2 8DP, UK
30 Corporate Drive, Suite 400, Burlington, MA 01803, USA

First published 2009

British Library Cataloguing in Publication Data
A catalogue record for this book is available from the British Library

Library of Congress Cataloging-in-Publication Data
A catalog record for this book is available from the Library of Congress

ISBN: 978-1-85617-717-7

For information on all Butterworth-Heinemann publications
visit our website at www.elsevierdirect.com

Typeset by Macmillan Publishing Solutions
www.macmillansolutions.com

Printed and bound in Italy

09 10 11 12 13 14   10 9 8 7 6 5 4 3 2 1

Contents

FOREWORD ix
ABOUT THE AUTHORS xiii

Section 1: The Marketing Infrastructure 1

CHAPTER 1 **Organisational Structures**... **3**
Introduction 3
The importance of organisational structures.................................. 4
References 16
Further reading 16

CHAPTER 2 **Quality Systems and Processes** **17**
The importance of quality systems.............................. 18
Quality models.. 19
PDCA cycle 24
Deming 14 steps... 26
Further reading 27

CHAPTER 3 **Measuring, Monitoring and Improving Marketing
Performance** **29**
Accounting measures 31
Productivity measures... 39
Relationship marketing and customer-related measures 41
Purpose 42
Market segment or niche... 42
Core message 42
Marketing communications 43
Sales conversion system 43
Internal measures of performance................................ 48
Innovation and learning measures of performance 50
Performance measures 52
Productivity analysis (inputs versus outputs)............................. 52
Comparative analysis (changes over time)............................... 53
Segmental analysis (analysis of markets) 56

v

Innovation audit...57

Competitor comparisons and benchmarking.............................60

Reference..61

Further reading 61

Senior Examiner's Comments – Section One 62

Section 2: Managing Marketing Teams 63

CHAPTER 4   **Management, Leadership and Establishing Teams 65**

Management roles...66

Leadership and management of teams 68

Leadership characteristics...70

Understanding leadership and management styles......................71

Leadership traits, skills and attitude 74

Teams 77

Groups versus teams 79

Creating and developing teams...79

Another stage?..85

Job analysis and job design..86

Competencies and standards that define a good manager.............86

Planning teams for effective performance 88

Sourcing and training teams...90

Induction and training 90

Internal recruiting 93

Recruiting externally...94

Munroe Fraser – 5-point plan 100

Interviews... 101

Do's and don'ts for successful selection interviewing: 106

Summary 106

Further study 107

Bibliography 107

CHAPTER 5   **Managing Teams 109**

Performance management and measurement............................ 110

Internal marketing.. 110

Knowledge management and communications 113

Management theories and performance 115

Job enrichment and job enlargement 119

Discrimination 119

International culture... 122

Virtual teams 129

Summary 132

Bibliography 133

CHAPTER 6 **Improving Team Performance** **135**

Introduction 136

Conflict in organisations...................................... 136

A four-category perspective of team problems 137

Developing the team............................... 144

Further study...................................... 145

Planning for change 145

Overcoming resistance through internal marketing.......... 152

Employee branding.............................. 159

Summary 169

Bibliography 169

Senior Examiner's Comments – Section Two.............. 171

Section 3: Operational Finances for Marketing **173**

Introduction **173**

CHAPTER 7 **Managing Marketing Finances** **177**

Introduction 178

The manager's role 179

The purpose of budgeting 182

Budget considerations 184

Setting the marketing budget 188

Information sources needed for budgeting 202

CHAPTER 8 **Budgeting and Costs** **211**

Negotiating marketing budgets (Syllabus Ref. 3.4).......... 212

Cost benefit analysis of marketing.......................... 216

Managing costs in marketing.......................... 224

CHAPTER 9 **Variance and Monitoring**........................ **235**

Budget variance.. 236

Evaluating performance of marketing operations 243

Senior Examiner's Comments – Section Three............ 251

FEEDBACK ON ACTIVITIES........................253

INDEX 255

Don't forget to look at the extra online support at **www.marketingonline.co.uk** which includes more free mini case studies.

Foreword

This unit is a different approach for CIM, representing a very practical approach to managing the human and financial resources that the marketer now has to face. It reflects the very real challenges and introduces the knowledge and skills required to effectively manage the marketing function.

The focus is about developing the marketer as a manager, by giving them the knowledge and understanding required to develop and manage the marketing infrastructure and the organisation's talent development, capability and capacity. This includes developing effective quality systems and processes to support compliance and approaches to measuring and monitoring marketing activities.

The unit also includes the development and management of marketing teams, which includes co-ordinating the human, financial and physical resources within the team effectively.

Finally, the unit includes developing a detailed understanding of managing the financial aspects of the marketing function and its associated activities to ensure that the financial performance of the function is consistent, reliable and effective.

The authors have taken a very practical approach to this book to ensure that in addition to understanding the theories, readers are be able to demonstrate how they would approach the management of the marketing function and its associated marketing teams. This includes effective resource and financial management, and also allows the reader to be in a strong position to achieve the following learning outcomes set by the CIM.

- Recommend how a marketing function should be structured to deliver competitive advantage, marketing and organisational success.

- Assess a range of approaches that can be used to manage the marketing function on a day-to-day basis.

- Prepare plans for showing how a team should be structured, selected, formed, managed and developed to demonstrate effective performance against objectives.

- Critically assess the organisation's resource needs and capabilities for the marketing team and manage its marketing activities effectively and efficiently.

- Prepare appropriate budgets and accounting documentation to support the financial management of the marketing function and associated marketing activities.

- Critically assess the ongoing financial situation, including manageability of the budget, financial stability and success of the marketing function.

The following text breaks this down into the three main sections:

SECTION 1 – THE MARKETING INFRASTRUCTURE (WEIGHTING 30%)
AUTHOR – FRANCIS NICHOLSON

This section of the book is concerned with establishing effective systems and processes to measure and improve marketing performance. It will describe how the marketing infrastructure impacts on the management activities that are explored in Section 2 (Managing Marketing Teams) of this CIM syllabus. Organisational structures are examined in detail along with the impact of the structure on work organisation, authority, relationships and job roles. It explores quality systems and processes, demonstrating how quality systems can be used to improve marketing performance.

Application of a range of methods for measuring marketing performance in different organisational contexts is dealt with, and you will therefore need to understand the models, concepts and theories in some detail to apply them to your studies.

Finally, this section will help you to determine which measures should be used in relation to organisational and marketing objectives, analysing the monitoring information resulting from those measures and make recommendations to improve marketing performance.

SECTION 2 – MANAGING MARKETING TEAMS (WEIGHTING 40%)
AUTHOR – RICHARD MEEK

This is the highest weighting section with a clear focus on how to improve marketing performance through people. This section of the book examines the role of the marketing manager as a manager of people and teams. It helps you to demonstrate an understanding of management and leadership approaches, tools, techniques and theories. It also assists in application of them practically within an organisational context. A key feature is encouragement to reflect on your personal approach to managing and leading others, and determine actions to improve both your own and your team's performance.

This section explores the whole spectrum of building high performing teams from team design and recruitment to operational management and performance management – the focus being on how to improve marketing performance through people.

The organisational context may vary, but the section places particular importance on consideration of the issues of working in virtual and international cross-functional teams and the complexities of diversity and culture, that many managers deal with on a day-to-day basis.

This section also examines how to build a high-performing team through effective team design and recruitment processes. It does not provide a detailed knowledge of employment law as this is not required of the marketing manager, but it does consider the impact of legislation throughout the recruitment process. When considering this element of the unit, it is important to take into account that this is leading towards building the organisations capacity and capability. Thus, it is essential to ensure that the right level of competency, combined with the right balance of individual talent is achieved to maximise the organisations potential to achieve competitive advantage. It explores aspects of performance management and sets objectives for individuals that are designed to meet with marketing and organisational objectives. Methods to measure individual performance and recommendations on how to improve individual performance are discussed together with the impact of the manager's approach on team member performance.

SECTION 3 – OPERATIONAL FINANCES FOR MARKETING (WEIGHTING 30%)
AUTHOR – FRANCIS NICHOLSON

This section of the text is focused on ensuring that the marketing function achieves its objectives within budget. It explores costing, budgeting approaches, cost management and financial measurement so that you will be able to make recommendations to improve marketing performance based on financial analysis.

A detailed section on budgeting and its role in the management and control of marketing performance is embedded in this section – we are not expecting you to be a qualified accountant to use it, rather just to have an understanding of the process with the ability to communicate successfully with an organisation's finance department. Importantly, it shows you how to apply the budgeting process within an organisational context and examine the costs associated with marketing activities. This will allow you to determine information sources that could be used to gather the necessary information to determine the costs. Finally, it will help you to prepare appropriate budgets, identify causes of budget variances and make recommendations to improve performance against budget, including a cost benefit analysis of marketing activities that considers both qualitative and quantitative measurement.

And finally, at the end of each section, there is a 'handy hints' from myself regarding assessment and direction for your studies, for that particular section of the unit, to help guide you through the assignment preparation.

NOTES ON THE ASSESSMENT

The assessment for this subject is a work-based assessment, integrated across the complete Managing Marketing unit, requiring you to apply learning in a synergistic way, bringing together various aspects of your studies to solve organisational problems or to develop new organisational initiatives.

The expectation is that you should produce a professionally presented document, which may be appropriate to use within your organisation or may be helpful in demonstrating to a potential employer your abilities to produce work to a high standard. The finished work should include appropriate theories and concepts, but these should be presented in a professional format appropriate for the chosen business context, rather than an academic report. Typically, the work produced will be appropriate for submission by a Marketing Manager to Senior Management.

It is expected that you will take a holistic view of the situation and tasks, producing an integrated piece of work that clearly demonstrates links between the tasks described in the assessment brief. These tasks are to be considered as an integrated whole rather than as a separate part, with each task having implications for the others. You will be rewarded for clear demonstration of the chain of actions proposed across all three units.

We hope you enjoy this very practical approach to managing the marketing function and we wish you good luck with your studies.

Andrew Sherratt
Senior CIM Examiner – Managing Marketing
2009–2010

About the Authors

Andrew Sherratt, MCIM, Chartered Marketer, Senior Examiner for the Managing Marketing unit, Principal of SPA Professional Academy – a CIM Accredited Study Centre. Andrew delivers marketing qualifications across the CIM levels in addition to operating as a business and marketing Training Consultant and visiting lecturer at IIB, Kiev following extensive experience of working in marketing for multi-national business to business organisations. In addition, Andrew is an active member of CIM, being on both branch and regional board committees.

Francis Nicholson is the Director of Education for the Institute of Internal Auditors – UK and Ireland. With 20 years of experience in education, especially in accounting, business and economics, he has taught across a wide spectrum of programmes. He is a case study writer for the CIM Postgraduate Diploma and is currently studying for a PhD in Business Ethics.

Richard Meek, Richard is a partner in a marketing consultancy with a range of clients from medium sized to large, international organisations. Marketing education has included teaching/training and writing for example for Financial Times Knowledge, News International, the IFS as well as texts in support of CIM exams. In addition, Richard is a Teaching Fellow in the Department of Marketing, Lancaster University where he teaches on a wide range of undergraduate and postgraduate courses, with a particular interest in employing simulations and role play.

The Marketing Infrastructure

CHAPTER 1

Organisational Structures

1.1 Critically evaluate the importance of organisational structures in delivering marketing value, focus and creativity including consideration of how the work of the marketing operations is going to be undertaken.

SYLLABUS REFERENCES

1.1:

- Functional structure
- Product/market structure
- Brand structure
- Territory structure
- Matrix structure
- International and multinational organisational structures

INTRODUCTION

Marketing infrastructure refers to all the resources and structures that are needed in order for marketing activity to take place. This includes staff, transportation, administration, marketing intelligence systems, communication, planning, quality assurance and budgets. Organisations require systems and processes for all of their operations, such as gathering and analysing marketing intelligence, developing the product mix, communicating value propositions, capturing potentially valuable leads through feedback (solicited or otherwise), increasing brand equity and building customer loyalty.

3

This raises the question of what are the most effective ways of organising marketing infrastructure. As we shall discover, there are a number of different types of organisational structures commonly used, and the choice is an important one. The structures fundamentally affect the ways in which resources are controlled, how authority is wielded and accountability distributed, where the sources of power lie, and so ultimately how an organisation delivers its mission. Often the structures have been adopted through a slow accumulation of change and development, but occasionally they are reviewed and may be redesigned to suit the emergent challenges of the external environment and the priorities of the organisation more effectively. In this section we will explore a number of different models. The form of organisational structure favoured will depend on many factors, such as size and age of organisation, market conditions, external environment, product mix, relationships with suppliers and buyers, skills of staff, technological innovation, competitor behaviour, organisational culture, and the preferred styles for decision-making and authority. Our focus will be on how differences in structures affect the ability of marketing to achieve its core purposes.

Systems and processes also require the means of determining the quality of their outputs. The elusive concept of quality has been the subject of much study giving rise to a number of different models for maximising effectiveness. Many of them have common features but they serve to emphasise different approaches. Typically they include metrics for gauging how well systems are performing. This, in conjunction with benchmark data and key performance indicators (KPIs), provides a detailed means for monitoring and measuring marketing performance. Finally, the purpose of quality management systems, performance indicators, benchmark data and various other forms of marketing metrics is to identify problems and opportunities for improvement as they arise and so drive the organisation even closer to maximising its successes.

THE IMPORTANCE OF ORGANISATIONAL STRUCTURES

Many organisations develop organically as they grow, responding to internal ambition and external conditions. Their structures often reflect this, having been built up over time, sometimes expanding, sometimes contracting. Occasionally – following the appointment of a new CEO, or as a result of a merger, or in response to adverse economic conditions, for example, but also through a deliberate desire to improve the arrangements that have arisen in an *ad hoc* fashion – organisations may undergo partial or wholesale restructuring. There are many variations to choose from, and senior managers must identify an appropriate form that best meets the priorities of their own particular organisation.

Organisational structures describe and determine the way work is arranged, how authority is exercised and the channels of communication that prevail, up, down and across the various divisions. The structures vary in a number of key dimensions and these will help us understand different organisational forms. These are shown in Table 1.1, reflecting Max Weber's *The Theory of Social and Economic Organisation* (1924) and the work of many of those who followed his modernist conception.

We tend to view bureaucracy in a negative fashion, but for Weber it was regarded as the desirable cohesive force that led to authority, control, order and efficiency. Generally, organisational activity is coordinated through hierarchy, structure and communication as well as the formal standardisation

Table 1.1	Dimensions of organisations
Dimension	**Description**
Size	In this context, size is a measure of headcount (although size of organisations may also be given by volume of sales, turnover or capital).
Differentiation	The amount of vertical differentiation is an indication of the number of levels of hierarchy (the more differentiation there is, the greater the number of levels), while the amount of horizontal differentiation or departmentalisation reflects the number of divisions.
Integration	The amount of vertical integration is the degree to which different levels of hierarchy operate in isolation or in unison, while horizontal integration is a similar measure for collaboration between divisions, reflecting the structures for accountability, communication and reporting.
Spans of control	The span of control is the number of staff that report directly to a given manager. In general, the greater the amount of vertical differentiation, the higher the number of levels of hierarchy and the narrower the spans of control.
Specialisation	Specialisation is the uniqueness or similarity of job and team roles arising from the division of labour.
Formalisation	Formalisation refers to the level of bureaucracy and the extent to which processes are prescribed in order to regulate activity.
Centralisation and decentralisation	In a highly centralised organisation, the authority is held among a small group of senior managers with limited autonomy for teams and divisions. In a decentralised organisation, power is more evenly distributed, allowing those lower down or further out from the centre to exercise a degree of power and control.

of processes. Later theorists, like Elton Mayo, recognised the importance of the human dimension as well. Managers should bear in mind that there are also informal structures that are equally important to understanding employee behaviour and for effecting change. The informal organisation accounts for the ways in which staff engage with each other, how messages are commonly communicated, and the lines of loyalty and dependency that exist through work-related social networks. Prior experience, cultural background, social conditioning and personal expectations all shape the organisation as it is understood by the individual. In some sense, the organisation does not exist beyond the ways in which it is encountered.

It is important that organisations as a whole and the divisions within them find the right structure to match their needs. An inappropriate structure may lead to difficulties in communication, unresponsiveness to external change, slow product or service development rates, unsatisfactory service to customers, unclear lines of authority and accountability, a lack of control, and ultimately in total failure. Structures play such an important role in determining operational effectiveness and efficiency that the marketing manager needs to take account of the dynamics of their own function as well as the organisation as a whole in order to take active and successful control.

Functional Structure

Functional organisational structures are arranged around the roles undertaken by individuals and teams. For example, a large manufacturing organisation may have the following major divisions:

- research and development
- production
- distribution
- human resources
- finance
- marketing and communications

These may be further subdivided. Marketing and communications, for example, may be arranged to include:

- sales
- advertising
- market research and intelligence
- public relations
- customer relations
- website management
- marketing administration

This is extended further into specific and individual job roles. The rationale for a functional arrangement is to maximise efficiency. The tasks needed by the organisation to deliver its mission are first identified and then grouped according to specialism. The skills needed to undertake the tasks determine the labour requirements of each division. There is a high degree of horizontal differentiation between teams, and probably high levels of specialisation as well. Managers and supervisors have authority over teams of staff undertaking similar or related roles, often leading to hierarchical and bureaucratic structures through the need to exercise control and to standardise activity. The larger the organisation, the greater these tendencies to formalisation and vertical differentiation. This may be regarded as the basis for the more traditional organisational form.

Functional structures are most ideally suited to organisations with a single product or service or with a portfolio of very similar items, and there are many advantages to such structures. They make efficient use of specialised skills through a highly evolved division of labour with minimal overlap and duplication. There is a high degree of accountability for staff and managers since roles are clearly defined and highly ordered. Reporting and communication lines follow the chain of command up and down the levels of authority. There are opportunities to specialise and to progress within the hierarchy. Individuals are likely to feel comfortable in the structure with a clear sense of their place in it. However, it can be difficult to achieve horizontal integration (coordination between divisions). A silo mentality may develop such that staff and managers are more interested in pursuing their divisional objectives than supporting broader corporate goals. Inefficiencies and even conflicts may ensue. Communication up and down the chains of command may be slow, and horizontally may be very difficult. Such structures also tend to be inflexible and unresponsive to a changing external environment.

For the marketing manager it may be advantageous to have all of the resources (staff and others) pooled together rather than dispersed between a number of different divisions. This should result in a more efficient use of budgets as it enables marketing activity to be tightly planned and closely monitored. The manager is more likely to be able to respond flexibly to changes in the external environment by moving resources between different campaigns and initiatives. In addition, some marketing activity needs to be focused on high-level corporate image, public relations and brand awareness, and so it is much more suited to a centralised function. However, with the marketing function separated from other departments, difficulties may arise in trying to achieve coordination and cooperation. If marketing is seen as the responsibility of a separate team, then production units and service providers may feel less inclined to support marketing activity. Horizontal communication between the marketing function and other divisions can be slow and ineffective, making it more difficult to respond to adverse variances and other problems as they arise. It may also create unrealistic expectations borne out of a misunderstanding of marketing, so that when sales are disappointing, for example, the production manager may ask for some more advertising as a quick fix.

Product/Market Structure

Another way of arranging staff and resources is around the various products or services that the organisation provides, or alternatively around particular markets by creating semi-autonomous units and profit centres acting as mini-businesses. A clothing manufacturer, for example, may organise its activities on the basis of menswear, ladies wear and children's wear, while a large local authority is likely to have such departments as:

- housing
- education
- children's services
- health and social care
- highways
- town planning

An organisation providing goods and services both on a business-to-business (B2B) and a business-to-customer (B2C) basis may divide its operations on these lines. Each of these divisions will need a functional team that may include administration, customer services, accounting, human resources, sales and marketing.

In this way, marketing is more fully integrated with operations. The function is closer to the action, better informed and better understood by staff. It will be easier to integrate operational and marketing plans, to set collective targets and performance indicators, and to respond more rapidly should variances arise. The total marketing resource will be divided between the products or markets, enabling marketing activity to reflect the particular needs of customers, based on appropriate characteristics and market factors. However, it may prove harder to ensure that marketing activity on an organisation-wide basis is sufficiently focused and integrated. Duplication of effort and overlaps in areas of responsibility may occur. Circumstances may change where resource needs to be reallocated to a particular area which often proves more difficult within such a structure.

A product or market structure may make expansion easier since the organisation can add new divisions to support new products or markets without radically altering the underlying structure. Autonomy may be high, with the product or market experts being empowered to make the decisions within their division. At the same time, accountability can be readily enforced as performance of individual products or markets should be relatively easy to identify.

Brand Structure

Smaller organisations may offer a single brand, while larger more established ones are likely to have a more complex profile with multiple brands, sub-brands, endorsed or joint brands, and a number of partnerships with other organisations. These organisations may choose to organise their activity and resources around their brands (Figure 1.1).

Brand management is of particular interest to organisations selling fast-moving consumer goods. A brand may be treated as a mini-business, requiring the full range of resources and services needed to support it that you would find in an organisation. By focusing the planning and decision-making processes around the brand, it is possible to achieve a coherence of vision with clear accountability. For example, the brand will require:

- market research
- product development
- production
- supply chain management
- logistics and distribution
- marketing communications
- customer service

This focusing of marketing infrastructure around the brand is illustrated in Figure 1.2.

In an organisation whose structure reflects the brand structure, the operations and resources are focused around the major brands in a fashion similar to that shown in Figure 1.2. There will be brand managers with responsibility for building brand equity. Budgets would also be built around the brands so that monthly management accounts reflect progress against budget, and other KPIs are all centred on individual brands and groups of brands.

While such models can be highly effective in building brands, care must be taken to ensure that the organisation does not lose its customer focus. Customer equity is ultimately more important than brand equity. While brands may continue to reflect the needs of customers, customer equity helps to reinforce the importance of relationships.

Territory Structure

An organisation may choose to divide itself by geographical regions, dividing the map into any suitable fashion. This is appropriate where the product

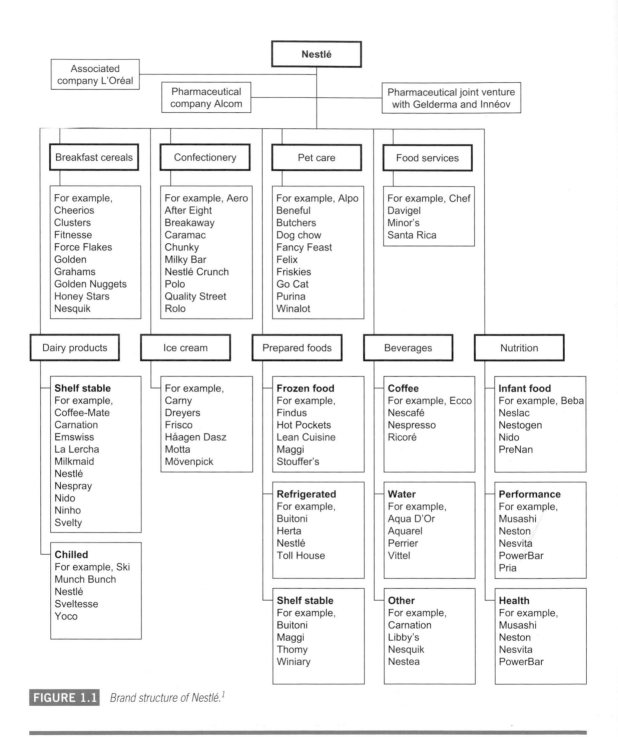

FIGURE 1.1   *Brand structure of Nestlé.[1]*

[1]*Sources*: http://www.users.telenet.be/vicky_michielsen/brandportfolio.htm, http://www.nestle.com/Brands/ BrandHome.htm and http://www.en.wikipedia.org/wiki/Aquarel

Brand Management Focus (The Brand Wheel)

FIGURE 1.2

Focusing resources on the brand.
Source: http://www.marketingminds.com.au/branding/brand_and_management.html

or services provided vary according to area (due to linguistic, cultural or regional preferences, perhaps). Alternatively, even with an undifferentiated product or service, a regional structure helps to subdivide the market, allocate resources and responsibilities and drive up performance through the use of KPIs, internal competition and reward schemes. In some cases, the organisation may be physically divided with plants, distribution centres and offices located across a number of regions. There may be a high degree of decentralisation of power from the head office to increase regional autonomy.

The English Football Association (FA) is an example of an organisation that is arranged on a regional basis. There are 43 affiliated county FAs that oversee activity in their regions, take charge of communications, membership, fixtures and registrations. Disciplinary matters are divided between the FA for senior clubs and local FAs for lower order clubs.

In a territory structure the marketing function may be fragmented between the regional divisions. In some cases, however, there may also be an element of marketing that is centrally coordinated, overseeing the regional marketing managers and their teams. Being distributed close to the operational teams on a regional basis makes it easier to respond to the needs of customers and to develop enduring and valuable relationships with them. There is still a need to ensure there is a balance that also recognises the interests of the organisation as a whole.

Matrix Structure

In a matrix structure, the horizontal divisions are diminished or in some cases removed completely to allow integration between functions. Individuals are given responsibilities that require them to work with members of other functions while still retaining some allegiance to their primary function. Cross-functional teams are formed – sometimes for specific tasks or projects, sometimes on a semi-permanent basis – with representatives from all the key areas. The team members continue to report to their line manager within their function but also to the leader of the cross-functional team. It is these horizontal and vertical relationships that form the matrix (Figure 1.3).

As with all organisational structures, a matrix is not simply a form but also a way of approaching the challenges of business. Complex tasks can be tackled in a highly collaborative fashion, ensuring cross-fertilisation of ideas and a high degree of coordination. The structure breaks down the tendency of other structures for individuals to work in silos, with allegiances up and down the hierarchy rather than across or to the organisation as a whole.

One of the first organisations to be associated with the matrix structure was Nasa which depended upon close cooperation of functions focused on specific, complex projects. Nasa found traditional, functional structures too bureaucratic, inflexible, politically charged and slow.

The focus for the cross-functional teams may vary considerably. In some organisations, it is on a product or market basis. In other words, a matrix structure may act as a combination of an organisation divided on functional grounds with a product/market structure laid over the top. Alternatively, the cross-functional teams may join forces in order to address a fixed term project, such as product development or change implementation.

FIGURE 1.3

A matrix structure.

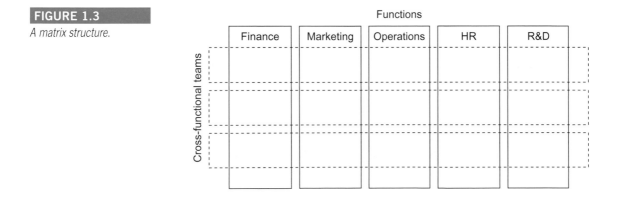

Three different kinds of matrix structures have been identified and described (Knight, 1977):

1. *coordination* where staff remain within their main function or department and cross-functional activity is achieved through integrated planning

2. *overlay* where staff are more formally part of two different teams, within their function and within a cross-functional unit, having two managers

3. *secondment* where staff will sometimes work within their functional divisions and sometimes within cross-functional teams but not simultaneously

Matrix structures are most appropriate for organisations operating in fast-changing environments where information, innovation and flexibility are vital. Creative, pharmaceutical and high-tech businesses fall into this category. The structures can be far more responsive to environmental change than more traditional hierarchical structures. Close collaboration between functions speeds up the process of communication, alerting staff and managers to opportunities and threats that arise while encouraging an organisation-wide perspective in reaching solutions, rather than working within silos. Vertical and horizontal channels are more readily accessed, also prompting more rapid decision-making. This is additionally linked to a more efficient use of resources by applying them to the area of greatest need and highest return. Technical experts and equipment may be shared across the organisation as well as budgets and other resources. As staff are working more closely on function-spanning activity, they will gain a more holistic picture and a greater sense of their contribution to corporate objectives. This should increase feelings of loyalty, morale and motivation. They will have more chance to influence decision-making and observe for themselves how this impacts on performance.

However, difficulties may arise as a result of staff reporting to two different managers, resulting in potential confusion and conflict. Staff may no longer know their position in the organisation so clearly and management may become diluted and less effective. The skills of the staff and managers – especially interpersonal skills – are very important to sustaining an effective matrix structure. A matrix structure may also prove to be expensive to maintain since the organisation is trying to support a functional structure plus additional reporting requirements on a horizontal basis.

International and Multinational Organisational Structures

The search for an appropriate organizational structure must balance the forces for local responsiveness against the forces for global integration.

Hennessey and Jeannet (2001)

It is estimated that there are over 35,000 multinational organisations (source: UN data). The revenues earned by the top 100 in 2008 topped $15 trillion, the largest earner being Wal-Mart with revenue of $379 billion.[2] Most structures evolve as organisations grow and this is especially pertinent to international and multinational operations. We should remind ourselves of the formal definition of a multinational organisation. The term refers to any organisation that operates in more than one country while being managed from its home country. Usually it is reserved for those that derive at least 25% of their turnover from countries other than their home base. Four different kinds of multinational organisations may be distinguished:

1. *Multinational* – a decentralised organisation operating in several countries while retaining a significant level of activity in its domestic market.

2. *Global* – a centralised organisation spreading its activities on a world scale chiefly to derive cost advantages.

3. *International* – an organisation that builds upon its parent firm's technology or research and development.

4. *Transnational* – organisations with a mix of the above models.[3]

The significance of this is not so much the precise definitions but the recognition that there are different models for operating in more than one country and these relate to organisational structures. The specific ways in which multinationals tend to grow are:

- *Organic growth* – year on year increases in revenues and profits and an expansion of operations.

- *Diversification* – expanding operations into new areas of activity (often through mergers and acquisitions).

- *Horizontal integration* – mergers and acquisitions with firms engaged in similar activities at the same level in the supply chain.

- *Vertical integration* – mergers and acquisitions with firms engaged in operations at earlier or later stages in the supply chain.

---

[2] *Source*: *Fortune Magazine*, 21 July 2008 quoted http://www.globalpolicy.org/socecon/tncs/tables/tncs2008.htm

[3] *Source*: http://www.businessdictionary.com/definition/multinational-corporation-MNC.html

Given the various ways in which organisations grow, there is no single model that describes the development of multinational and international organisational structures. However, some studies have identified some common characteristics and patterns. For example, the findings of Hollensen (2004) are illustrated in Figure 1.4.

As the organisation gains more experience in international activity and commits more resources overseas, it is likely to develop from *ad hoc* arrangements (stage 1) to a more highly structured functional structure (stage 2). Progressing further, as it extends its reach into multiple regions, a multinational typically forms divisions on a geographical basis (stage 3) with managers having responsibility over single or groups of countries. With further advances in the scale and complexity of international operations, this develops even further into a focus on products and markets (stage 4), enabling the business to reflect more precisely local variations in preferences and needs and so build valuable long-term relationships with

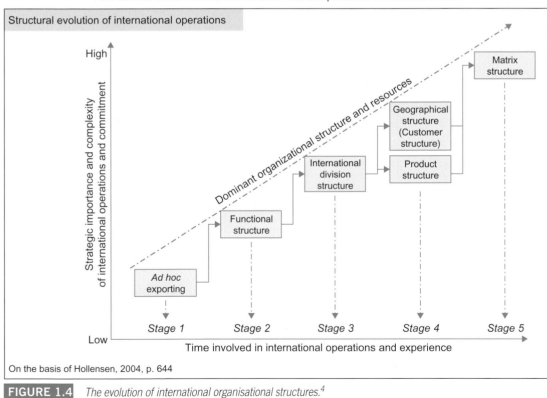

How can the structural evolution of international operations be characterized?

On the basis of Hollensen, 2004, p. 644

FIGURE 1.4   *The evolution of international organisational structures.[4]*

---

[4]*Source*: http://www.rainerbusch.de/mo_13_1-imorg.htm

its customers. At its most advanced, a multinational typically reaches a matrix structure (stage 5) in an attempt to increase it flexibility and responsiveness to changing market conditions by sharing expertise and maximising the speed of communications and decision-making.

Sometimes international matrix structures are described as 3D as the cross-divisional activity spans multiple functions, products or markets, and countries. There are many different ways of arranging activities and resources. For example, products may be developed and managed globally, while functions (human resources, marketing, finance, etc.) are duplicated for each significant geographical region, mindful of culture, legislation, custom, economic conditions and so on. Overlaying this structure, a regional manager may have responsibility for the local market.

For the marketing manager operating in an international environment, there is the need to complement their skills in strategy, planning, budgetary control, communication, information management and so on with additional expertise in such matters as multi-cultural understanding, geographical knowledge, global economics, international politics and legislation. The structures of large multinationals can be incredibly complex and potentially very expensive to maintain. Individuals are likely to require strong interpersonal skills to thrive and prosper.

ACTIVITY 1.1

Referring to your own organisation, or one with which you are familiar, describe the organisational structure. You should refer to size, differentiation, integration, formalisation, spans of control and centralisation/decentralisation.

What benefits does this structure provide for the effective operation of the marketing function? What barriers or hindrances does the structure also give to marketing?

REFERENCES

Hennessey, D., Jeannet, J.-P., 2001. Global Marketing: Strategy and Cases, fifth ed., Houghton Mifflin Company, Boston, MA.

Hollensen, S., 2004. Global Marketing: A Decision-Oriented Approach. Prentice Hall, Harlow.

Knight, K. (Ed.), 1977. Matrix Management: A Cross-Functional Approach to Organization. PBI-Petrocelli Books, New York.

FURTHER READING

Boddy, D., 2008. Management: An Introduction. Prentice Hall, Europe.

Hatch, M.J., 2006. Organization Theory, second ed., Oxford University Press.

Quality Systems and Processes

1.2 Critically assess the requirements of developing effective and efficient quality systems and processes to support compliance including evaluating and assessing the relevance of key quality concepts.

1.2:

The importance of quality systems
Quality models:

- Total Quality Management
- European Foundation of Quality Management
- ISO 9001
- Six Sigma
- ISO 14001
- PAS2050
- Benchmarking

PDCA cycle
Deming 14 steps for improving quality

Quality is the totality of features and characteristics of a product or service that bear on its ability to satisfy stated or implied needs.
Kotler and Armstrong (2001)

A system is an organised set of processes that are grouped together with the aim of achieving some collective purpose. Quality is a natural aim of

17

organisations but it can be elusive. To describe products or services as being high quality is common but what does it really mean? High performance, durable materials, elegant design, attention to detail, attentive and responsive staff, fitness for purpose and value for money may all form part of a conception of quality. In order to be confident of delivering quality, most organisations adopt systems and processes that reduce failure rates, ensure consistency of output, focus activity towards the customer and provide a means of gauging the quality of the service delivered. There are many similarities in such schemes and they are not without critics. There is always a danger that by committing time and resources to meeting the demands of a particular model, the attention of staff and managers is taken away from more important operational and strategic matters. The interest of quality systems and processes to marketing managers should be high, given the importance of brand value and organisational reputation in building long-term relationships, securing loyalty and maximising lifetime customer values.

THE IMPORTANCE OF QUALITY SYSTEMS

Quality systems may be applied to specific functions or activities, or to a whole organisation. Their importance is to maximise effectiveness which is essential for competitive or organisational advantage and delivering value for money.

> Quality systems may be applied to:
>
> - individual teams and divisions
> - targeted processes and systems in administration, production, finance, distribution, communications, etc.
> - products, brands or services
> - one-off projects and initiatives
> - the whole organisation.

Given the elusive nature of quality, it is helpful to have historical data, targets and benchmarks with which to compare actual performance. Most models emphasise the need for a coordinated, embedded and holistic approach. Quality is not something that you add to a product or service like packaging or a separate feature, rather it often arises from the approaches taken to delivering it at all stages. It is not something that remains static either, and managers need to keep attuned to new challenges and changing demands from inside and outside of the organisation. Technology may contribute but it also needs a set of quality processes in itself for managing the inputs it makes to the value chain.

Another common feature of most quality models is the need to take a systematic and sustained approach. Quality is not achieved quickly and requires the support of managers at all levels for the long term. The desire of management to control is one of the major drivers for quality metrics, but caution should always be exercised to ensure that the data measures what is required and can be collected without undue time and expense. Managers need metrics that are representative of the current state of things, indicating trends and allowing forecasts to be made so as to underpin effective decision making and control.

QUALITY MODELS

Total Quality Management

Total quality management (TQM) was very popular in the 1970s and 1980s and while it may have since peaked in popularity, it is still a very persuasive model and holds sway in many organisations even today. The influence of the TQM philosophy can be seen in much of the subsequent thinking in quality systems and processes.

TQM, as the name suggests, strives for quality in all processes. Indeed, its philosophy maintains that anything less than this is inefficient as it results in higher levels of waste, rejected items, failures and customer dissatisfaction. It requires the buy-in by all levels of the organisation led by the senior team and a suitable set of metrics by which to gauge success or otherwise.

European Foundation of Quality Management

The European Foundation of Quality Management (EFQM) created a quality model in 1992 as the basis for European Quality Awards, and these are still awarded to organisations deemed to have demonstrated high levels of quality of their systems and processes. However, the application of the model has gained more widespread usage as a framework for benchmarking, self-assessment and improvement.

The EFQM model recognises five enablers for quality:

- leadership
- people
- partnerships
- resources
- processes

In order to produce excellence in performance, customer satisfaction leadership and society, EFQM advocates:

- being result-focused
- being customer-focused
- providing consistent leadership
- embedding excellence into systems and processes
- investing in the development of individuals
- maintaining a continuous process of improvement and innovation
- developing and sustaining partnerships
- a well developed sense of corporate social responsibility[1]

ISO 9001

The International Organisation for Standardisation (ISO) defines a series of standards for business sectors. There are over 17,000 sets of standards relating to everything from agriculture to wood technology. The advantage of universally accepted statements is that they standardise:

- language and terminology, including documentation, symbols and labelling
- requirements for safety and pollution
- compatibility of components, including dimensions, weights and measures, and performance

ISO 9001 is the standard for quality management. It covers the processes relating to production and service delivery together with the controls that need to be in place to ensure that customer satisfaction is maximised. The benefit of adopting the standards is that it helps organisations identify and define the key roles and responsibilities in quality management. By following the quality processes described in the standards, an organisation should be rewarded by achieving cost savings from improved productivity and reduced wastage and defects. The benefits to customers will be in the form of high levels of correct order fulfillments within time. In addition, once an organisation has been accredited, it will be able to declare its adherence to ISO 9001 which will signal to customers, suppliers and other stakeholders that its quality management processes meet recognised international standards.

In order to apply for accreditation, an organisation should first familiarise itself with the requirements of the standards and how they impact on routine operations and activities. The standards need to be adopted, integrated

---

[1]See http://www.efqm.com

into stated policies and procedures, and embedded in operation manuals. There also needs to be a process for confirming achievement of the standards. Compliance with the standards must to be confirmed by the work of compliance assessors or internal auditors. At this point, the organisation may apply for accreditation through an audit by a third party. If successful, the organisation is then issued a certificate of registration in acknowledgement. Periodic audits will be used to determine ongoing compliance.

ISO standards are not without their critics. Firstly, the philosophy rests of the assumption that it is possible to improve quality through the adoption of a generic set of standard processes. Given the richness and diversity of activity, it seems unlikely that a single approach to documentation, control, corrective action, audit and continuous improvement could be effective. Admittedly, there are a number of industry-specific variations for IT, telecommunications and car manufacturers amongst others. The process of documentation, and seeking and maintaining accreditation can be time consuming and expensive, and some have argued that it may act as a distraction from genuine quality management by focussing the attention on the wording rather than the principle of the standards. It may reduce the sense of responsibility for quality if managers believe that it has been 'taken care of'. Slavishly following the standards may make them blind to genuine problems in their own organisation. It is not clear how much stakeholders are impressed by a certification like ISO 9001. What often happens is that there is a trend towards gaining accreditation for new initiatives – like the Charter Mark, Investors in People and so on – but their very success creates a diminution in the perceived value. If everyone has the certificate, it no longer provides a mean of distinguishing between competing organisations.

Six Sigma

Motorola developed the principle of the six sigma method. It aims to remove processes that cause defects and damage customer satisfaction on the basis that it is cheaper to prevent failures than to fix them or discard rejects. The model takes its name from a mathematical symbol used in statistics for standard deviation, that is, a measure of spread around the mean in a normal distribution. When the spread of performance between the average and the minimum required standard is six times the standard deviation, then the number of items falling outside of acceptable tolerance is negligible (in fact, less than 3.4 in a million). The quality of output is so high and so consistent that the incidence of failure is tiny. (Figure 2.1)

In common with other models, like TQM, six sigma requires full commitment from the whole organisation with support from the highest level to be successful. It is a scientific model with a heavy focus on quantitative data.

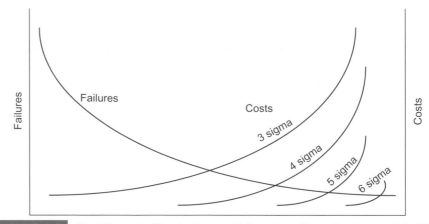

FIGURE 2.1 *The falling costs of the six sigma model (based on a diagram by Johnson, et al., 1997).*

It is particularly suited to production and financial outcomes. Champions are needed to generate and sustain enthusiasm for the model. Motorola claim to have saved $17 billion as a direct result of the six sigma model since they adopted it in 2006[2].

ISO 14001

ISO 14001 is a set of environmental management standards first introduced in 1996. The comments made earlier in relation to ISO 9001 are equally relevant here. The rationale and process for implementation are the same. So too are the potential advantages and pitfalls. The standards cover:

- management systems for environmental control
- auditing processes for environmental management
- methods for measuring performance
- labelling
- life-cycle assessment
- environmental factors in production[3]

PAS2050

BSI Standards Solutions produced Publicly Available Standards (PAS) 2050 *Assessing the life cycle greenhouse gas emissions of goods and services* in 2008 at the joint request of Defra and the Carbon Trust. Unlike the ISO standards, PAS standards, as the name implies, are available for free.

---

[2] For more information see http://www.isixsigma.com
[3] For more information see http://www.british-accreditation.co.uk

The philosophy is very similar to that of ISO standards. The standards contain benchmarks for emissions and help organisations find means to reduce them. They enable the user to make an assessment of the total greenhouse gas emissions that are released in the natural life cycle of their goods and services and to compare this with other available materials, means of production and delivery[4].

Benchmarking

There are a large number of agencies who can provide external marketing benchmarks appropriate for your organisation, enabling you to compare your performance with industry standards or norms. External benchmarks are potentially very powerful in helping an organisation set targets for improvement. However, they must be used with care. A comparison is only valuable if one is comparing like with like and it is hard to find two identical organisations with matching goals, product portfolios, tactics, market profiles and so on. Even when a reasonable comparison is possible, one might still wonder at the value of it. Pursuit of performance to match a particular benchmark may be inappropriate and may result in undue focus on a given aspect of activity at the expense of other more pressing matters. At best, benchmarks should only be part of an overall model for quality. Historical performance and an organisation's own internal targets are equally important.

Benchmarks for marketing exist pretty much for every metric that the marketing manager may choose to use to guide them towards making improvements. This might include benchmarks for the staffing of marketing for example, including:

- *Headcount* – how big are marketing functions in organisations of comparable size and similar profiles?
- *Staff turnover* – how long, on average, do members of staff stay within marketing functions?
- *Salaries and wages* – what are the average rates of pay within marketing departments in the sector?
- *Staff satisfaction* – how well do members of marketing teams rate their employer?
- *Staff development* – what is the typical spend on training and upskilling?

Similar benchmarks may also be used for project appraisal, responsiveness to media campaigns, average lifetime customer value, average customer

---

[4] For more information see http://www.bsi-global.com

purchase, gross ratings points, rate of new product acceptance, conversion rates from enquiry to sale and so on.

It is important not to ignore the use of internal benchmarks as well. Performance within one function, or within one geographic region, may be used to help benchmark performance elsewhere in the organisation. These have the added advantages of being readily and freely available, and being completely transparent to the prospective user.

PDCA CYCLE

The PDCA cycle (plan, do, check, act) was made popular by Deming and is implicitly or explicitly part of many other quality systems. For example, the six sigma model incorporates a cycle of define, measure, analyse, improve and control, which is just a variation of PDCA. It can also be found in other similar cycles such as the standard scientific approach and Kolb's learning cycle. A key to such cycles is that they form an iterative process such that the outcome informs the next cycle on a continuous basis, each time perfecting the process a little more. It is deceptively simple and incredibly powerful.

When applied to business processes the PDCA cycle allows managers to analyse activity in order to identify the causes of defects and failures of customer satisfaction. If adopted as a cyclical approach, it then allows feedback to be used to ascertain the success of changes made in reducing the number of defects. (Figure 2.2)

At the *plan* stage, the aim is to develop business processes so that they lead to improvements in outputs. At the *do* stage, the new or revised processes are implemented and performance is measured. At the *check* stage, the performance is analysed to help inform any future changes. At the *act* stage, further revisions are identified and agreed.

Deming's principal interest was in production. It is possible to refine the PDCA cycle using a secondary loop within the *do* segment to illustrate the relationship of operational activity as a sub-process within a larger cycle of strategic development. (Figure 2.3)

Quality assurance within marketing may be viewed as a PDCA cycle. The performance indicators described elsewhere in this section are vital if a systematic approach is to be taken to raising the effectiveness of marketing activity. Being able to demonstrate the value that marketing adds to the strategic PDCA cycle is a further desirable outcome of using such a model.

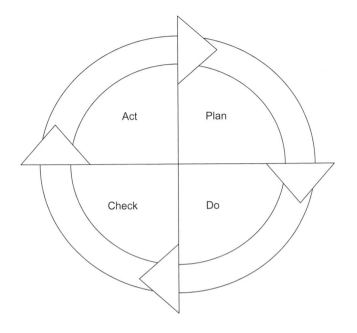

FIGURE 2.2
PDCA cycle.

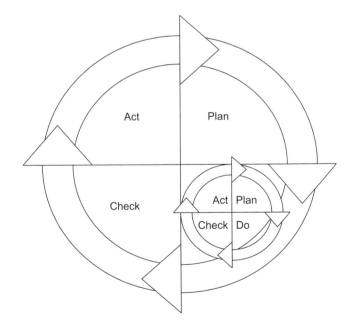

FIGURE 2.3
Nested PDCA cycles illustrating operational activity as a sub-process within strategic development.

Deming's approach to quality may be given as follows:

Quality may be defined as the result of work efforts divided by costs.
Where the focus is on quality, quality tends to increase over time and costs fall.
Where the focus is on costs, the costs tend to rise over time and quality falls.

DEMING 14 STEPS

In addition to popularising the PDCA model for quality improvement, Deming has given his name to an annual award in the United States for quality and productivity. He has also been hugely influential in Japan where he taught for many years, and his name is used for prizes awarded in that country. In his book *Out of the Crisis*, Deming set out 14 steps that lead to improved management. In doing so, he set out the framework for what become TQM and other similar models of quality. The following steps are paraphrased from his original work.

1. Create a 'constancy of purpose' for improvement, focusing on long-term excellence, competitiveness and survival rather than short-term profits.

2. Adopt a new approach ('a new philosophy') that embraces change.

3. Stop relying on inspections to achieve quality, rather ensure that quality is built in.

4. Choose suppliers based on price and quality, and establish long-term, trusting relationships.

5. Keep on improving every process, and in this way reduce costs.

6. Make training on the job a standard part of everyone's daily routine.

7. Adopt and institute leadership.

8. 'Drive out fear' so that individuals are motivated by a desire to succeed rather than through threats and coercions.

9. 'Break down barriers' between individuals and departments to facilitate cross-functional working.

10. Get rid of slogans, targets and 'exhortations', as they do not help to improve quality because quality is usually the result of processes not individuals.

11. Remove numerical quotas for staff and managers, and use leadership instead.

12. Encourage pride in workmanship and remove performance management systems that rate individuals.

13. Foster a lively self-improvement programme for all staff and managers.

14. Put everyone in charge of achieving the desired transformation of the workplace.

ACTIVITY 2.1

Consider a marketing function with which you are familiar. Select one of the quality models described earlier. Describe the steps you would take, assuming you were the marketing manager, to introduce the quality model into the marketing function.

What difficulties might you encounter in trying to introduce and implement the quality model?

What benefits would accrue from introducing the quality model?

FURTHER READING

Boddy, D., 2008. Management: An Introduction. Prentice Hall, Europe.

Hatch, Mary Jo., 2006. Organization Theory, second ed. Oxford University Press.

Johnson, W.C., Chvala, R., Voehl, F., 1997. Total Quality in Marketing. CRC Press LLC.

Kotler, P., Armstrong, G., 2001. Principles of Marketing, ninth ed. Upper Saddle River: Prentice Hall Inc.

CHAPTER 3

Measuring, Monitoring and Improving Marketing Performance

1.3 Determine innovative and effective methods of measuring and monitoring marketing performance for marketing operation, marketing activities and effective resource management.

1.4 Critically analyse monitoring information and recommend ways to improve marketing performance.

SYLLABUS REFERENCE

1.3:

Accounting measures

- Profit and loss
- Balance sheets
- Cash flow
- Budgetary control

Productivity measures

- Inputs versus outputs

Relationship marketing and customer-related measures

- Retention
- Satisfaction
- Communication

Internal measures of performance

- **Recruitment**
- **Retention**
- **Attitude**
- **Performance**
- **Communications**

Innovation and learning measures of performance

1.4:

Productivity analysis (inputs versus outputs)
Comparative analysis (changes over time)
Segmental analysis (analysis of markets)
Innovation audit

- **Organisational climate**
- **Current performance**
- **Policies**
- **Practices**
- **Cognitive styles**

Competitor comparisons and benchmarking

Marketing has a fundamental role to play in any organisation by helping it realise its strategic objectives. It is also a *boundary spanning activity*, meaning that it projects messages about the organisation, its products and services to the external environment, as well as drawing information and intelligence from that environment in order to understand what is going on. It is natural that managers are keen to see the impact made by marketing as it is so closely associated with its core purposes – delivering goods and services, maximising returns on assets and investments, securing long-term financial viability and rewarding investors and shareholders.

As well providing a means by which an organisation may gauge its successes, marketing is also a mechanism for identifying changes in trading conditions, monitoring competitor actions, observing patterns of customer behaviour and forecasting future outturns. Potential problems or the crystallising of risks can be detected promptly to enable remedial action to be taken.

In driving the market and informing the organisation about prevailing conditions, marketing performance is a central concern. In this section, we will examine ways in which performance can be measured. In the following section, we will see how this is used to build improvements.

ACCOUNTING MEASURES

Accounting measures of marketing performance reflect the financial impact that its activities have. They can be analysed according to:

- *Profit and loss* – the impact on incomes earned and costs incurred.

- *Balance sheets* – the impact on assets and liabilities.

- *Cash flows* – the impact on money moving into and out of the organisation.

- *Budgetary controls* – the impact on the monitoring and management of income and expenditure.

We shall explore each of these accounting measures in turn.

Profit and Loss

Organisations can measure a wide range of marketing metrics such as loyalty, brand awareness, customer satisfaction and so on (as we shall see below), but the reason why these measures are important is that they lead to sales and income. Sales are possible only, of course, if customers are aware of an organisation's products and services, are able to differentiate them from those of its competitors and are willing and able to pay for them, and so marketing is hugely important in this area.

In accounting terms, the Profit and Loss account (sometimes referred to as the Trading and Profit and Loss account or the Operating Statement) is a record of the incomes earned and the expenses incurred for a given period. It is common to record incomes and expenditure on a monthly and a cumulative basis during the year, culminating in a statement for all 12 months.

The profit or loss made is simply the difference between the incomes and the expenses. Where incomes are greater the excess is referred to as a profit, where expenses are greater the deficit is referred to as a loss. (Many not-for-profit activities refer to 'surplus' and 'deficit' in place of 'profit' and 'loss' but for our purposes the terms are interchangeable.)

It should be noted that incomes earned are not the same as monies received from sales, as much business is conducted on a credit basis (buy now and pay later). For the purpose of profit and loss, we record sales income at the point the sale is made, not when the money is received. The same is true of expenses. They are included at the point they arise rather than when they are paid (Figure 3.1).

	£
Sales	187,000
Less: *Expenses*	98,500
e.g. Salaries and Wages	
Light and Heat	
Advertising	
Depreciation	
Postage	
Etc.	
Profit	£88,500

Marketing costs (promotions, advertising, PR events, salaries and wages, agency costs, webpage development, etc.) will appear as expenses in the profit and loss statement. It is common to express the marketing cost as a percentage of turnover or of the total costs, enabling managers to make comparisons with other functions, with previous years, with budgets, with benchmark data and with external organisations and competitors. This single measure is useful as a high-level indicator but it is a very simple indicator of marketing performance. The marketing manager will be interested in how activity impacts on sales and what return is achieved for particular expenditure.

Metrics relating to profit and loss may be focused internally as well as in comparison with the market (Table 3.1).

Information can be broken down to reflect the contribution made by products, brands, regions, retail outlets, sales representative, market segment, etc. If an organisation wishes to measure the impact and effectiveness of particular campaigns, it needs to identify which sales have occurred as a result. It cannot be assumed that all increases are due to advertising. The use of coded order forms, sales promotion reference numbers, surveys asking customers where they heard about the organisation and other techniques are used to help marketing managers assess the value of a given event or campaign.

The information derived from the profit and loss data can be used to inform strategies for competitive positioning, product development, pricing, promotion and so on, which themselves will require suitable metrics to measure their impact. The relationships between price, profits and volumes of sales may be described by using cost–volume–profit diagrams covered in Chapter 8.

Return on (marketing) investment is measured by:

$$\text{ROI (or ROMI)} = \text{profit or surplus/investment} \times 100\%$$

Table 3.1	Marketing metrics linked to profit and loss	
Profit and loss items	**Internal measures**	**External measures**
Sales	Number of units Value of sales Percentage changes in sales Comparison with budgets	Percentage market share Comparison with competitor performance Comparison with sector averages Share of wallet
Expenses	Cost of marketing (by activity and by campaign) Marketing as a proportion of total costs	Comparison with competitors Comparison with sector averages Share of voice
Profits	Value of profit Movements in profit Comparison with budgets	Benchmark data for profit margins relevant to sector Trends in market performance
Ratios	Profit as a percentage of sales Expenses as a percentage of sales Marketing as a proportion of sales Return on Investment (ROI) Return on Marketing Investment (ROMI) Marketing spend per lead Sales acquisition cost	Benchmark data and competitor performance

For example, we may be interested in evaluating the ROI of an email or direct mail campaign. Suppose the following data were available:

- Number of mailouts 10,000
- Response rate 5%
- Conversion rate of responses 25%
- Cost of initiative (staff time, design, postage, etc.) £1,000
- Average profit or surplus made on each sale £12

We can analyse this data and calculate a return on investment. 5% of 10,000 = 500 of the contacts who responded and of these 25% = 125 made a purchase. The average cost of each response is £1,000 divided by 500 responses, £2, and the average cost per purchase is £1,000 divided by 125, £8. The 125 sales generate £12 profit each or a total of £1,500. Therefore, an investment of £1,000 has generated a £1,500 profit and an overall surplus (after deducting the cost of the campaign) of £500. This return of £500 is 50% of the investment of £1,000, so ROI = 50%. This figure could be used to compare other campaigns and other options to determine whether it represents the most effective way of spending £1,000.

If an organisation aims to increase its incomes, it should do so on the basis of a planned growth strategy. It is possible to gain additional sales in a way that actually reduces profitability, and while this might be sustainable in the short term it cannot be continued indefinitely. Penetration pricing and loss leaders may help to raise awareness and secure larger market share but this must ultimately lead to new, profitable income streams. Even in the public and not-for-profit sectors, where the aims are principally around value for money and organisational advantage and where it may be acceptable for one profitable activity to subsidise a loss-making one, survival depends upon at least balancing income and expenditure in the long term.

Growth, therefore, should follow a number of key considerations:

- What is the level of penetration in existing markets?

- Is growth possible from existing markets by increasing customer loyalty and lifetime values?

- Is growth possible by attracting new customers for existing products and services by making adjustments to the marketing mix?

- Is it possible to take market share away from the competition by identifying and exploiting competitor's loyalty gaps?

- Are there any potential new markets large enough to make the necessary investment worthwhile?

- Are those markets likely to grow, stay the same or shrink in the long term?

In fact, using the Ansoff matrix, growth in sales and revenues may occur through four main strategies:

- *Market penetration* – increasing the sales value of existing products to existing customers or customers within the existing market by selling more of the same and so gaining a greater share of the market and wallet and increasing the lifetime value of customers.

- *Product development* – modifying existing products or introducing new ones to existing markets.

- *Market development* – selling existing products or services to new customers, such as new geographical regions or new population segments.

- *Diversification* – introducing new products to new markets.

The high-level strategy for growing the customer base together with the associated risks and costs needs to be determined before a revenue improvement plan could be devised. Whilst finding new customers, maintaining existing customer loyalty must remain a priority. Both are sources of revenue, but generally (depending on the sector) it is easier (and cheaper)

Table 3.2	Potential risks and revenue improvement tactics for growth strategies	
Strategy	**Risks to consider**	**Potential revenue improvement tactics**
Market penetration	■ A price war with competitors ■ An inability to match demand ■ Market becomes saturated	■ Competitive pricing to shift the break even point while increasing volume of sales to improve profit ■ Use of customer loyalty and reward schemes to encourage repeat purchase and improve lifetime values ■ High profile promotion leading to increased and sustained sales activity ■ Targeting high growth markets to benefit from rising sales ■ Squeezing out competitors through aggressive marketing and secure the loyalty of their customers
Product development	■ Insufficient demand for the new product ■ Other suppliers introduce similar products ■ Demand for new product substitutes existing demand for existing products	■ Using technology to introduce new product features and charging a premium price (price skimming)
Market development	■ Disaffecting as many existing customers as new ones generated	■ Utilising (or developing) new channels of distribution to access other customers ■ Introducing multiple pricing strategies to appeal to different potential market segments
Diversification	■ Over-stretching resources ■ Uncertainty about new product and new customers	■ Entering into a strategic alliance to share risks (and revenues) until viability is confirmed

to secure repeat custom from the customer base than to sell to new ones. Table 3.2 illustrates some of the risks and potential revenue improvement tactics that may be deployed when seeking growth.

Balance Sheets

Balance sheets provide a schedule of the assets held and the liabilities owing by the organisation at a given moment in time. They are typically drawn up at the end of the year but may also be produced at any point.

Asset refers to all items of positive value held by the organisation. Long-term (or fixed) assets include tangible items such as premises, motor vehicles, machinery, computer equipment and investments, as well as intangible ones such as copyright, patents, goodwill and reputation, although this latter group may not always be listed on the balance sheet. Short-term (or current) assets are those subject to frequent change as part of normal activity and are not normally held for more than one year, such as stocks of finished goods, raw materials and work in progress, money in the bank and the till (cash in hand), and amounts owed to the organisation by customers who made purchases on credit (known as debtors).

Liabilities are amounts owed by the organisation to other parties, including suppliers (known as creditors) and investors (shareholders, banks and others).

The balance sheet is so-called because it balances, showing that the value of the organisation (its total net assets) is equal to the investment in it by the owners (sole trader, partners, members or shareholders). The profits generated are added to the shareholders' funds as this is owed by the organisation back to the owners (Figure 3.2).

The marketing function may have its share of assets (vehicles, equipment, furniture, stocks of collateral, etc.) and the most effective way of gauging its performance using the balance sheet is by the return on assets (ROA).

FIGURE 3.2	
Simple balance sheet.	

	£
Fixed assets	208,390
e.g. Land and Buildings	
Plant and Machinery	
Motor Vehicles	
Computer Equipment	
Office Furniture	
Current assets	56,400
e.g. Stock	
Debtors	
Cash at bank	
Cash in hand	
Less: *Current liabilities*	48,200
e.g. Creditors	
Bank overdraft	
Less: *Long term liabilities*	23,000
e.g. Loans	
Total net assets	£193,590
Represented by:	
Share capital	£193,590

ROA = profit or surplus made/value of assets deployed × 100 %

This calculation can be made for the organisation as a whole, or for the marketing function or for specific initiatives. It looks at how well the assets have been used. For example, if Figures 3.1 and 3.2 relate to the same organisation, we can see that £193,590 of assets have been used to generate £88,500 of profit. This is a ROA of 46%. To answer the question whether this is any good, it is necessary to compare this result with other opportunities in which the assets could have been put to use, targeted performance, previous results and benchmarks for the sector.

Cash Flow

As opposed to profit and loss which measures incomes when they are earned and expenses when they arise, a cash flow shows money flowing in and out of an organisation. This is an alternative and equally important view of performance and highlights the crucial dimension of timing. Many organisations experience cyclical patterns of activity due to public holidays, religious festivals, changes in the weather and school calendars. While it may be possible to rely on large sales earned over a relatively short period to generate a profit for the year as a whole, it is desirable to spread cash inflows more evenly, at least so that they match outflows a little better. Generally, organisations find that they are committed to fixed monthly costs (salaries, rent and rates, light and heat, leasing, hire purchase, etc.) regardless of sales. If money does not flow in, they will need to draw upon reserves or may even need to borrow, thus adding to costs. Ideally, the cash flowing into the business each month should be enough to cover the necessary outgoings. This is what keeps an organisation solvent.

To illustrate this, suppose a business has the following earnings and expenditure for the months from November to June (Table 3.3).

Let us also suppose that credit customers are given two months in which to pay while all supplies are made on credit which must be settled within one month. Assume the cash balance at the start of January is £6000. The following table shows the cash flow for the six months from January to June (Table 3.4).

For the purposes of the cash flow, the receipts and payments have been put in the month in which they occur. For example, the receipt of £3000 from debtors in January relates to sales made (on two months' credit) in November. Also, the payment of £5200 to creditors in January relates to the purchases made in December (on one month's credit). The closing balance of cash at the end of each month is equal to the opening balance plus the inflows minus the outflows. This then becomes the opening balance

Table 3.3	Income and cost items							
	November	December	January	February	March	April	May	June
Sales								
Cash	1800	3000	1300	1000	1800	2500	4000	5500
Credit	3000	6100	3000	2600	3200	5400	8900	15000
Costs								
Purchases	2200	5200	2600	1500	2700	3900	6500	11600
Fixed costs	3800	3800	3800	3800	3800	3800	3800	3800

Table 3.4	Cash flow statement					
	January	February	March	April	May	June
Cash inflows						
Cash sales	1300	1000	1800	2500	4000	5500
Debtors	3000	6100	3000	2600	3200	5400
Total inflows	4300	7100	4800	5100	7200	10900
Cash outflows						
Creditors	5200	2600	1500	2700	3900	6500
Fixed costs	3800	3800	3800	3800	3800	3800
Total outflows	9000	6400	5300	6500	7700	10300
Cash flow						
Opening balance	6000	1300	2000	1500	100	–400
Inflows	4300	7100	4800	5100	7200	10900
Outflows	9000	6400	5300	6500	7700	10300
Closing balance	1300	2000	1500	100	–400	200

for the next month. The closing balance is initially positive but is declining until it becomes negative in May, becoming positive once more in June. In this case, the organisation deals with seasonal variations. There have been higher sales over the winter holidays, followed by a decline and then an increase again up to summer. Fixed costs remain the same each month, and although purchases vary with the level of sales, the timing of inflows and outflows does not prevent the reserves of cash dropping. Some form of borrowing is required for May (such as an overdraft), incurring additional costs as a result.

Marketing activity should understand the importance of cash flows. Marketing itself is a cost-and cash-outflow but more importantly it is responsible for attempting to create the most beneficial patterns of sales and sale income. In our example, the organisation may decide that a price promotion is required to stimulate extra demand in Spring to compensate for falling sales.

Budgetary Control

Much is said about budgetary control in Chapters 7 and 9 and its relationship to marketing performance. The main purpose of budgeting is to enable managers to exercise control over financial resources through monitoring and variance analysis. Marketing managers need to focus on their expenditure against plan but also respond to variances elsewhere in the budget, especially in sales. The degree of analysis should be appropriate to the organisation and might include a breakdown by product, brand, region or market segment. Control implies effective and timely decision-making which requires speedy information of the right kind.

PRODUCTIVITY MEASURES

Historically, productivity was used as one of the earliest measures for marketing performance. The approach took manufacturing as a model and examined how much output could be achieved from a given unit of input. *Marketing Productivity Analysis* is typical of this approach (Sevin, 1965) in which products and activities are analysed for profitability. As the discipline developed, other non-financial measures were included among inputs and outputs, increasing both the value of and the difficulties inherent in the analysis.

Inputs Versus Outputs

Productivity is a measure of the ability to transform inputs into outputs. The greater the productivity, the greater the outputs in proportion to the inputs. Marketing is interested in the productivity of the organisation as a whole, especially the areas of production or service delivery. We can also measure the productivity of marketing activity itself. In simple terms, the value that marketing adds is calculated by working out the additional sales made as a result. It may not always be easy to determine, but in principle there should be a direct and positive relationship between marketing inputs and outputs in sales. The inputs include investment, knowledge, skills, understanding, information and time, as well as the easier costed dimensions of design, materials, printing, postage, agency fees, IT support, etc. The outputs may range from cash flow, profit, number and value of sales, and market share. There may be complications in determining the value of some of these. For sales of specific products and services, it is reasonably straight forward (provided, there is a sophisticated cost accounting process that attaches direct and indirect costs to products). Where the output is about developing customer relationships, building brand value, raising awareness and increasing loyalty, it becomes less clear.

To measure inputs, we need to find a way of counting the cost of the work done. Resources and materials can be calculated readily. The most common way of calculating the value of the time taken to make plans, generate ideas, produce copy, monitor, report and so on is by using a standard fee per hour, depending on the grade of staff involved. A major proportion is simply salary. We can decide how many hours of productive time an employee should use per year and divide this into their salary, resulting in a rate of so much per hour. We can add a percentage on top of this to account for overheads (light, heat, depreciation, rent, etc.). In such matters, utility supersedes accuracy. There is no point adding to the costs by spending hours calculating what that cost is. An approximation based on sound estimates and a good working model should suffice.

To measure outputs, it is necessary to have metrics that we can count, such as:

- the growth in sales

- the number of leads generated

- the number of new names and contact details added to the database

- the number of times the organisation's name has been mentioned in the media

- the number of column inches in the trade press

- the number of positive responses to customer surveys

- the number of new customer loyalty cards issued

- the number of people who can recognise the organisation or the product name after it has appeared in adverts

To improve, productivity implies that more outputs are produced for fewer inputs, but several caveats must be taken into account.

- *Quality* – Not every hour of input is as effective (or as valuable) as any other. Not all publicity is good publicity. Marketing activity depends on being structured in its development, targeted, sophisticated and tailored.

- *Risk* – There are no guarantees that the inputs will deliver the planned outputs. What may be seen as short cuts of increasing productivity may also carry higher risk. Those risks include the risk of productivity actually falling and risks to damaging reputation. For example, greater press coverage may be achievable through shock tactics and high-profile stunts in advertising, press releases and PR events. However, such things can easily backfire and end up having the opposite effect from the one intended.

- *Focus* – It is possible to spread a marketing budget very thinly across multiple products, campaigns, launches, communications, promotions and events until it is not enough to make an impact anywhere. It is often more effective to limit oneself to fewer but better resourced activities, concentrating on those of greatest strategic relevance and potential for return.

- *Diminishing returns* – Doing more of the same will not necessarily generate more of the same outputs. Attention spans are short, demands made on people's time are immense, familiarity breeds contempt and boredom quickly sets in. Sometimes less is more. Change, innovation and progression command more attention.

Productivity is important because improvements lead to reduced unit costs and greater profit margins.

RELATIONSHIP MARKETING AND CUSTOMER-RELATED MEASURES

One approach to measuring performance is to commence with a self-assessment of current activity. Many agencies, publications and websites offer surveys that can be used for this purpose. They usually allow some form of scoring or ranking a series of criteria or questions. A common way of scoring answers is by using a Likert scale, such as:

5 Strongly agree

4 Agree

3 Neither agree nor disagree

2 Disagree

1 Strongly disagree

The outcome of such a survey can then be used to formulate a plan for improvement.

The following is an example of a marketing performance self-assessment taken from an online survey:[1]

PURPOSE

1. I have a clear purpose and vision for my business.
2. I have business objectives that are specific, measurable, achievable, relevant and timely.
3. My company is structured and organised to carry out effective marketing.
4. I have strong marketing expertise within the company (or its key advisors).
5. I have an effective marketing planning process that maximises profits by identifying, attracting and keeping valuable customers.

MARKET SEGMENT OR NICHE

1. I have identified a valuable market opportunity that I could "own".
2. I clearly understand my market size and its future potential.
3. I monitor my key competitors.
4. I have a definition that effectively describes my target customer groups, especially the high value ones.
5. My strong understanding of my target customer groups needs, desires and requirements has driven the development of my solutions, benefits and features.

CORE MESSAGE

1. I have developed a simple and powerful core message that is focused on solving the customer's problem.
2. It is as clear and concise as it could be.
3. It is distinctive from the competition.
4. The benefits and features are compelling for my target customer groups, especially the high value ones.
5. It works equally well to attract new customers, get existing customers to buy more and to keep customers for longer period.

---

[1] *Source*: http://www.brandnewwaysme.com/marketingpi.html

MARKETING COMMUNICATIONS

1. My core message effectively reaches my target customer groups.

2. My communications have real impact and attract customers to come to me.

3. They generate high repeat sales.

4. They encourage high levels of referrals.

5. I am making the best use of the marketing communication options available (e.g. advertising, direct marketing, publicity marketing, networking, seminars, public speaking, newsletters, customer magazines, web marketing).

SALES CONVERSION SYSTEM

1. I have a marketing and sales system that converts a high percentage of sales prospects to customers.

2. I use new technology systems to automate the process and to capture vital data.

3. My system enables me to evaluate the performance of each step or activity and for different customer groups or channels.

4. I can accurately forecast future sales and profits.

5. I can determine which marketing activities give me the best results (highest profits) for each pound spent.

In this case, the lower scoring statements indicate areas that require attention. Such assessments can be useful as they focus on areas that need development. It is not a precise science and can only be effective if the assessment is made objectively and with a good understanding of the dimensions that are included.

Another related model describes marketing performance at a number of different levels, such as low, medium and high or poor, good and excellent, and then invites the user to identify the one that most closely matches their own organisation (Table 3.5).

Retention

Tactics for maintaining the loyalty of existing customers while aiming for growth might include building customer relationships, offering loyalty schemes, and providing other perks and benefits. Organisations may offer regular customers targeted (but not intrusive) contact, preferential access to

Table 3.5	Self-assessment of marketing performance[1]		
	Weak performance	**Average performance**	**Outstanding performance**
Product innovation	We follow the example set by others	We follow the needs of our customers	We lead the market
Product/service quality	We do the minimum to meet customer needs	We give the customers what they want	We exceed customers' expectations
Organisational structure	We operate a hierarchical or functional structure	We operate a divisional structure	We operate a matrix structure
Market strategy	Our strategy is product led	Our strategy is market led	Our strategy is to be the market leader
Market segmentation	We do not segment the market (mass marketing)	We target market segments	We target individual customers (niche marketing)
Pricing policy	We aim to deliver lowest prices	We aim to deliver highest quality	We aim to deliver highest value

[1]With acknowledgements to http://www.steinermarketing.com/marketing_performance.htm

information, advance notice of special offers and promotions, and the privileged provision of additional services, such as insurance, lines of credit and saving schemes.

In implementing measures to improve performance, we can take advantage of the brand value cycle. This model is usually described as having five or six stages (Figure 3.3).

The steps may be explained as follows:

- *Assessment* – research the market to identify the customers' attitudes with existing brands, what they are communicating, how they could be improved and so on.

- *Development* – develop brands and devise appropriate strategies for product positioning.

- *Marketing infrastructure* – arrange marketing infrastructure in a way that supports and reinforces brands through planning, processes, structure, distribution, communication and so on.

- *Delivery* – apply the brands consistently in the market.

- *Monitoring and evaluation* – maintain a continuous review of customer responses to brands.

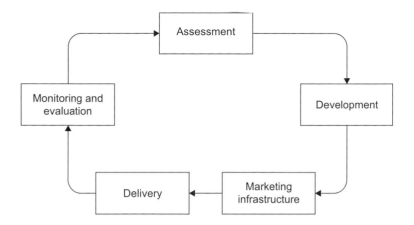

FIGURE 3.3

Brand value cycle.

Brands and branding are of great importance to organisations and their customers. For the customer, brands make it easy to identify products and services through recognisable logos, packaging, presentation, communication and delivery, thus speeding up the process of decision making and purchasing. This is true for B2B and B2C transactions. Trusted brands reduce the risk involved in procurement. Brand loyalty also adds to a customer's satisfaction with the product or service as it adds to the perceived value. For the supplier, the brand has real value because it can be reflected in the price the buyer is prepared to pay. The brand also serves as a short cut to communicate a proposition requiring lower levels of promotion and generating faster recognition and adoption rates. These benefits can be carried over into new but related brands which are subsequently cheaper to launch.

Brands, then, add directly to revenues by being part of the commodity sold and also have a favourable impact on costs. Understandably, organisations work hard to increase and protect brand value.

Satisfaction

Customer and consumer satisfaction can be classed as demand-side metrics for gauging marketing performance. In recent studies consumer satisfaction was found to be used as a measure by 68% of UK companies as a marketing metric while customer satisfaction featured for 45%[2]. Satisfaction is important because it is related to retention, sales and life time values. It is also true that happy customers promote products, brands, services and organisations to others by word of mouth and personal endorsement, leading to customer acquisition and further sales.

---

[2]Ambler, T., Kokkinaki, F., Puntoni, S., 2004. Assess Marketing Performance: The Current State of Metrics. Centre for Marketing, 01-903.

Typically satisfaction can be measured by asking customers to respond to the following kinds of questions:

- Are you completely satisfied with your purchase?

- How likely are you to make a similar purchase again in future?

- Would you recommend the product, service or organisation to friends?

There are a number of customer satisfaction indices used around the world, such as the UK Customer Satisfaction Index (UKCSI),[3] derived from asking questions such as these and then enabling organisations to be ranked and changes to be measured. The score is calculated between 0 and 100. The American Customer Satisfaction Index (ACSI)[4] is very similar, linking:

- Customer loyalty
- Customer complaints
- Perceived value
- Perceived quality
- Customer expectations.

A series of three questions on satisfaction, expectation and performance are each graded 1 to 10 by sample consumers and then results are compiled to produce a percentage rating. Table 3.6 illustrates an extract from ACSI published data.

The extract in Table 3.6 shows customer satisfaction ratings for sectors of the US economy based on over 200 companies. It also shows how ratings have moved in the last 12 months and in comparison with readings first taken in the 1990s. So while Hyundai's satisfaction rating rose 24% in the last 12 years, Delta Airline's fell by 21%.

Communication

Engaging with customers is a key dimension to the activity of marketing and so one of importance for marketing performance. Customers engage with the product, brand, organisation and with each other in various different ways, but a communications strategy will deliver a planned series of messages and interactions. This may be done with the assistance of technology. Interactive communication such as blogs, discussion forums, online user panels, online accounts, personal greetings, reminders and buying suggestions, emails and SMS texting may all be used to ensure the customer continues to engage with the organisation. In addition, static webpages,

---

[3] See http://www.instituteofcustomerservice.com
[4] See http://www.theacsi.org

Table 3.6	Extract of ACSI statistics[1]		
Sector	2008	% change in year	% change since first year
e-commerce	80	−2	6.4
Finance and insurance	76	0.7	−3.2
Retail trade	75.2	1.4	−0.7

[1]Figures taken from http://www.theasci.orgwww.theasci.org fourth quarter results for 2008 dated 17 February 2009.

such as product information, contact details and FAQs are also common. Mailouts may also be used, keeping customers updated on the details of their personal account, advising them of forthcoming promotions, seeking feedback and in general staying connected.

Clearly the purpose of communication is to foster loyalty, encourage sales and maximise lifetime values. Encouraging customers to engage with others is a way of gaining word of mouth advocacy at no real cost.

In order to set metrics, an organisation needs to be able to measure an appropriate dimension:

- the number of recorded visits to a website
- the number of clicks on a certain web item
- the number of repeat visits as well as the number of first-time visitors
- the number of communication made (letters, brochures, emails, texts, etc.)
- the contributions to an online survey
- the number of readers of a blog

Engagement has been proposed as a marketing metric with four components:

1. *involvement* – measuring communication links an individual has with the organisation
2. *interaction* – measuring the depth of involvement
3. *intimacy* – measuring the affection the individual has for the brand
4. *influence* – measuring the likelihood that the individual may persuade others to buy the brand[5]

---

[5]Haven, B., 2007. *Marketing's New Key Metric: Engagement*. Forrester Research Inc.

Table 3.7	Suitable metrics for different levels of customer engagement[1]
Level of engagement	**Suitable metrics**
Involvement	Number of website visits
	Duration of visits
	Number of pages viewed
	Key words used for searches
	Navigation routes taken through site
Interaction	Contribution to blogs and discussion forums (frequency, quantity, topics)
Intimacy	References made to products, brands and organisation on organisation's own or third party sites
	Opinions expressed in customer service calls
Influence	Information forwarded to friends
	Encouragement made to others
	Product advocacy

[1]Based on Haven, Brian, 2007. Marketing's new key metric: engagement. *Forrester Research Inc.*

In other words engagement can be measured on four different levels, depending upon the sophistication of the metrics used, moving from purely quantitative to more qualitative and evaluative (Table 3.7).

Capturing such information becomes harder the deeper the level of engagement one is trying to measure. While web analytics will provide the necessary data on *involvement*, a combination of market intelligence, surveys and direct contact with customers is necessary to measure *influence*.

INTERNAL MEASURES OF PERFORMANCE

Collecting data in order to measure marketing performance does not need to be an expensive and time-consuming business. It quickly becomes counter-productive if vast amounts of time and resources are diverted to research, analysis, monitoring and reporting. Organisations often overlook the potential of readily available information from internal sources. In many cases, it is the internal measures that are the most important. It is interesting and sometimes useful to know how individual performance compares with sector averages and with particular competitor organisations. Indeed, such measures provide a necessary reality check on strategic thinking. However, once the vision, mission, objectives and tactics are set, the focus should be on how well marketing is performing against the measures the organisation has set for itself. Every organisation is sufficiently unique for it to be necessary to treat external comparisons with a certain amount of qualification. What matters ultimately – to customers, shareholders, suppliers, staff, managers and other stakeholders – is how well it is doing to deliver its value propositions.

The key to collecting data is to incorporate it within routine activity rather than having to run additional processes for capture. MkIS, customer databases, web analytics and technology generally make this an awful lot easier. Care and attention are required when planning data capture in order to ensure that the required information is clearly defined and recorded at the most appropriate time. The secret with all data capture is getting it right first time. It is inefficient to go back to source materials to extract useful details that could – and should – have been recorded initially.

A series of metrics can be used based on internal sources. Table 3.8 illustrates some examples.

Table 3.8	Measuring marketing performance from internal sources	
Dimension	**Appropriate metrics**	**Comments**
Recruitment	■ Number of new customers ■ Cost of customer acquisition ■ Lead conversion rate	The marketing funnel as a concept illustrates the move of potential customers through to becoming leads and then finally customers. Knowing the dynamics of this process including the number of customers gained in any particular period is fundamental to implementing effective marketing strategies. Measuring the cost of conversion and comparing with previous results also shows whether it is becoming easier or harder to secure new custom.
Retention	■ Customer retention rate ■ Customer loyalty ■ Churn rates (customer defection) ■ Lifetime customer values	The frequently repeated maxim that it is cheaper and easier to secure new sales from existing customers than it is to attract new customers is almost certainly true in most markets. One of the present trends is for a general decrease in loyalty. The Internet makes it easier for customers to be informed of other available suppliers and prices, and switching costs have been minimised. Organisations have to work

(Continued)

Table 3.8	(Continued)	
Dimension	**Appropriate metrics**	**Comments**
		harder to keep their customers by providing value, by understanding their customers, by engaging with them and by rewarding loyalty.
Attitude	■ Customer satisfaction	Customer satisfaction levels are an indicator of likely loyalty. Satisfied customers will return for repeat purchases, thus increasing lifetime value and reducing the ratio of marketing costs to sales. Happy customers also promote goods and services to other potential customers, ensuring the organisation benefits from cost-free word of mouth promotion. Knowing how highly customers regard the organisation helps the organisation to make adjustments to the promotional mix or even just to provide information to answer questions and resolve misunderstandings.
Performance	■ Lifetime values ■ Average spend per customer ■ Average spend per visit ■ Profit ■ Value of sales	In the end, the aim of all marketing activity is to secure improved financial performance and long-term survival of the organisation. The ultimate criteria for measuring the effectiveness of marketing is a return in the form of increased sales and profitability.
Communications	■ Website analytics ■ Number of mailouts and emails ■ Analysis of customer service enquiries	Metrics for communications and customer engagement are discussed above.

INNOVATION AND LEARNING MEASURES OF PERFORMANCE

One of the four quadrants of the Balanced Scorecard is learning and growth (see Chapter 8). This highlights the importance of focusing on development, innovation and change as part of the overall monitoring of performance. Learning is not just staff development and training (although this is important). It is also a matter of the organisation learning, responding more effectively to customer needs by changing its manner of engagement. Metrics may include targets for staff satisfaction, appraisal, and personal and professional development, but should also reflect a more holistic dimension.

Table 3.9	Organisational goals and possible innovation and learning targets
Organisational goal	**Possible innovation and learning targets**
To raise the level of skills of staff	▪ Total spend on training and development ▪ Number of days of on-the-job and off-the-job training ▪ Investment per member of staff
To be recognised as an equal opportunities employer	Equal opportunity measures (gender, ethnicity, age, etc.)
To raise staff loyalty and morale	▪ Staff satisfaction surveys ▪ Staff turnover ▪ Average number of days taken as sick leave
To retain the knowledge and experience of the best staff members	▪ Number of internal promotions ▪ Amount of cross-functional activity
To improve staff performance	▪ Number of staff achieving performance-related bonuses ▪ Revenue per employee
To remain at the forefront of innovation	▪ Spend on research and development (compared with competitors) ▪ Number of new products introduced

In describing the quadrant, Kaplan and Nolan described three distinct areas of focus:

- information capital
- organisation capital
- human capital

As always, measures of performance should link to the strategic objectives, to what is important to the organisation and its stakeholders, and this is exactly what the Balanced Scorecard model promotes. We should be interested in how the organisation must change and innovate in order to deliver its core purpose and satisfy its objectives. Table 3.9 illustrates some organisational goals with possible innovation and learning targets.

ACTIVITY 3.1

Consider a large marketing initiative with which you are involved or with which you are familiar. Select a range of suitable metrics for measuring its performance. Make sure you cover a range of different measures, such as productivity, accounting measures, and learning and growth. For each of the chosen metrics, state from where and how you would draw the required data and any difficulties that might arise from doing so. How might you respond to disappointing results if the performance measures revealed lower outcomes than expected?

PERFORMANCE MEASURES

In this section, we examine how information collected from various performance measures may be analysed to enable managers to take decisions resulting in positive change.

PRODUCTIVITY ANALYSIS (INPUTS VERSUS OUTPUTS)

We have already noted above that productivity may be measured fairly easily when an organisation or function is engaged in the process of converting tangible inputs into tangible outputs (see section 1.3). Productivity can be expressed very simply as a ratio of outputs to inputs. Productivity improves when more outputs are generated per unit of input.

$$Productivity = outputs/inputs$$

Sophisticated cost accounting techniques are required to enable the organisation to allocate and apportion direct and indirect costs to the unit of input. As an organisation moves from single to multiple inputs and outputs, it becomes more difficult to gather the data, and when delivering services rather than products, one must account for time, skill and knowledge as well.

It should always be remembered that such productivity measures are only intelligible when we make comparisons – with previous years, budgets, competitors and sector benchmarks. The trends in productivity are probably more important than the absolute value. We can usually find some measurable unit even when analysing a service provider, public sector or not-for-profit organisation, such as bed occupancy, room utilisation or professional time. The analysis may be conducted for individual processes, divisions or functions, whole organisations or a sector of the economy, provided it is possible to identify a recognisable unit of input and output. Natural efficiencies (known as economies of scale) may be gained through larger scale activity but not always, and sometime diseconomies occur that serve to reduce productivity.

Figure 3.4 illustrates a typical pattern.

Where the graph becomes steeper in the middle section, the ratio of outputs to inputs is higher, showing greater productivity. Productivity then peaks as diseconomies begin to emerge and more units of input are required to generate output. Optimum efficiency is achieved at or close to point X.

There are two alternative approaches to improving productivity (although they are not exclusive): reducing the costs of inputs or increasing

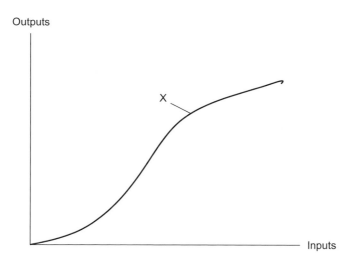

Outputs

X

Inputs

FIGURE 3.4
*Relationship between
inputs and outputs.*

the volume or value of outputs. This is not as easy as it sounds, since scaling back on the costs associated with production or service delivery is liable to have a negative qualitative impact on outputs.

Within the marketing function, various techniques may be tried to get 'more bangs for your bucks' (Table 3.10).

Improving productivity, then, is about finding the best return on the investment, that is marketing. It requires a search to lower costs as well as maximise returns. The process for customer acquisition needs to be highly targeted while the process for customer retention can be tailored and personal. Those customers (new and existing) with the greatest potential for lifetime values need to be prioritised. It is common in customer relationship management to categorise customers in such a way that high value ones are afforded extra careful attention, for good reason. The focus on retention and loyalty allows for cross-selling as well as word of mouth advocacy.

COMPARATIVE ANALYSIS (CHANGES OVER TIME)

In all our considerations of targets, benchmarks and actual performance so far, we have stressed the need to consider trends and variations over time rather than just absolute values. In order to understand and interpret variations, it is necessary to use time series analysis to distinguish between:

- random variations
- seasonal variations
- underlying trends

Table 3.10	Strategies for improving marketing productivity
Productivity improvement method	**Explanation**
Quality management	In section 1.2, we noted several times that it is cheaper to reduce the number of defects occurring than to reject them. The implementation of quality models should improve productivity by identifying and eliminating inefficiencies. The whole process of setting goals and targets, monitoring performance and identifying scope for improvement is designed to increase efficiency (doing something cheaper) and effectiveness (doing something better).
Moving from customer acquisition to customer retention	In a general sense, shifting the primary focus from customer acquisition to customer retention is designed to capitalise on the lower costs associated with increasing lifetime values rather than attracting new leads and converting them. This is not to suggest that customer acquisition is not important but rather to prioritise keeping existing customers ahead of any growth strategy.
Moving from mass marketing to segmented and niche marketing, to individual customer and account marketing	Target marketing enables organisations to focus on the most likely prospects, reducing wasteful activity on those groups with the highest conversion costs. Blanket coverage and a scattergun approach are almost certainly less efficient, both because it will hit people with limited interest and those on the receiving end will feel less attracted by generalised messages.
Cycle time reduction	An analysis of processes and operations can reveal the incidence of idle time which may be shortened or eliminated. The gaps between the end of one activity and the start of the next can be the cause of inefficiencies. It may require a more holistic approach to planning with overlapping cycles or it may be a question of deploying staff skills in a different arrangement.
Management accounting techniques	To improve productivity, it is important to be able to measure it and to have an appreciation of costing. Understandably the Chief Finance Officer (or equivalent) is keen to know what contribution marketing makes to the bottom line. Hard financial targets – including return on investment, return on assets and the contributions to cash flow, profitability and share value – provide a much more convincing argument for not cutting the budget than more rarefied discussions of brand awareness and public profile. To achieve this, the marketing function needs to be able to identify and apportion its costs to units of activity. Overheads (staff time, rent and rates, light and heat, depreciation, etc.) need to be included through a suitable basis (usually time). Armed with a reasonably sophisticated model, the marketing manager is much more able to gauge productivity and any changes to it over time.
Benchmarking	There are many sources of benchmarking data that the marketing function can use to help it set appropriate targets. When used with proper discernment they can add real

(*Continued*)

Productivity improvement method	Explanation
Table 3.10 (Continued)	
	value to performance management. Comparison with sector averages may highlight that an area of activity requires careful analysis if it is widely divergent. Benchmarks help to answer the question 'what should our productivity be?'
Staff training and development	It is always important to involve staff in sharing goals for improving productivity rather be seen to be imposing a potentially threatening system for measuring and assessing their work. Ideally the marketing team should be involved in agreeing targets and suggesting opportunities for improvement. If linked to appraisal and professional development, this should lead to higher levels of commitment and motivation towards achieving those goals.
Research and development	R&D does not need to be solely about product innovation and manufacturing techniques. We have seen that in virtually all quality models there is a need to review existing practice and to test new approaches before implementing them on a wider scale. Most models take a cyclical approach so that innovation is a continuous process. R&D (either internal or an outsourced service) can provide a consultancy resource to the marketing function, exploring ergonomics, integrated operations, productivity trends, technology, skill requirements and processes, and bring their knowledge and experience of other systems to bear.
Technology	Technology – especially information technology – can be used both in the delivery of marketing and in gauging its productivity. Developing models for efficiency, building up a database of historical performance, monitoring and analysing activity, linking operations that may be isolated bureaucratically or geographically, carrying out continuous auditing and producing timely reports are all made easier through the use of technology. Analytical tools, databases and marketing intelligence all come together in the Marketing Intelligence System (MkIS) and if used properly this can be a considerable benefit to monitoring and improving productivity.

Sales, profitability, productivity and other measures are likely to be subject to change over time. Some of these may be purely random and need to be eliminated. Random (or stochastic) effects are more likely to be apparent with smaller samples or over shorter time periods. Using comparative data, it is possible to identify positive and negative movements that are purely random and to smooth out the data. Seasonal variations occur in a repeated cycle, often annually, due to patterns of weather, public and school holidays, festivals and religious observance as well as longer economic or political cycles. From previous records such variations should be predictable and should be included in forecasts and planning. After random and seasonal variations have been identified, the remaining pattern is the underlying trend – upwards, downwards or no change.

SEGMENTAL ANALYSIS (ANALYSIS OF MARKETS)

Market segmentation is a common approach taken to achieve target marketing. The total market population is divided according to certain characteristics that can be associated with a likely appetite for a particular variation of the marketing mix. The assumption is made that, although distinct from the rest of the market, the segment itself is undifferentiated, at least in respect of the relevant characteristic, and as such it can be targeted by a common marketing strategy. The marketing mix suitable for a given segment may only vary in respect of one aspect, such as price, compared with other segments. It is the analysis of the market segments that allows the organisation to develop the right mix in order to maximise sales.

Segmental analysis may be made according to a number of broad categories of characteristics, such as:

- lifestyle
- economic status
- geographical
- demographic
- psychographic

Narrow distinctions – or niche markets – can also be defined. A highly sophisticated form of segmentation is used by political parties to identify likely voting behaviour and susceptibility to canvassing so that they can target their resources in areas where it is likely to have the greatest impact. Segmentation is used to improve performance. It moves the organisation away from mass marketing and allows a more carefully targeted approach. It is conducted through a top-down approach – by which the total market is divided and subdivided according to appropriate distinguishing features – or a bottom-up approach – where market segments are constructed from recognisable types of customers. Segmentation may also be made on the basis of groups of products or services.

Having designed activity around segments it is then possible to monitor performance of those same divisions of the market. Many organisations report their earnings by segment in the annual accounting statements. For example, when KCOM published its accounts for 2007/8 it included the segmental analysis as shown in Table 3.11.

Table 3.11	Segmental analysis from KCOM's annual report[1]					
	Revenue		Operating margin		EBITDA	
	2008	2007	2008	2007	2008	2007
	£'000	£'000	£'000	£'000	£'000	£'000
Segment:						
Integration & Managed Services	278,431	270,959	54,435	59,852	8,649	19,030
Telecoms & Internet Services	244,356	222,667	143,324	133,066	62,849	58,421
Information Services	14,132	13,630	7,605	7,322	4,065	3,684
Other	(19,622)	(24,136)	(1,920)	(19,532)	(6,263)	(10,163)
Continuing activities before exceptional items	517,297	483,120	203,444	180,708	69,300	70,972

[1]Source: http://www.kcom.com/investorcentre/annualreport/2008/financial_statements/notes/note4.asp

The items listed as 'other' are a share of head office overheads and EBITDA is the profit before other items have been deducted (EBITDA stands for earnings before interest, taxes, depreciation and amortisation). In this case, the segmentation has been made on the basis of products and services.

INNOVATION AUDIT

Innovation is important to an organisation, especially in competitive markets, because maintaining advantage very often depends upon responding to change rapidly and flexibly. The opportunities for innovation occur at every point. This includes, among many possibilities:

- new products
- new processes
- new approaches
- new ideas
- new channels
- new suppliers

- new quality models
- new partners
- new working arrangements
- new layouts
- new markets

The purpose of an innovation audit is to help organisations improve their creative and entrepreneurial skills. It follows a structured process of identifying strengths and weaknesses through analysis, interviews, surveys and other techniques. Some audits also include self-assessment questionnaires to take an initial indication of present activity. The audit should show how innovation is currently being fostered within the organisation and what the inhibitors are. It should help the organisation benchmark its approach to innovation against recognised best practice. The outcome of the audit is usually in the form of a report of the findings together with recommendations for developing innovative capabilities further.

The main components for innovation – and hence for innovation audits to focus on – are:

- organisational climate
- current performance
- policies
- practices
- cognitive styles

The organisational climate determines the degree of encouragement for innovation. The 'tone at the top' sets the vision for the rest of the organisation. To succeed, innovation requires its own strategy that is linked to the organisation's business goals. An audit would need to identify from staff at all levels the extent to which innovation is encouraged. Traditional, hierarchical organisations tend to have a high degree of formalisation and bureaucracy, requiring that operations follow strict procedures with little scope for innovation. This climate may also apply to the ways in which senior managers tackle strategic planning and problem solving. While such an approach may be low in risk and avoid the possibility of being blamed for deviating from protocol, it may also lead to stagnation. This in turn may erode the organisation's ability to compete or deliver its primary aims. To some extent, the licence to innovate is also a licence to make mistakes. Certain management styles may resist allowing such a possibility but that is how organisations, as well as people, learn and develop. The growth and learning quadrant of the Balanced Scorecard reflects the importance of positive change. There is nothing wrong with taking risks, provided they are understood and that appropriate measures have been taken to mitigate them.

The innovation audit will attempt to measure the *current performance* in respect of new approaches. To do this, it will need to consider questions like:

■ How are ideas generated?

■ Who is involved in the problem solving process?

■ Does the organisation follow structured techniques for stimulating innovative responses?

■ What is the ratio of new ideas to ones implemented or of prototypes to launch?

There are a number of techniques for generating new ideas and stimulating innovative approaches. Common ones include:

■ brainstorming
■ synectics (what if)
■ mind mapping
■ role play
■ analogy and metaphor
■ six thinking hats
■ horizon scanning
■ six questions (who, why, where, what, when, how)
■ lateral thinking

Formal *policies* highlight the ways in which innovative approaches have been enshrined in the organisation and its operations. It is one thing for the CEO to declare that novel and creative thinking is encouraged if in practice the policies of the organisation make this difficult. Policies cover all aspects of organisational activity. They may reveal implicit or explicit support for innovative approaches, either by creating a more relaxed environment where staff feel that is okay to try new approaches or by a proactive support of innovation. The policies will impact on key aspects such as:

■ communication
■ planning
■ group work
■ accountability
■ allocation of resources
■ authorisation

Successful innovative organisations need frameworks in which progressive and alternative ideas may be proposed and implemented. This does not mean that accountability is removed, rather that senior managers (the ultimate risk owners) have delegated some of their responsibilities for creativity to others further down the chain. At all levels, there needs to be a balance between structured activity and greater openness to change.

Practices under scrutiny through the innovation audit include the processes for evaluating new proposals. Creativity is often stifled because proposals do not conform to expectation.

Innovation as an approach fits better with certain *cognitive styles* of personality and behaviour. It is more effective when an individual or team regards innovation as a natural and continuous process. Someone with an active desire to search for new ways of approaching situations should be one of the people to consider for being an innovation champion. They also need the courage to be different, to be tenacious and to learn to accept that sometimes new approaches will fail.

Some of the cognitive styles can be learnt, and innovative organisations provide training and development opportunities for their staff to develop the good habits and techniques. It is also important to ensure that problem solving teams have the right balance of personalities. There are a number of techniques and models used to profile team roles, one of the most popular and well-known being Belbin. Belbin's team roles include a plant, the name given to a creative problem-solver. However, a team of plants is unlikely to succeed since they tend to be too preoccupied in new ideas and may not be any good at developing or communicating them. Sometimes people need someone else to be asking searching questions in order to stimulate their creativity. Plants need coordinators, shapers, teamworkers, completer-finishers and others to complement their cognitive style and turn the innovative idea into a workable solution.[6]

COMPETITOR COMPARISONS AND BENCHMARKING

A lot has been said in the previous sections about the use of benchmarks and the value of comparisons with competitors. These are of value if taken as part of a wider perspective and must be treated with an appropriate degree of circumspection. While interesting the comparisons may not of themselves be very revealing. Organisations are unique in their size, shape, aims, history, culture, skills, ambitions, appetite for risk, performance, etc., and so at best we may look at similar firms with similar profiles. This can be helpful in setting targets or judging how well the organisation is performing. However, there is a danger that it can become a distraction. Trends over time and comparisons with internal targets may be more important and more useful.

---

[6]For more on Belbin's team roles refer to http://www.belbin.com

Guidelines for competitor comparisons and benchmarking may be summarised as follows:

- The use of competitor data and benchmarks needs to be part of a planned and systematic approach to performance management, based on a genuine need for making external comparisons rather than relying on internal targets and historical results. Specific high-priority areas of activity should be selected for making such comparisons where there is an accepted urgency for driving improvements.

- The competitors selected need to match the organisation as closely as possible, with consideration given to the sector, size, vision, strategic priorities and product portfolio. More than one competitor should be used for comparison purposes to reduce bias.

- Comparisons should be made and assessed over a period of time in order to establish trends.

QUESTION 3.2

Construct a survey that might be used with (a) staff and (b) senior managers as part of an innovation audit within an organisation with which you are familiar. What other indicators would you use to help you analyse the extent to which new ways of thinking are encouraged by the organisational climate, by its policies and practice and by the cognitive skills of the staff involved?

REFERENCE

Sevin, C., 1965. Marketing Productivity Analysis. McGraw Hill, New York.

FURTHER READING

Clark, B., 1998. Measuring performance: the marketing perspective. In: N., Andy, W., Daniel (Eds.) Business Performance Measurement: Theory and Practice. Cambridge University Press.

Senior Examiner's Comments – Section One

For Section 1, the assessment will require you to analyse the structure of the marketing function of an organisation to demonstrate the understanding of how it fits within the larger context of the organisation. You will need to include critical evaluation of the current organisation and marketing structure in order to generate value through marketing activity. Consideration may have to be given to the analysis of current processes for marketing and development of these to ensure compliance with best practice, emphasis should be paid to how the marketing function should use quality systems and ensure compliance with these along with the benefits gained.

The expectation of the assessment for this section is that you will consider the objectives of the marketing operation and how the structure and processes currently used enable or hinder the fulfilment of the objectives, recommending ways to improve, measure and monitor performance. The recommendation of appropriate improvements is of key importance throughout the assessment. You will be expected to evaluate measures, while also needing to develop your own measures, demonstrating how to be creative and innovative in terms of ensuring that marketing provides value for money (VFM) for the organisation.

It is expected that you will take a holistic view of the situation and tasks, producing an integrated piece of work that clearly demonstrates links between the tasks described in the assessment brief. These tasks are to be considered as a whole rather than as separate parts, with each task having implications for the others.

Managing Marketing Teams

CHAPTER 4

Management, Leadership and Establishing Teams

2.1 Critically evaluate the differences between management and leadership and identify the role of an 'operational marketing manager'.

2.2 Determine the needs for and show how to establish and build synergistic and harmonious marketing teams including preparing a plan to show how teams should be structured to deliver organisational and marketing objectives.

2.3 Propose a range of approaches for the sourcing of a team, including consideration of recruitment, training and development to provide the right balance of competency and skills.

2.1:

- leadership traits, skills and attitude
- leadership and management styles, for example, Action-Centred Leadership, Transactional Leadership, Transformational Leadership, Situational Leadership, the management styles continuum
- the scope of leadership – providing strategic direction
- the manager's role – planning, organising, co-ordinating, controlling, communication, teambuilding, coaching, networking, developing the functions of the marketing manager – information, value creation, communications
- reflect on personal approach to management and leadership and produce a personal development plan

2.2:

- *structuring the team* – the team audit, functional roles, team roles
- *team development and talent management* – stages in team development, team cohesiveness, high-performance teams, the manager's role
- job analysis, job design, job enlargement, job enrichment
- competency development requirements
- flexible working practices assess and apply a range of team theories, for example, Belbin's team roles, Tuckman's stages of team development

2.3:

- *recruitment channels* – internally and externally
- *selection tools* – job description, person specification
- *selection techniques* – assessment centres, interviews
- *on-boarding* – induction
- training and development
- outsourcing of jobs/projects
- *recruitment evaluation* – determining recruitment effectiveness
- legal considerations when recruiting

MANAGEMENT ROLES

Management is one of those words that is in such common use that people think they share a common view of its meaning. Mintzberg (1973), based on researching the work of managers (confined to chief executives), concluded that they adopted a variety of roles during the day (Figure 4.1 and Figure 4.2), essentially this consisted of a mass of fragmented activities, constant interruption, pressure for immediate answers and reliance on word-of-mouth messages. Managers value 'soft' information, often acquired through gossip, hearsay and speculation. Consequently, important information for the organisation is held, not necessarily in the memory of its computers but, in the minds of its managers. Mintzberg offered a view of management based on 'roles'.

Each of the ten roles covers a different aspect of managerial work. The ten roles form an integrated whole but different managers are likely to give greater prominence to different roles as well as relative emphasis depending on work aspects considered. For example, sales managers tend to spend relatively more time in their interpersonal roles, while production managers tend to devote more attention to the decisional roles. Any single

Role category	Role	Indicative behaviour
Interpersonal	Figurehead	Performs ceremonial and symbolic duties such as greeting visitors, signing legal documents
	Leader	Sets the strategic direction of the organization, motivates managers and other staff
	Liaison	Maintains information links both inside and outside the organization
Informational	Monitor	Seeks and receives information, scans periodicals and reports, maintains personal contacts
	Disseminator	Forwards information to other organization members, sends memos and reports
	Spokesperson	Transmits information to outsiders through speeches, reports and memos
	Entrepreneur	Initiates improvement projects, identifies new ideas, delegates responsibility to others
Decisional	Disturbance Handler	Takes corrective action during disputes or crises, resolves conflicts among subordinates, adapts to environmental crises
	Resource Allocator	Decides who gets resources, scheduling, budgeting, sets priorities
	Negotiator	Represents department during negotiation of contracts, sales, purchases, budgets

FIGURE 4.1

Mintzberg's managerial roles.
Source: Mintzberg (1973).

manager is likely to emphasise different roles depending on the aspect of their work considered. Mintzberg found that the amount of time spent in each of the three main categories of roles varied with the level of the manager. For example, first-line supervisory positions are likely to have more decisional roles (at a day-to-day operational level). Senior managers spend more time on interpersonal roles. Middle managers tend to be more occupied with informational roles. Roles will also change with culture and organisational size.

Mintzberg and other management researchers (e.g. Kotter) found that managers in fact spent relatively little time working on the classical perspective of marketing management, analysis, planning, implementation and control. They came to this conclusion quite simply by following them around all day. Gaining information from the world around, for example, becomes a more important role, the more senior the manager as informal discussions with other senior managers and experts are the best way of building a view of the longer term environment in which the business must compete. Without this input it is really difficult for senior manager to build a future view beyond the time frame of standard research reports.

LEADERSHIP AND MANAGEMENT OF TEAMS

Not all leaders are managers and not all managers are leaders. However, managers can be leaders and vice versa. Managers and leaders will both have some activity in common. However, what distinguishes a leader from a manager is more a question of the balance of activities that comprise a job. There is an expectation that leaders engage in activities that support their central function of focusing on the strategic direction of the organisation.

John Kotter (2001) makes a distinction between leadership and management. Management is about coping with complexity by planning and budgeting (usually for one month/ year ahead) while he states that leadership, by contrast, is about coping with change by setting a direction though visions and strategy. The distinction is brought out in the present era of rapid technological change, changing demographics, economic turbulence and increasing levels of competition. He brings this distinction home by using an example of a peacetime army which works well with sound administration and management throughout but with leadership concentrated at the top of the hierarchy. In contrast, a wartime army requires competent leadership throughout as he states (p. 86) that no one has worked out how to manage people into battle, they have to be led. Kotter discusses more differences between leadership and managers and some more of these ideas are summarised in Table 4.1

Gosling and Mintzberg (2003) provide a refreshingly different perspective on what management is. Rather than a collection of attributes in which one management writer's list is fairly similar to any other, they consider

Table 4.1	Based on the ideas from Kotter (1991, p. 86)	
	Managing – coping with complexity	*Leading/leadership* – coping with change
Complexity	Managed through planning and budgeting Establishing detailed approaches to achieving the plan	Setting direction through visions and strategies
Developing the capacity to achieve the plan/vision	Organising Staffing Creating organisation structure and job roles Suitable recruitment Communicating the plan Delegation	– Communicating the vision/ new direction – Selecting the appropriate people to whom the vision should be communicated who can create the groups of likeminded people to commit to its achievement
Ensuring that the plan or vision is achieved	Controlling, problem solving, monitoring formal and informal targets	Motivating and inspiring people to achieve success

the problem of trying to reconcile some long standing, seemingly incompatible, management mantras. For example:

Be local and be global.

Change perpetually and maintain order.

Make the numbers (i.e. achieve your performance targets) while nurturing your people.

Their conclusion is that some of these objectives are mutually exclusive. The answer lies in how the manager should think in trying to address these and many other seemingly irreconcilable problems that they must resolve as managers. To do this requires the manager to have various mindsets. These are the tools which she or he must learn to be great managers. The five mindsets they came up with are termed:

1. The Reflective MindSet
    Make time for digesting (i.e. processing and learning from) your experiences.

2. The Analytical MindSet
    Analysis is all around us from industry analysis (i.e. the context in which we compete) to relationship analysis (e.g. 360 degree feedback). The main problem here is too much analysis. To use Gosling and Mintzberg's example – the marketer can be so busy studying consumers that they miss the sale. The focus with this mindset is to move beyond the analysis of the obvious, to test the assumptions on which the analysis is based. This can lead you to questioning, for example, why the organisation has decided to launch a new product or the basis of resourcing a new marketing campaign based on the assumptions behind optimistic forecast which no one thought to question. Forecasts often become a perceived reality only disproved when a different outcome is achieved.

3. The Worldly MindSet
    This is in contrast to the global perspective that sees the world as a homogeneous landscape and ignores difference. A worldly mindset sensitises managers to look out for local differences and issues. This ranges from consumers in the market and how they consume, to the supply chain and manufacturing operations

4. The Collaborative MindSet
    Leaders do not necessarily do, or command to be done, 'things' that the organisation does. However, they do set up

structures and processes to enable things to be 'done'. To do this successfully requires an understanding about how people collaborate to work effectively. Gosling and Mintzberg (2003)explain this effectively when they ask who manages self managing teams (p. 60)? People in teams must collaborate within the team and between teams: successful leaders setting up these teams must understand how this collaboration works.

5. The Action MindSet

This is perhaps most curiously named as it is more about a call to sensitivity than a call to action. In other words, be sensitive to change and that which requires changing for the benefit of the organisation and to ensure that the unchanged continues to prosper. In other words do not simply focus on that which needs to be changed but also apply leadership to the unchanged organisation. It too needs leadership.

Extending Knowledge

Kotter's writing on the distinction between leaders and managers is well worth reading. He takes an applied approach and writes this in an easy to read style.

Kotter, J.P., 2001. What Leaders Really Do. Harvard Business Review – BEST OF HBR Breakthrough Leadership, December.

ACTIVITY 4.1

(a) Think about Kotter's war example and provide your own example that contrasts a situation in which you 'managed' with one in which you 'led'.

(b) Obtain a copy of Kotter's Harvard Business Review paper and provide an example of how you already apply these ideas to your work. Where you do not already do this, consider how you *could* apply these ideas. Are there any experiences that you need to have at work to help you to complete this activity effectively? Discuss with you manager.

LEADERSHIP CHARACTERISTICS

Five Characteristics of Leadership

- *Challenging the process* – encouraging others to develop new ideas and judicious risk taking.

- Inspiring a shared vision about the future.

■ *Enabling others to act* – encouraging collaboration, co-operation, building teams and empowering others.

■ *Modelling the way* – planning and reviewing progress and taking corrective action in a way that gains the respect of others; being clear about values and acting in a manner consistent with them.

■ Recognizing and celebrating others' achievements.

Source: Kouzes and Posner (2002)

UNDERSTANDING LEADERSHIP AND MANAGEMENT STYLES

Various perspectives of leadership styles exist. A selection is presented below and these include so-called *situational perspectives* (often termed contingent models) in which managers adapt their approach to influencing others dependent on the context in which they do this and will change their approach accordingly. Models of this type include 'Action-Centred Leadership and Tannenbaum's management styles continuum'. Another general approach considers leadership from the perspective of the *characteristics and traits* of leaders. This includes the five (big) traits identified by McCrae and John (1992) and the contrasting transactional–transformational leadership perspective.

Situational Perspectives Models

Action-Centred Leadership

John Adair's (2002) Action-Centred Leadership model is based on three parts:

1. Defining the task

2. Managing the team or group

3. Managing individuals

People need to be briefed properly about the objectives that need to be achieved, what needs to be done, why, how and when. The extent to which all of this needs to be spelled out by the leader or manager will depend on the people involved, the work context and the nature of any particular task. In a situation where there is an expectation that tasks will be delegated, there is no need to go into great detail about how something should be done because this will be the responsibility of the person carrying out the task. The purpose of the business is to deliver something of value to people.

The leader is responsible for ensuring that the marketing task determines what that value is, and then organises work in the most effective and efficient way to deliver it (see Figure 4.1).

Core Functions of Leadership

Adair sets out the core functions of leadership that are central to the Action-Centred Leadership model (see Figure 4.2):

Planning	Seeking information, defining and allocating tasks, setting aims, initiating, briefing, setting standards.
Controlling	Maintaining standards, ensuring progress, ongoing decision-making.
Supporting	Individuals' contributions, encouraging team spirit, reconciling, morale.
Informing	Clarifying tasks and plans, updating, receiving feedback and interpreting.
Evaluating	Feasibility of ideas, performance, enabling self-assessment.

The Action-Centred Leadership model, therefore, does not stand alone; it must be part of an integrated approach to managing and leading. There should be a strong emphasis on applying these principles through training (Table 4.2).

Tannenbaum and Schmidts' (1973) Leadership Continuum

Tannenbaum and Schmidts' (1973) leadership continuum perceives of leaders as operating in a variety of ways from a completely authoritarian, autocratic approach (point 1 below) to a more inclusive, consultative, democratic approach (point 7 below). This is a more sophisticated perspective in which the tendency to behave operates in a continuum. The leader will be located at a point on this continuum depending on attributes (including personality) intrinsic to them, forces or characteristics intrinsic to their staff and forces operating in the business environment or a specific situation.

FIGURE 4.2

Functions of leadership.
Source: Adair (1992);
Adair, J. (2002) Team
Leadership, London: Pan.

1. The manager decides and announces the decision. The manager reviews options in light of aims, issues, priorities, timescales and so on, then decides the actions and informs the team of the decision. The manager will probably have considered how the team will react, but the team plays no active part in making the decision.

2. The manager decides and then 'sells' the decision to the group. The manager makes the decision as above, and then explains reasons to the team, particularly the positive benefits that the team will enjoy from it. In doing so, the manager is seen by the team to recognise their importance and to have some concern for the team.

3. The manager presents the decision with background ideas and invites questions.

    The manager presents the decision along with some of the background which led to it. The team is invited to ask questions and discuss with the manager the rationale behind the decision, which enables the team to understand and accept or agree with the

Table 4.2	Adair's leadership checklist		
Key functions	**Task**	**Team**	**Individual**
Define objectives	Clarify task Obtain information Identify resources and constraints	Assemble team Give reasons why Define accountability	Involve each person Gain acceptance
Plan and decide	Consider options Establish priorities Plan time	Consult Encourage ideas Agree standards	Listen Assess abilities Delegate Agree targets
Organize	Establish control Brief plan Obtain feedback	Structure Answer questions Prepare and train	Check understanding Counsel Enthuse
Control and support	Maintain standards Report progress Adjust plan if necessary Set personal example	Co-ordinate Maintain external co-operation Relieve tension	Guide and encourage Recognize effort Discipline
Review	Evaluate results against objectives Consider action	Recognize team's Success Learn from setbacks	Appraise performance Identify further training Needs Aid personal growth

decision more easily than in 1 and 2 above. This more participative and involving approach enables the team to appreciate the issues and reasons for the decision, and the implications of all the options. This will have a more motivational approach than 1 or 2 because of the higher level of team involvement and discussion.

4. The manager suggests a provisional decision and invites discussion about it.

    The manager discusses and reviews the provisional decision with the team on the basis that the manager will take on board the views and then finally decide. This enables the team to have some real influence over the shape of the manager's final decision. This also acknowledges that the team has something to contribute to the decision-making process, which is more involving and therefore motivating than the previous level.

5. The manager presents the situation or problem, gets suggestions and then decides.

    The manager presents the situation, and maybe some options, to the team. The team is encouraged and expected to offer ideas and additional options, and discuss implications of each possible course of action. The manager then decides which option to take.

6. The manager explains the situation defines the parameters and asks the team to decide. At this level, the manager has effectively delegated responsibility for the decision to the team, albeit within the manager's stated limits. The manager may or may not choose to be a part of the team which decides. While this level appears to gives a huge responsibility to the team, the manager can control the risk and outcomes to an extent, according to the constraints that he stipulates. This level is more motivational than any previous and requires a mature team for any serious situation or problem.

7. The manager allows the team to identify the problem, develop the options and decide on the action, within the manager's authority limits. The team is given responsibility for identifying and analysing the situation or problem; the process for resolving it; developing and assessing options; evaluating implications and then deciding on and implementing a course of action.

LEADERSHIP TRAITS, SKILLS AND ATTITUDE

Five Basic Group Traits

What makes an effective leader? Most successful leaders can operate in different organisations and this suggests that there are attributes linked to the individual that makes a good leader. Leadership traits has a precise meaning in terms of the ideas presented from psychology, in contrast to the more general usage of this term. What types of characteristics can this include in the context of discussing leadership? McCrae and John (1992) identified five basic groups of traits which could be considered as some of the basic building blocks of personality. In their paper on this subject, they affirm that 'The five-factor model can be profitably used in most applied settings' (1992: p. 206). They labelled these five traits (to some extent integrating the ideas of many researchers) as extraversion, agreeableness, conscientiousness, neuroticism and openness. Generally positive values on all factors are found in leaders, except 'neuroticism, where low levels are desirable (Table 4.3).

Transactional Leadership, Transformational Leadership

Large changes have been, and will continue to, take place in the work environment with the influence of globalisation, market forces and technologies which in turn affects work force behaviour and expectations. Van Eeden and Cilliers (2008), pp. 253–255) suggest that changes are taking place in cultural patterns, role definitions, structures, policies, procedures and technologies, and that leadership is central to successful organisational transformation. They are not alone in contending that the transactional–transformational model of leadership provides a valuable framework for exploring the role of the leader in a changing work environment. Many, they suggest, support the view that transformational leadership provides an ideal of leadership, given contemporary developments in the global business world including doing business internationally and in multicultural environments.

Before describing the characteristics of the transformational leader we should consider the characteristics of the contrasting, transactional leader

Table 4.3	Five main personality traits
Factor (trait) category name	Adjectives describing the trait (Note that the trait heading embraces a variety of personality attributes which are classified under the heading)
Extraversion	Active, assertive, energetic, enthusiastic, outgoing, talkative
Agreeableness	Appreciative, forgiving, generous, kind, sympathetic, trusting
Conscientiousness	Efficient, organised, planful, reliable, responsible, thorough
Neuroticism	Anxious, self-pitying, tense, touchy, unstable, worrying
Openness	Artistic, curious, imaginative, insightful, original, wide interests

Source: McCrae and John (1992).

in this view of leadership. In transactional leadership, the leader clarifies what followers need to do as their part of a transaction (successfully complete the task) to receive a reward or avoid punishment (satisfaction of the followers' needs) that is dependent on completion of the transaction (satisfying the leader's needs). There are two management approaches engaged in by people adopting this leadership style namely active or passive management. In the case of *active management by exception*, the leader looks for mistakes, irregularities, exceptions, deviations from standards, complaints, infractions of rules and regulations, and failures, and he or she takes corrective action before or when these occur. *Passive management by exception* implies that the leader is reactive and waits to be informed about errors and deviances before taking action.

Transformational leaders, in contrast, move followers beyond their self-interests for the good of the group or organisation. In an ideal form, they achieve a position in which followers respect, admire, and trust the leader and emulate his or her behaviour, assume his or her values and are committed to achieving his or her vision. The leader shows dedication, a strong sense of purpose and perseverance, and confidence in the purpose and the actions of the group that helps to ensure the success of the group and gives followers a sense of empowerment and ownership. He or she behaves morally and ethically. In addition, he or she acts as a mentor giving personal attention, listening to others' concerns and providing feedback, advice, support and encouragement. The leader furthermore designs appropriate strategies to develop individual followers to achieve higher levels of motivation, potential and performance providing support and monitoring progress (van Eeden and Cilliers, 2008, p. 255).

Knowledge work will dominate the twenty-first century. It requires more envisioning, enabling and empowering leadership, all of which are central to transformational leadership (Bass, 1997). Leaders must move beyond the transactional reward–punishment exchange relationship to develop successful organisations in the twenty-first century. In contrast to the transactional leader, who requires subordinates to comply with his or her direction, transformational or charismatic leaders operate in a different way. The transformational leader motivates, inspires and energises staff and ensures that they understand the vision for the future of the organisation. This need not be done in some high-octane, major organisational event but can operate at a much more subtle, low-key and continuous way from talking to individual members of staff, presence at meetings, through to the image that the leader projects for the organisation that motivates employees to deliver that vision. Steve Jobs of Apple in the United States and Richard Branson of Virgin in the UK are two of the better known examples of this type of leader.

The transactional–transformational leadership framework can be extended to describe teams and group effects as well as how whole organisations differ. People jockey for positions in a transactional group, whereas they share common goals in a transformational group. Rules and regulations dominate the transactional organisation, while adaptability is a characteristic of the transformational organisation.

The Scope of Leadership – Providing Strategic Direction

An important role of leadership is providing strategic direction. This is something that really cannot be outsourced and must be controlled closely by the leader. One contrasting perspective in which to view strategic direction is connected with transactional–transformational leadership styles. To some extent, this is also connected to a relative emphasis on efficiency or effectiveness.

Too many leaders operate at the transactional level where they are brought in to 'sort out' the organisation. Most commonly this means a focus on increased efficiency, slashing costs, selling weak performing brands and businesses, getting rid of staff and selling assets. According to Montgomery (2008, p. 57) 'the challenge [of a leader] is a matter not of unearthing an existing purpose but of forging one'. So when Lou Gerstner put together strategic direction for IBM, he decided that it would no longer focus on the invention of technology but on its application. Similarly Steve Jobs transformed Apple in the late 1990s when its strategy was to focus on high end, differentiated computers even though the market was telling the company (through sales and share price) that this was of decreasing interest. On returning to the company as the CEO, Steve Jobs declared the focus to be as a passionate design company that believed technology would change the world.

ACTIVITY 4.2

Identify the leadership style and strategic approach in your organisation. You could focus either on the CEO of the group or where this makes more sense of your business area. To what extent does your leader combine leadership style with an efficient/effective focus?

TEAMS

Introduction

Organisations operate within the external marketing environment. They must align themselves with this environment if they are to maintain long-term competitiveness. The complexity of the marketing environment means increasingly that work is undertaken and implemented by teams rather than by individuals. Teams must work effectively and they too must adapt to the changing requirements of the business environment. This is crucial if marketing strategy is to be implemented fully and effectively. For this to happen, it requires positive action within the organisation to foster a culture of interdependency and to maximise employee contribution.

Strategic choice theory suggests that the general strategy and direction of change adopted by an organisation is determined by a powerful individual or group and that they design an organisational hierarchy in order to implement it.

> *The structure they design is supposed to be largely a self-regulating one in which people are assigned roles and given objectives to achieve that will realize a given strategy.*
>
> Stacey (2003, p. 32)

Teams are formed, or exist, to solve organisational problems. They must have clear aims and objectives, comprise an appropriate mix of individuals and be managed to ensure that they make an effective contribution. This does not happen automatically, but requires planning, performance evaluation and strategies to improve the performance of sub-optimal teams when this is diagnosed.

Teams – What are They?

We perhaps assume that we all share a common definition of teams. To clarify our thinking on this subject a definition is helpful:

> *A team is a small number of people with complementary skills who are committed to a common purpose, performance goals, and approach for which they hold themselves mutually accountable.*
>
> Katzenbach and Smith (1994)

The workplace, or functional, role played by individuals is the basis on which they are recruited, in particular if they are specialists.

Work roles may be defined as:

> *The mix of tasks and responsibilities undertaken by individuals or executed within teams.*
>
> Belbin (2004)

Management literature is concerned with teams only in as much as this helps us to understand organisational effectiveness. In other words, how effective were organisations in solving problems and implementing their solutions; that is, how effective were they in their work? In a text written after reflection on his definitive work on teams, Belbin (2000) concluded that the balance of emphasis was too uneven. It tended to focus too much on teams and hardly at all on work. In *Beyond the Team*, Belbin changes his emphasis to focus on the type of work undertaken and how this affects the social arrangements within the organisation for undertaking and completing work. It is useful to remember that the context in which a team operates affects how the team performs and the relationships that develop.

GROUPS VERSUS TEAMS

A high degree of commitment and loyalty is required for people in organisations to operate effectively as teams rather than simply groups. Katzenbach and Smith (1994, pp. 88–89) make the distinction between groups and teams. They suggest that a working group (common in bureaucratic, hierarchical structures) linked to formal work roles is based primarily on individual contributions. Performance is assessed by measuring each individual's contribution. There may still be a co-operative attitude in which individuals discuss issues and problems to improve individual work.

Group performance is the sum contribution of individual members; however, team performance is synergistic. The team achieves more than could be achieved with individuals working essentially on their own, even in a co-operative spirit. The main difference is that teams include mutual accountability, in addition to individual accountability. On other dimensions, the differences between teams and groups tend to be of degree, for example more information sharing, more joint task and target setting and performance review.

Formal groups, or teams, within an organisation may be permanent (e.g. marketing department) or temporary (one-off project to set up a CRM system). They must have clear goals and tasks and their purpose within the organisation is 'to find solutions to structured problems' (Stacey, 2003, p. 68). They may take various forms and can even be autonomous, self-managing and democratic and may even be charged with designing their own approach to a given problem. This is in contrast to the traditional command and control perspective of groups within the organisation operated more along military lines, with edicts from senior management and organisational design focused on reporting and control.

CREATING AND DEVELOPING TEAMS

People obviously implement organisational strategy within the context of organisational structures. In the past, they operated within highly regimented, hierarchical units. As layers have been stripped out of organisational hierarchies, rigid structures and work groups no longer exist. Flatter organisational structures have resulted in a greater degree of self-management. As structures have become flatter, people are forced to work in fluid, rather than permanent, teams. To understand how strategy may be implemented effectively therefore requires the study of management teams and team management.

Marketing Team Types and Contexts

New teams increasingly cut across traditional functional structures and can upset organisational balance on all key attributes unless they are well managed. Piercy (2002) sees changes required in organisational processes to align the organisation 'to market' and these will result in:

- Changes in organizational hierarchies
- Increasing dependence on high-performing, temporary, multi-functional teams organized around market segments
- Process re-engineering
- Transnational networks of organizations
- Learning organizations
- Increased emphasis on key account management

Source: Adapted from Piercy (2002, pp. 235–236).

Forming a team, or teams, to complete a major task within the organisation may be compared with the external activities of building collaborative networks. Successful internal collaborative networks, just like their external counterparts, are about informal processes based on trust, information sharing, joint decision-making and collective responsibility. Ever more frequently, requirements for effective market-led implementation require multi-functional teams that operate across conventional internal boundaries and even external boundaries, as networks including suppliers, distributors and customers are required to solve customer-focused problems.

Extending Knowledge

How to transform marketing from its traditional approach to a relatively new approach of organizing marketing in order to 'go to market'. See Chapter 5 'Total integration: processes and teams take over from departments' in Piercy, N.F., 2002. Market-led Strategic Change: A Guide to Transforming the Process of Going to Market, third ed. Butterworth-Heinemann, Oxford.

Team Diversity and Team Success

Discussion of success of teams has developed beyond classical roles considered by Belbin to include the impact of diversity within the team on the success of team functioning. Such diversity issues concern both demographic diversity – that is, the degree to which team members vary, for example, in terms of age, gender and ethnicity – and diversity in terms of functional specialism. Pelled et al. (1999), on reviewing the literature on diversity in group performance, found that no conclusive influence was evident. Some studies linked diversity to successful performance while others have linked it to unsuccessful performance. Their own conjecture was to suggest an indirect influence on performance through conflict. They suggested that two types of conflict existed:

1. *Task conflict* – is where group members disagree about task issues, including goals, procedures, key areas in which to focus for decision-making and appropriate choices for action. Factors that tend to reduce task conflict include repetitive, routine tasks as well as the length of time the group has been together.

2. *Emotional conflict* – describes the outcome rather than the causes of conflict in that it focuses on interpersonal clashes, which are characterized by negative attributes such as anger, frustration and so on.

Source: Pelled et al. (1999, p. 2).

Pelled et al. concluded that 'task conflict' and its resolution leads to enhanced performance, while emotional conflict tends to diminish performance.

Team Skills, Characteristics and Roles

Belbin (2004), in his research at Henley, concluded that there were only a few ways that people could contribute to teamwork. The essential contributions comprised the following:

- Co-ordinating the efforts of the team
- Creating ideas
- Motivating and driving the team forward
- Exploring resources
- Evaluating options
- Organizing the work
- Following up on detail
- Supporting others
- Providing expertise

Belbin as well as other authors have defined important team roles and assign individuals to these roles based on established personality theories, as illustrated in Table 4.4. Some role names have been amended to fit in more readily with modern approaches to work. Fluid/flexible teams brought together for the life of a task/project result in the term 'Chairman' being replaced by 'Co-ordinator'. Flatter organisational structures rather than rigid hierarchies result in the use of the more appropriate term 'Implementer'. Finally, 'Completer-finisher' has been reduced to 'Completer' to avoid confusion with 'Implementer'.

Please note that Belbin (2004) still employs the original, rather than the amended, terminology (Table 4.4).

ACTIVITY 4.3

Investigate resources available at Belbin Associates' website.

Belbin's work has spawned a website with this as its focus. Visit Belbin Associates' website at http://www.belbin.com/index.htm.

ACTIVITY 4.4

Determine your team role.

Online at http://www.belbin.com – only possible if you have purchased the second edition of Belbin's text (2000).

Stages in Team Development (Tuckman)

There is broad support for the assertion that teams go through various stages after formation. As long as any dysfunctional behaviour does not develop, team performance grows over time, however, not at a constant rate. This is not simply because people, and therefore teams, vary in their effectiveness over time. It is related to a generalisable pattern of development in which performance initially improves at a relatively slow rate as team members get to know each other socially and in terms of the skill set they possess. As team learning develops about task issues, the project and how to co-operate in achieving its objectives, a phase occurs in which performance increases rapidly. In contrast, towards the end of the life of a project team, the rate of development slows down as diminishing returns set in.

A significant advance in thinking on effective teams was the realisation that this was not a static situation but a dynamic process. Team members interact with one another over time and similarly develop competencies and varying degrees of conflict, both resolved and unresolved. Consequently, a perspective of teams is required that takes on board this dynamic process. Various theories of team development have been suggested, the most widely discussed and applied is the theory proposed by Tuckman in which he

Table 4.4	Belbin's team roles		
Belbin's named roles	**Characteristics**	**Positive qualities**	**Allowable weaknesses**
Company worker (amended to 'Implementer')	Conservative, dutiful and predictable	Organising ability, common sense in practical work, hard-working and self-disciplined	Lacks flexibility, unresponsive to unproven ideas – tends to stick to the orthodox
Chairman (amended to 'the Co-ordinator')	Calm, self-confident and controlled	Accomplished in encouraging and obtaining contributions from team members without judgement. A strong sense of objectives	No more than ordinary in terms of intellect or creative ability. Tends to take credit for the effort of the team
Shaper	Highly strung, outgoing, dynamic	Has great drive and a readiness to challenge inertia, ineffectiveness, complacency or self-deception	Prone to provocation, irritation and impatience
Plant	Individualistic, serious minded, unorthodox	Possesses 'genius', imagination, intellect and knowledge	Inclined to disregard practical details. Tends to be preoccupied with ideas and has a strong sense of their ownership
Resource investigator	Extroverted, enthusiastic, curious, communicative	Good at developing contacts and exploring opportunities. Possesses an ability to respond to challenge	Liable to lose interest once the initial fascination has passed
Monitor-evaluator	Sober, unemotional and prudent	Judgement, discretion and hard-headedness	Lacks inspiration or the ability to motivate others
Team worker	Socially orientated, rather mild-mannered and sensitive	Possesses an ability to respond to people and situations and to promote team spirit	Indecisive at moments of crisis
Completer-finisher (Amended to 'Completer')	Painstaking, orderly, conscientious and anxious	A perfectionist with a capacity to follow through. Delivers on time	A tendency to worry about small things. A reluctance to 'let go' – perhaps somewhat obsessive

suggests that team performance goes through four stages of group development over time. These he labelled forming, storming, norming and performing. Later he added a fifth stage which was termed 'adjourning', when a team that had been formed for a project was disbanded upon completion.

Two factors are important in determining, and describing, progression of a team through these stages. These are the resolution of interpersonal relationships and of task activities. In essence, the model by Tuckman describes these two issues, as groups progress through the different stages (Figure 4.3).

Tuckman, working with another colleague, added a stage referred to as 'adjourning' in which the group works on finishing off the project. The project is disbanded and some emotional baggage will result. This may be highly positive, where group members focus on the success of the team, or

---

Forming

Everyone in the embryonic team is yet to feel emotionally attached to it. Members tend to feel a certain degree of anxiety as roles and relationships within the team are established. Inevitably they will compare the new team with the former teams they have been members of.

Group members make an initial assessment of interpersonal relationships and norms within the group. The focus on task is to identify what these are, where task boundaries are and the sort of information required to complete the task(s).

Storming

In this phase, people finally understand their function within the team and team relationships settle. It is possible that in this phase, subgroups start to form and the potential for conflict can foment.

Group members begin to know each other. There may be some conflict not only over leadership but also over how the leader will operate. Members of the group struggle to varying degrees for individual autonomy. Individuals may in fact display a lack of commitment to the demands of particular tasks that they do not favour.

Norming

In this stage, group bonding, team spirit and cohesion develop. Their level of commitment to each other, and to the team, increases. People feel sure about their team identity and role. Group 'norms' literally begin to develop to the extent that the cliched phrase 'That is the way we do things around here' becomes appropriate.

As problems over the demands of particular tasks, and task allocation, have been resolved, conflict diminishes and is more likely manifested in greater cohesiveness in group functioning. Task co-operation and mutual support develops.

Performing

The team has fully committed to achieving its goals. They are flexible and collaborate freely and willingly. Now that people feel comfortable with each other and their work role, they can devote a substantial amount of emotional as well as physical energy to the project. This creates a wonderful environment in which creativity can thrive.

This is the most effective in terms of task activity and interpersonal relationships. The latter are established and almost taken for granted, operating in the background. The focus of activity is on completion of task activity.

FIGURE 4.3 *Tuckman's four stages of team development.*

it may be negative, due to the loss of friendships and emotional work ties established during the term of the project.

ANOTHER STAGE?

All organisations wish their teams to remain at the 'performing' stage. However, the management writer John Adair, in his book *Effective Team-building* (1986), has identified a further stage (dorming) that can come after performing.

This may be regarded as a stage of relative complacency, where people prefer to live on past successes rather than to devote their energies into further innovations and successes. In a sense, team members become institutionalised within their own team and become focused on processes rather than on outcomes.

Each team stage has recognisable characteristics. Sometimes, problems arise during a team stage and other times in the transition from one stage to another.

The Tuckman model is not the only model of team development and it does suffer from some limitations. Perhaps the most important is that not all teams progress through all stages. The model is really an idealised version. With that in mind it still provides a very helpful means of considering team dynamics and progression towards an ideal, highly effective team.

ACTIVITY 4.5

Applying team roles

Consider a team in which you work with all the people in the team. What are your individual roles?

Now answer the following questions:

1. Who establishes team objectives?
2. Who co-ordinates most of the work?
3. Who provides most of the creative ideas?
4. Who takes most of the decisions?
5. Who acts as a mediator/peacemaker in times of internal dispute?
6. Who is the main motivator in the team, providing encouragement and support?
7. Who looks after communication?
8. Who is able to provide constructive criticism and is able to do this in a way that is accepted without conflict?

9. Who is good at overcoming difficult issues and situations?
10. Who takes responsibility for controlling and monitoring work?

If most of your answers focus on the leader, then the team is probably at the forming or storming stage. If most of your answers are focused on the team, then your selected team is very likely to have reached the performing stage.

JOB ANALYSIS AND JOB DESIGN

Job analysis is 'any systematic procedure by which one describes the way a job is performed, the tasks that constitute a job, anchor the skills and abilities necessary to perform a job' (Friedman and Harvey 1986, p. 779). There are various methods that can be used to conduct a job analysis. This for example includes the job analysis interview and the 'task analysis inventory' approach that involves the use of a structured questionnaire listing a large number of tasks for which respondents identify the frequency of performance as well as the importance of each task in their job. Job qualifications include the skills and abilities needed to succeed in the job, and these are often derived through job analysis (Table 4.5).

ACTIVITY 4.6

Job analysis and job design
Find out the approach your organisation takes to job analysis and role definition. Is there a formal approach taken to this as discussed above, including a summary questionnaire that post holders have in the past completed? Perhaps this is currently being undertaken and a full list of post characteristics is being assembled. Alternatively there may be no formal procedure. In this situation, the identification of the need for a new member of staff is based on an inability to cope with the level of work and a manager, or managers, will quickly agree on a list of characteristics required on an informal basis and quickly advertise this.

Is there or what is the list of traits, knowledge and experience required? Identify the characteristics specified in:

(a) Sales and marketing for a senior and a junior management position and compare these two posts.
(b) Another department/specialism with which you frequently work – also including a senior and a junior management position.

COMPETENCIES AND STANDARDS THAT DEFINE A GOOD MANAGER

There are many sets of management competences and organisations sometimes develop their own or use generic management standards. Although the following example is taken from an NHS document it could be applied to many different sectors and contexts.

Table 4.5	Example specification of characteristics specified for a sales post

Traits	Knowledge/experience

■ Integrity
■ Self motivation
■ Concern for ethics
■ Tact
■ Responsibility
■ Creativity
■ Achievement orientation
■ Ambition
	■ Experience in handling large accounts of
	  – company operating strengths/weaknesses
	  – company products and/or services
	  – company procedures
	  – customer's company personnel and personalities
	■ Experience in planning and goal setting of
	  – company personnel and personalities
	  – customer's industry

As an effective manager, you should be able to:

■ Lead a team effectively
■ Identify and set objectives
■ Communicate clearly
■ Manage resources and plan work to achieve maximum benefits
■ Make sound decisions in difficult situations
■ Know when to seek help and do so when appropriate
■ Offer help to those you manage, when they need it
■ Demonstrate leadership qualities through your own example
■ Manage projects
■ Manage change
■ Delegate appropriately – to empower others, to improve services and to develop the skills of the people you manage – without giving up your own responsibilities
■ Consider and act upon constructive feedback from colleagues.

Source: Management for Doctors (February 2006).
www.gmc-uk.org/guidance/current/library/management_for_doctors.asp

The following case study provides an example of a modern conception of management.

CASE STUDY

Siemens

Siemens AG is a global electrical and electronics business employing half a million people around the world. A key pillar of the Siemens' business strategy is the way it manages, develops and motivates its employees.

Fit42010 is Siemens' global Strategy. The four cornerstones of this programme are People Excellence, Operational Excellence, Corporate Responsibility and Portfolio. The business strategy that relates to people management is referred to as People Excellence. The vision is: 'To provide a people experience at Siemens that generates unequalled engagement, commitment and capability, delivering exceptional customer value and organisational goals'.

People Excellence encompasses five key areas:

■ Acquisition – Attraction, selection, integration, entry-level talent

- Identification – Performance Management Process, Succession planning, expert and functional careers, diversity and work–life balance
- Development – Management, graduate and trainee development
- Deployment – Performance management process, job evaluation
- Engagement – Leadership feedback, upward feedback

and consists of four main elements:

- achieving a high performance culture
- increasing the global talent pool
- strengthening expert careers
- Siemens' Leadership Excellence Programme (SLE)

Central to People Excellence is the building of a high performance culture. Feeling part of a successful team is part of the engagement process. Siemens wants its employees to be involved in the business and to feel part of its success. Employees therefore need to know how they fit into the business. Targets for individuals are related to targets for the whole business. A high performance team is one in which all members of the team work towards shared targets and have a sense of shared responsibility for the results the team achieves.

Siemens' talent management philosophy involves making sure that every employee is provided with the guidance and support to achieve their full potential. Everyone has talent and matching talent with task is a business priority and source of competitive advantage. People Excellence supports the business by providing a framework to match talent with task – enabling people to make the best use of their talents, whatever they might be.

By applying the Talent Management philosophy managers are expected to engage and motivate employees throughout the organisation, regardless of hierarchy or organisational boundaries. Talent Management enables job enrichment, where individuals are encouraged to take on extra tasks and responsibilities within an existing job role to make work more rewarding. It also promotes job enlargement, where the scope of the existing job is extended to give a broader range of responsibility, plus extra knowledge and skills development. Talent Management is a global philosophy that is a key part of supporting each of the elements of the Siemens' business strategy.

ACTIVITY 4.7

The case study identifies a number of key themes in modern conceptions of management, for example, fostering a non-hierarchical culture, customer focus, team working, listening, responsive and fast moving. However, this may be the theory of how management should be practised, an issue for all organisations is whether any of the theory is translated into practice and managers are held accountable for ensuring that it happens.

How would you characterise management in your own organisation? Is it like this or is there a gap between the theory and the practice? If the latter, why does this happen?

PLANNING TEAMS FOR EFFECTIVE PERFORMANCE

Belbin (2004, pp. 124–125) concludes that team design should be guided by five interlocking principles:

1 Members of a management team can contribute in two ways to the achievement of team objectives. These are high performance in a functional role in drawing on their professional and technical knowledge and performing effectively in their team role. Belbin

clarifies that this describes a pattern of behavioural characteristics where the manager interacts with others in the team.

2 Each team needs an optimum balance in both functional and team roles. The ideal blend will depend on the goals and tasks that the team faces.

3 The effectiveness of a team will be promoted by the extent to which members correctly recognize and adjust themselves to the relative strengths within the team. This includes both expertise and ability to engage in specific team roles

4 Personal qualities fit members for some team roles while limiting the likelihood that they will succeed in others.

5 A team can deploy its technical resources to best advantage only when it has the requisite range of team roles to ensure sufficient teamwork.

Putting a Team Together

The process of putting a team together must be based on information on the individual in order to ensure that he/she fits organisational requirements. Principal sources of information for this include:

- Psychometric tests
- Self-perception questionnaires
- Colleague-completed assessment of 'perceived team role' capability
- Information gained from staff attending in-company training courses

Belbin also cautions us to ensure that recruitment (or internal reshuffling) does not simply recruit more similar people without achieving a balance in team members in terms of the 'team' as well as functional roles that they perform. With an increase in the number and variety of teams being utilised by organisations, there is an increasing need to understand what in fact makes a team function effectively.

Recruitment

One common mistake in recruitment is to select people to fit in with the organisation. The perspective taken is often concerned foremost with organisational culture rather than role. The former approach is focused on the status quo while the latter takes account of the need for evolution and development in team performance. One aspect of effective team performance probably includes further empowering team members. This increases work scope.

Recruitment that focuses on the team role that must be filled, taking account of existing skills and roles, is likely to be most successful.

> **Extending Knowledge**
> See Belbin (2004) for a full discussion on planning an effective team in Chapter 11 'Designing a team' and Ahmed and Rafiq (2002, pp. 86–87) on empowerment and recruitment.

SOURCING AND TRAINING TEAMS

Introduction

All large organisations have developed human resource management (HRM) departments, and their managers can rely upon the existence of clear personnel policies and back-up through every aspect of concern to personnel management. For many managers, however, there is likely to be little formal support and it is left to them to recruit, select and manage. Even for managers with HRM support, there is a need to understand fully the systems and procedures so that they have sufficient understanding to be able to exert control as needed. In this, the relationship with HRM is exactly the same as with any other specialist function.

The process involves clearly defined stages, and the use of a systematic approach should ensure that you do not overlook anything important and, significantly, it will reduce the area of subjective judgement where people's biases, prejudices and weaknesses can creep in. This supports the most effective recruitment process and minimises individual bias in the recruitment process, which also supports compliance with legal requirements.

INDUCTION AND TRAINING

Every organisation should have an induction programme that provides all the information that new employees and others need, and are able to assimilate, without being overwhelming or diverting them from the essential process of integration into a team. All new employees need some form of introduction to the organisation and the job. A well-planned system of induction provides regular training and/or development sessions. For example, large department stores have a continuing programme of induction with a new course starting every week and special provision for part-time workers. This leaves individual managers in the position of receiving staff who have at least received training that is specific to their job. Some training, such as health and safety awareness, should be given to all employees.

In larger organisations, line managers may take responsibility for monitoring and encouraging each individual at their place of work and for off-the-job training. However, there may be a specialist training and development section that is usually part of the Human Resources Department.

Trends in Induction

Changing Content

- Moving away from being purely about the practicalities of an organisation to discussing culture and values. For example, an online induction and e-learning programme has been developed to introduce the culture for new HR staff in the NHS, and Tesco also uses e-learning for its annual 40,000 new recruits.

- Involving a wide range of personnel in the programme development to ensure that the content continues to match the organisation profile; out-of-date or badly produced material is depressing.

- More awareness of socialisation issues and using induction sessions for cross-function team building.

Procedures

- More written procedures to provide evidence of induction programme, for example, for Investors in People, ISO 9000.

Evaluation

- Holding post-induction reviews, either formally or informally.

- Using statistics (e.g. on early leavers) to monitor the effectiveness of the induction process.

INSIGHT

Without a good induction new employees get off to a bad start and never really understand the organization itself or their role in it. This may lead to:

- Poor integration into the team
- Low morale, particularly for the new employee
- Loss of productivity
- Failure to work to their highest potential

In extreme cases, the new employee leaves, either through resignation or dismissal; the results of our most recent recruitment and retention survey showed that 19 per cent of leavers had less than six months' service. Early leaving results in:

- Additional cost for recruiting a replacement
- Wasted time for the inductor
- Lowering of morale for the remaining staff
- Detriment to the leaver's employment record
- Having to repeat the unproductive learning curve of the leaver
- Damage to the company's reputation

Source: Chartered Institute of Personnel and Development (2006) Recruitment, retention and labour turnover survey 2006. CIPD, London. Available at: http://www.cipd.co.uk/surveys

All new employees should receive an individual induction programme that reflects their specific needs. A typical allocation of induction tasks would be as follows:

- *Line manager/supervisor* – explain the departmental organisation, the requirements of the job, the purpose and operation of any probationary period and the appraisal system.

- *HR* – cover the housekeeping aspects for a new starter (possibly on arrival, certainly on Day 1) such as completing employee forms, taking bank details, explaining the induction programme.

- *Safety officer* – explain health and safety issues.

- *Section supervisor or a nominated colleague* – provide an escorted tour of the department and introduce fellow workers; then give day-to-day guidance in local procedures for the first couple of weeks.

- *Senior manager(s) and/or HR* – give an overview of the organisation, its history, products and services, quality system and culture.

- *Training officer (or line manager)* – describe available training services, then help to develop a personalised training plan. Provide details of other sources of information during induction such as the company intranet or interactive learning facilities.

- *Company representatives from trades unions, sports and social clubs etc* – give details of membership and its benefits.

- *Mentor or 'buddy'* – sometimes inductees are allocated a colleague, not their line manager or anyone from personnel, to help speed up the settling-in period.

The Benefits of Training and Development

- *Improved motivation* – Individuals see their skills base extending and their promotion prospects being enhanced.

- *Lower turnover* – Opportunities for self-improvement, leads to people staying longer in one employment.

- *Higher levels of performance* – Trained and motivated staff are more likely to give of their best, which, in the end, justifies the training budget.

INSIGHT

The Polestar Group is the United Kingdom's leading commercial printer and the fourth largest in the world. The Group aims to be the most innovative and profitable printers in Europe. This means that its staff need to be trained to use the latest high-tech digital equipment. Polestar's employees experience training at work that includes the following: induction training – training in new ways of working, technology and software multiskilling – employees are trained to do several different interrelated jobs learning management, organizational and leadership skills developing skills through a wide range of personal enhancement programmes.

Skilled print workers are in short supply, and the average age of the workforce is high. Polestar has developed a training programme called 'Printdynamics' which is designed to both attract and retain good workers. It is an interactive CD-Rom and online training package that offers comprehensive coverage of the print industry. It guides the trainee through the different print processes. Ensuring that employees are multi-skilled leads to increased job satisfaction and flexibility. Ongoing training often results in improved productivity by eliminating waste and avoiding delays.

Source: http://www.technicalmarketingltd.com/VNO/Polestar/presspack.html

INTERNAL RECRUITING

Internal recruiting has traditionally been done by a manager appointing or promoting people. Some organisations use formal internal advertising to find the best candidate. They will advertise on notice boards, via intranets or newsletters.

Not everyone agrees with formalised internal recruitment:

- Employees may think it is an empty exercise, believing decisions are already made.
- Some managers anticipate problems in succession planning if they must use open internal markets.

To avoid problems, businesses can bring someone impartial – managers from other departments, someone from HR – into the procedure. Internal recruitment can be efficient because:

- The person and the firm know each other.
- Savings on commercial advertising rates for recruitment can be made.

Employees are motivated because they can see the possibility of progression.

Whilst there is a cost in building on existing skills internally, this can be more reliable and less expensive than external recruitment. On the down side:

- Good people outside could be overlooked.
- Unsuccessful internal candidates can feel slighted.
- Entirely new skills may need intensive training.

CASE STUDY

McDonald's

Recruiting, selecting and training for success

McDonald's employs on a large scale. A typical McDonald's employs about 60 people. Most are hourly paid. Managers and office staff are paid a salary. For each job there is a job description which describes the duties of the job and a person specification that describes the skills and personal qualities needed for the job.

Hourly paid workers are recruited through adverts in restaurants, job centres and career fairs. Interviews are planned using the McDonald's interview guide. Candidates are rated on a scale. Jobs are offered to those with higher ratings. The management department recruits managers. They come from two main sources. Over half are promoted hourly paid workers. Most of the rest have degrees. People can apply online, via a recruitment hotline or by post. The online process includes a psychometric test. A good first-stage interview is followed by two days on site called 'On the Job Experience'. If the OJE is a success there is a final interview after which it is decided whether or not to appoint. Those who are successful are inducted into the business. The Welcome Meeting gives an outline of the company. It includes the job role and food, hygiene and safety training. Standard policies and methods of doing things are explained. The meeting also covers administration, benefits and training. McDonald's provides for workers to further their careers through a development programme.

McDonald's puts great emphasis on on-the-job training. Staff are given a training card on which to record their achievements. They are expected to check with their managers to ensure progress is properly recorded and that they gain experience in all work areas. New employees are teamed up with a 'buddy', a member of the training team. Job rotation is practised and there are 19 work areas to which staff can be assigned.

Observation and questioning are used to assess staff and two observations must be passed before someone is regarded as 'competent'. Restaurant managers spend a lot of time on a one-to-one basis with new recruits. Managers have training responsibilities and can spend 60 per cent of their time on the floor with the crew. Their own training involves learning everything a crew member needs to know and further classroom work.

Source: http://home.comcast.net/~nelson1397/mcdonaldscase.htm

RECRUITING EXTERNALLY

Businesses could choose to search using the following media:

- Advertising in papers, magazines or locally
- Employment agencies
- Executive 'headhunters'
- Job centres
- Colleges/universities
- Careers fairs

These are all useful, but there are some disadvantages:

- Companies might be overlooking and frustrating talented internal candidates.
- External recruitment can be expensive.

Advertising and the Use of Agencies

The concepts of positioning, segmentation and targeting apply just as much to recruitment as to any other form of advertising. The agency's job is to translate your needs into shortlisted candidates. The aim is to design an advert so that only those who have a realistic chance of being successful apply for the position. It is as important for unsuitable candidates to rule themselves out as it is to encourage eligible people to apply. Having a large field of candidates is of little use if many of them would stand little chance of being appointed.

E-recruitment

E-recruitment is becoming a more important tool in the 'war for talent' environment. Research conducted by DEMOS3 looks at the trends that will shape the recruitment industry for years to come. Recommendations included:

- Companies should align human resources, public relations and marketing, and be clear on core organisational values.

- Companies should find ways to connect with the passive job seeker.

- Companies should broker and make use of peer-to-peer relationships.

- Companies should use Web 2.0 technologies (such as blogs, web-based communities and hosted services including social-networking sites) to build personalised relationships online.

Creating relationships with potential employees is important, the key way being through employer brand. In order to maximise a brand's potential to attract the right people, it must express core organisational values and messages and be found in the right places.

Social Networking and Blogs

A number of organisations have started to make use of recruitment 'blogs' (or online diaries) from employees as part of the information they offer to potential candidates about working for the organisation (e.g. based on the experiences of graduates on a development scheme). This is a potential way to build relationship with would-be candidates – and to feature different areas of a company and its vacancies.

Advantages of Using E-recruitment

E-recruitment has the potential to:

- Speed up the recruitment cycle and streamline administration.

- Allow organisations to make use of IT systems to manage vacancies more effectively and co-ordinate recruitment processes.

- Reduce recruitment costs.

- Reach a wide pool of applicants.

- Reach a niche pool of applicants.

- Make internal vacancies widely known across multiple sites and separate divisions.

- Provide the image of an up-to-date organisation, reinforcing employer branding and giving an indication of organisation culture.

- Offer access to vacancies 24 hours a day, 7 days a week reaching a global audience.

- Be a cost effective way to build a talent bank for future vacancies.

- Help handle high volume job applications in a consistent way.

- Provide more tailored information to the post and organisation, for example, case histories of the 'day in the life' or self-assessment questionnaire or quiz to assess fit with role.

- Be spontaneous for candidates as ease of use means there is the ability for applications to be instantaneous.

Disadvantages of Using E-recruitment

The disadvantages to using e-recruitment include the potential to:

- Limit the applicant audience as the Internet is not the first choice for all job seekers.

- Cause applications overload or inappropriate applications if care isn't taken drafting the job profile/specification.

- Exclude those who do not want to search for a new job online.

- Attract fewer of those unable to fully utilise technology, for example, certain disabled groups.

- Give rise to allegations of discrimination, in particular the use of limited keywords in CV search tools.

- Make the process impersonal, which may be off-putting for some candidates.

- Impact on the 'cultural fit' dimension of recruitment.

- 'Turn-off' candidates, particularly if the website is badly designed or technical difficulties are encountered.

- Lose out on candidates, especially if your own website is below the search engine ranking of your competitors.

- Provide too little or inappropriate information, for example, corporate recruitment guidelines might not be written in a web-friendly style.

ACTIVITY 4.8

What are the recruitment methods used in your organisation for:

- Marketing jobs?
- Sales jobs?
- Administrative jobs?

Applications

After the closing date, a long list of possible candidates can be drawn up. From the long list you can use your personnel specification to compile a shortlist. It is good practice to respond to all applicants, but some organisations feel they cannot afford it. Applicants are consumers in the marketplace so it is important to create a favourable impression with everyone who applies for a job.

Job Description

A job description is the focus of any employee's relationship with the employer. In establishing what the job is, the manager provides the foundation for all the stages of recruitment, selection, training and appraisal that follow. The job description describes the tasks and responsibilities which make up the job. As well as being a prerequisite to the recruitment process, it provides a standard against which the performance and development needs of the post-holder can be assessed. It also enables the department to focus on the characteristics of the post rather than those of the previous occupant. Job descriptions have several standard components, provided in greater detail as needed:

- *Job title* – Accurate titles reflecting the function and level of the job; modest duties should not have grand titles. 'Engineer' should only describe a qualified engineer.

- *Position* – Stating the job title of the person to whom the employee is responsible as well as those who report to the job holder.

- *Areas of responsibility* – Stating the overall purpose of the job; the principal role of the job holder and the expected contribution to achieving objectives.

- *Main tasks* – Identifying the tasks, grouping together related ones. Includes the objective or purpose of each task but not how it is done.

- *Description of tasks* – In short numbered paragraphs, with no more than two sentences per description; gives details of measures of work involved and proportion of time involved for any task; descriptive headings used to group together related tasks.

- *Special requirements* – Equipment, tools, special skills.

- *Location* – of the job and travelling needed.

- *Special circumstances* – Lifting, dangerous or unpleasant conditions, night work, overtime, weekend working.

- *Challenging aspects of the job* – This can be useful in attracting applicants.

- *What is the overall purpose of the job?* – Describe in one sentence, for example, 'to assist the Head of Department in the efficient running of the departmental office'.

- *What are the main tasks of the job?* – Try to use active verbs, for example, 'producing', 'planning', rather than vague terms such as 'deals with', 'handles'.

- *What are the main responsibilities involved?* – 'Responsibilities' define the scope of the job, for example for managing staff, materials, money and so on.

- *The key result areas of the job and the standards expected* – These may include such aspects as the degree of precision required and/or the consequences of error.

- *With whom does the post-holder work?* – These may include other staff, students and so on.

- *Terms and conditions of the post* – Unsocial hours, necessity to work regular overtime and any restrictions on periods during which annual leave can be taken and so on.

The job description provides a basis for drawing up a 'person specification', that is, the skills and experience required to carry out the duties of the job.

The Person Specification

Purpose – The person specification forms the basis of the recruitment process from the advertisement through to the final interview stage. It describes the skills, aptitudes and experience needed to do the job and should be based on the job description, rather than a subjective view of the sort of person you would like to see filling the job. Generally, person specifications are laid down under standardised headings.

Qualifications and training:

1 *General education* – It may be more appropriate for applicants to have certain levels of literacy or numeracy rather than academic qualifications. If qualifications are stipulated, equivalent qualifications that would be considered must be included.

2 *Specific training* – For example, vocational certificates, professional qualifications and apprenticeship certificates.

Knowledge – This is knowledge without which the job cannot be done, for example, of computer systems. It should not include knowledge that can be imparted in an induction programme.

Experience – Either directly relevant or similar experience in a different environment might be considered. The type, range and depth of experience should be qualified (e.g. staff supervision). Specifying length of experience is usually unhelpful as some people learn more in a shorter time than others will learn in a longer time.

Skills and abilities – This includes such aspects as the ability to communicate effectively, numeracy, analytical skills, attention to detail and so on. However, these skills must be clearly measurable as part of the selection process.

Special requirements – This should only form part of the specification where it is relevant to the job, for example, a special type of driving licence if fork lift truck driving is to be part of the job, or a need to travel and stay away from home. The required characteristics are then entered against the appropriate heading, and subdivided into essential and desirable categories. The candidate who meets both the essential and desirable criteria will do the job particularly well, but obviously this person may be hard to find. Training and development may be needed in some areas. The person specification should be realistic. Too high an ideal will mean that potentially good candidates are excluded.

EXAMPLE

The following advertisement is for a marketing manager working for a leader in online recruitment.

Advertisement for a marketing manager

This is an opportunity to be part of one of the most highly regarded companies in an exciting and fast-moving industry. We are currently looking for a passionate Marketing Manager with heaps of initiative to oversee all marketing activities and communications. You'll be responsible for devising and implementing the company's annual marketing plan and helping to ensure continued growth in our client, user and subscriber numbers.

The Person
You must have:

- At least 3–4 years of experience in a similar marketing role.
- Extensive experience of planning, buying and monitoring online marketing expenditure, aimed primarily at candidates, including spending time with major search engines.
- Experience of devising and executing trade marketing campaigns to new and existing clients.
- Experience of managing a marketing budget of several hundred thousand pounds.
- Ideal, but not essential, are exposure to and understanding of the (a) accountancy and finance sectors, (b) the online recruitment industry and (c) some exposure to search engine optimization.

You must be:

- Enthusiastic, with a hands-on approach to marketing.
- Self motivated and adaptable with a can-do attitude.
- An excellent communicator, with creative, accurate written skills.
- Able to act as part of a wider management team, interfacing with all parts of the business especially sales.

MUNROE FRASER – 5-POINT PLAN

This focuses more upon a candidate's career to date as an indicator of future potential.

1 *Impact on others* – Whether a person's appearance and demeanour are important.

2 *Qualifications and experience* – Skills and knowledge required.

3 *Innate abilities* – How quickly and accurately a person's mind works.

4 *Motivation* – The kind of work that appeals to a person and the amount of effort they are prepared to put into it.

5 *Emotional adjustment* – Capability of working with others.

ACTIVITY 4.9

Using one of the sets of headings identified above, draw up a person specification for the Media Relations post below:

1 *Job purpose*
The Media Relations Executive will work in conjunction with the company's senior executives to develop and implement a comprehensive

communications strategy. This will require building sound media contacts to ensure positive media coverage for the company's activities.

2 *Tasks*

a Conduct a comprehensive review of media relations and provide a diagnostic report for the Board of Directors.

b Develop and implement a company media relations strategy.

c Provide a quarterly analysis of media coverage with recommendations to improve coverage.

d Arrange and publicise corporate events and host media representatives.

e Anticipating and responding to events by issuing press releases, giving professional advice and guidance to other company managers.

f Co-ordinate press conferences as necessary.

g Provide in-house training on media relations and skills to company staff according to need.

h Establish robust relationships with key media representatives.

INTERVIEWS

In relation to the focus of an interview, there are three principal interview models:

■ *Biographical interview* – exploring the candidate's experiences.

■ *Behavioural interview* – eliciting information about how applicants have behaved in similar situations.

■ *Situational interview* – comprising a series of job-related questions.

Many interviewers (or organisations) prefer to use one technique, but these different models can be useful in different situations and an interview can combine all three aspects.

With regard to the process of interviewing there are, again, various models that can be used, for example, panel interviews.

Panel Interviews

Panel interviews can provide a better picture of a candidate than a one-on-one interview. There is more chance to think about a candidate's responses because the interviewer is more of an observer than a participant. This increases the validity of the assessment. In most one-on-one interviews, the interviewer is often thinking about what question to ask next, rather than listening to a candidate's answer. Many people hate these sort of interviews and find them a bit of an endurance test. To do well you will need to identify the important figures on the panel and which role each is fulfilling. The chairperson is easy to identify as they will generally make the introductions. You will also need to identify the person whom you will be working for directly – make sure you give them plenty of eye contact. When you are talking to the panel, remember that you are talking to all of them and not just the person who posed a particular question – your answer has to be the correct one for each panel member! If there is one particular panel member who everyone else seems to agree with, you should make sure you impress him or her.

Source: http://www.alec.co.uk/interview/panel.html

The Interview Room

It is essential that candidates be made to feel relaxed so that a proper assessment of their suitability for the job can be made. In the case of interview panels, care should be taken to ensure that the candidate is not seated too far away from the interviewers so as to feel isolated, nor so close as to be able to read the interviewers' notes.

Planning the Interview

For an interview to succeed, it should be conducted in an orderly, empathetic but efficient manner. It is recommended that interviewers should undertake the following preparation:

- Compare the candidate's application form with the person specification and pick out the points which need investigating further, for example, experience, qualifications, gaps in a career history and inconsistencies.

- Once the interview panel has done this, they should then prepare a plan of how the interview is to be conducted to ensure that nothing is omitted.

- Questions need to be planned. These should be designed to probe the selection criteria of the person specification, namely a candidate's knowledge, ability and experience. Other questions should be aimed at a more general assessment.

- Where a candidate is attending an interview and they have informed you of any disability that they have, which may affect them during the interview process, it is a requirement of the Disability Discrimination Act to carry out 'reasonable' adjustments to ensure they can perform to their maximum potential, for example, if access is a problem for a candidate, the interviews should be held in a room accessible to all.

- Identify key questions pertinent to the job that is asked of all candidates. This ensures that they have been asked equivalent and relevant questions.

- Allocate the subjects to be explored. Each interviewer can cover different areas, for example, work experience and training.

- The candidate should have an opportunity to ask questions and interviewers should be prepared for the more obvious ones, such as hours of work and annual leave.

Objectives for an Interview

Interviewers should be clear on the objectives of the interview:

- To find out whether a candidate is suitable for the job advertised

- To find out whether the job and the department/organisation are suitable for a candidate's needs (an aspect which is often overlooked)

- To fairly select the most suitable candidate

Conducting the Interview

The interviewer should control the focus of the interview:

- Introduce the members of the panel. Start the interview slowly, to allow the candidate to relax.

- Explain the structure of the interview and what it is trying to achieve.

- Give an overview of the context of and brief background for advertising the job.

- Put the candidate at their ease and begin your questioning by identifying areas that are familiar, for example, his/her present job, before working through to the candidate's thoughts on the job for which he/she has applied.

Finishing the Interview

Once the interviewers have obtained all they need from the interview, they should check that the candidate has no further questions and then signify the end of the interview. They should then:

- Tell the candidate when he/she can expect to know the outcome.
- Check the candidate's expenses are covered, if appropriate.
- Thank the candidate for attending the interview and see him/her out.

Key Points

- Remove as much stress from the interview as possible.
- Ask open-ended questions.
- Ascertain all relevant facts, and probe ambiguous or vague answers.
- Listen to what the candidate has to say.
- Provide information relevant to the job.
- Provide opportunities for the candidate to ask questions.
- Tell the candidate when they can expect to know the outcome of the interview.

The Interview Assessment

- When a succession of candidates is seen over a period, it is essential to record accurate views on each immediately after each part of the process.

- Never allow interviewers to rely on memory.

- The interview assessment allows each of your defined categories to be rated and a justification noted. This greatly facilitates the discussions that must take place at the end of the session as the shortlist is constructed or the successful applicant is identified.

- Do not allow any sharing of views about candidates until after individual assessments have been recorded in writing.

Debriefing

Arrange a debriefing to:

- Shortlist or reject candidates.
- Make improvements to the recruitment and selection procedures.
- If possible, provide advice to the unsuccessful candidates – this is good for public relations and is used routinely in the public sector.

CASE STUDY

The recruitment process at Apple

In marketing, you have the unique opportunity to work on revolutionary products from concept to launch with the best creative minds in the industry. Working with the most creative people in the business on breakthrough products is as satisfying as it is challenging. Our marketing department is comprised of the best and brightest, and we're always looking for stand-out talent to add to our team.

The Marketing division spans a variety of different disciplines including: Developer Relations, Events, Graphic Design, Marketing Communications, Product Marketing, Public Relations, Research and Analysis, Worldwide Markets. Take a look at our website at www.apple.com. Explore the site and get to know our products. If you're a Software Engineer, make sure to visit our Developer site. Interested in Sales? Learn how our customers are using our products in creative ways in the Education, Pro, and Business sections. Make sure you take the time to explore the website, it will tell you a lot of what you need to know about Apple and our customers.

Try our products in person at one of our retail stores or resellers. Listen to music on an iPod. Ask questions of one of the Mac Specialists. When you're at home, download our iTunes software to your Mac or PC and check out the iTunes Music Store. It's important that you familiarize yourself with our products to see what makes Apple unique. Once you're in the interview, relax and be yourself. The interview process is designed for us to make sure that we're a good fit for each other, which means that you should ask questions of us in addition to answering the questions that we ask you. Come prepared to discuss a variety of topics, not just your past experiences and accomplishments. And don't forget, we don't have a dress code, so wear clothes that make you comfortable.

Source: http://www.apple.com/jobs/marketing/interview.html

Numerical Critical Reasoning

Numerical critical reasoning tests look at how well you can reason with numbers and understand information presented in a numerical form. In this sort of test, you are presented with information followed by a number of questions. The task is to select the right response from a range of possible responses.

Drawbacks of Selection Interviews

There is some doubt that an interview is the most appropriate mechanism for assessing candidates' suitability with accuracy, witness:

- First impressions are often lasting impressions; decisions tend to be made early on in the interview.

- Interviewers may prefer candidates who are like themselves, which may lead to discrimination.

- There is a danger of the interviewer only hearing information which supports preconceptions or first impressions.

- Interviewers can get jaded and confused if too many interviews are held in one day – early interviews get forgotten and later ones are less effective.

ACTIVITY 4.10

- How have those who have interviewed you performed in their role?
- What would you have done differently?
- What was good/bad about the best/worst interview you've ever had?

DO'S AND DON'TS FOR SUCCESSFUL SELECTION INTERVIEWING:

- Do prepare thoroughly.
- Do check the organisation's policies.
- Do watch for inconsistencies between verbal and non-verbal behaviour.
- Don't make decisions based on a gut reaction.
- Don't break your schedule.
- Don't allow interruptions.
- Don't talk too much.

Working with diversity is an important skill for managers and team members, and they need to have good cultural and interpersonal awareness. The differences amongst individuals and groups should be acknowledged, accepted and valued. Working with people in different countries raises particular issues of cultural awareness.

SUMMARY

Teams differ in many ways, including size, purpose, type of work performed, structure, leadership, influence and decision-making ability. It is important to recognise that teamworking is not the best solution in every situation, and teams are not always more effective and efficient than individuals working to solve a problem. However, in many business situations, the ability to work in teams is valuable and teams can accomplish more than individuals who plough their own furrow. Criteria for an effective team were identified. An effective team has cohesion and a common purpose. Recruitment and selection guided by a personnel specification and proper preparation for interviews is of key importance. There are a wide range of selection procedures that can be used depending on the nature of the job and its importance to the organisation.

Recruitment and selection can be expensive but so can appointing the wrong person to a post.

FURTHER STUDY

Read Boddy, D., 2005. Management: An Introduction. Pearson Education, Harlow. Chapter 4, 'The international context of management' and Chapter 15, 'Teams'.

BIBLIOGRAPHY

Adair, J., 2002. Inspiring Leadership: Learning from Great Leaders. Thorogood, London ISBN 1854182072, ISBN-13: 978-1854182074.

Bacal, R., 2002. The six deadly sins of team building, http://www.work911.com/articles/teambuidingsins.html

Bass, B.M., 1997. Does the transactional–transformational leadership paradigm transcend organizational and national boundaries? American Psychologist 52 (2), 130–139.

Belbin, R.M., 2000. Beyond the Team. Butterworth-Heinemann, Oxford ISBN 0750646411.

Belbin, R.M., 2004. Management Teams: Why they Succeed or Fail. Butterworth-Heinemann, Oxford ISBN 0750659106.

Friedman, L., Harvey, R.J., 1986. Can raters with reduced job descriptive information provide accurate position analysis questionnaire (PAQ) ratings? Personnel Psychology 39, 779–789.

Gosling, J., Mintzberg, H., 2003. The five minds of a manager. Harvard Business Review 81 PART 11, pages 54–63.

Katzenbach, J.R., Smith, D.K., 1994. The Wisdom of Teams. McGraw-Hill, New York ISBN 0875845819.

Kotter, J.P., 2001. What leaders really do. Harvard Business Review – BEST OF HBR Breakthrough Leadership.

Kouzes, J.M., Posner, B.Z., 2002. The Leadership Challenge, third ed. Jossey Bass, San Fransisco.

McCrae R.R., John O.P., 1992. An introduction to the five-factor model and its applications. *Journal of Personality* 60 (2), 175–215. Published Online: 28 April 2006 Journal compilation © 2008 by Blackwell Publishing.

Mintzberg, H., 1973. The Nature of Managerial Work. Harper & Row, New York ISBN 0060445564.

Montgomery, C.A., 2008. Putting leadership back into strategy. Harvard Business Review January.

Pelled, L.H., Eisenhardt, K.M., Xin, K.R., 1999. Exploring the Black Box: An Analysis of Work Group Diversity, Conflict and Performance. Administrative Science Quarterly 44 (1), 1–28 March.

Piercy, R.M., 2002. Market-led Strategic Change: A Guide to Transforming the Process of Going to Market. Butterworth-Heinemann, Oxford ISBN 075065225X.

Stacey, R.D., 2003. Strategic Management and Organizational Dynamics. Prentice-Hall, Harlow ISBN 0273658980.

Tannenbaum, R., Schmidt, W.H., 1973. How to choose a leadership pattern: should a manager be democratic or autocratic – or something in between? Harvard Business Review 37 (2), 95–102.

Tuckman, B.W., Jensen, M.C., 1977. Stages in Small-group Development Revisited. Group and Organanizational Studies 2 (4), 419–427.

van Eeden, R., Cilliers, F., 2008. Leadership styles and associated personality traits: Support for the conceptualisation of transactional and transformational leadership. South African Journal of Psychology 38 (2), 253–267 ISSN 0081-2463.

CHAPTER 5

Managing Teams

LEARNING OUTCOMES

2.4   Plan how the work of the team will be undertaken establishing priorities and critical activities required to meet marketing and organisational objectives and with customers in mind.

2.5   Propose approaches to manage and co-ordinate the work of teams and individuals to create effective working relations including appropriate levels of consultation, taking into account the balance of skills and activities available.

2.6   Propose approaches to manage and co-ordinate the work of remote teams to create effective working relations.

SYLLABUS REFERENCES

2.4:

- performance management and measurement – marketing strategy and individual objectives, communicating standards, techniques to measure performance against objectives and standards
- internal marketing – aligning internal communications with external communications, managing knowledge.

2.5:

- characteristics of effective teamwork/high-performing teams
- management skills and techniques – communication, motivation, empowerment, involvement, delegation, task allocation, feedback, running effective meetings, listening, assertiveness, group decision-making
- assess and apply a range of management theories, for example, McGregor's Theory X/Y, Maslow's Hierarchy of Needs, Herzberg's

Motivation-Hygiene Theory, McClelland's Motivation Needs Theory, Vroom's Expectancy Theory
- job enrichment/enlargement
- preventing discrimination and valuing diversity – equal opportunities and employment law
- reflect on personal approach to team management and produce a personal development plan
- flexible working practices

2.6:

- managing international teams, cultural considerations, for example, Hofstede's Cultural Dimensions, Trompenaars' Cross-Cultural Communication
- managing virtual teams – benefits and constraints

KEY DEFINITIONS

Job enlargement refers to increasing the motivational value of a job through the performance of a greater number and variety of similar level tasks (Lawler, 1969).

Job enrichment involves adding tasks, for example, related to planning and controlling work that are typically performed by someone higher up in the organisational hierarchy, for example, a supervisor or a more senior manager (Lawler, 1969).

PERFORMANCE MANAGEMENT AND MEASUREMENT

Marketing implementation is concerned with translating marketing plans into action. The marketing plan is the vehicle for communicating the strategy within the organisation and addresses the issues of 'what' should happen and 'why' it should happen. Implementation is concerned with 'how' the strategy should be carried out, 'who' is to be responsible, 'when' things will take place and 'where' things will happen. Too often in organisations the implementation stage is overlooked and as a result a 'good strategy' can fail. It is important that organisations devote as much time and energy to the implementation of plans as they do to creating marketing strategies. Implementation is planned to be undertaken by ever smaller groups of people in an organisation, down to teams and ultimately individuals.

INTERNAL MARKETING

This is discussed in detail in Chapter 6. Interest here is in making wider connections between internal marketing, strategy, planning and implementation and connecting this with implementation at the level of the individual.

The Internal Marketing Plan

The internal marketing plan should take the same format as an external marketing plan with objectives, strategy, market segmentation, marketing mix programmes and evaluation.

Internal Market Segmentation

Internal markets could be segmented in a number of different ways such as by job function, role or location. However, these methods may not always be the most appropriate especially when working with smaller numbers of people. It may be more useful to segment according to the extent to which people are likely to accept any required, or proposed, change. Jobber (2001) suggests that three different segments can be identified:

1. *Supporters* – likely to gain from the change
2. *Neutrals* – will neither gain nor lose
3. *Opposers* – likely to lose from the change or are traditional opponents

A separate marketing mix (approach) can then be developed for each of these segments (individuals). It may also be possible to identify influential individuals that are opinion leaders.

The development of a market orientation is a key ingredient of successful implementation. Without a customer-centred philosophy it is likely that any new strategy will encounter problems. Jobber (2001, p. 649) suggests the following process for ensuring the successful execution of the marketing plan:

1. Gain the support of key decision-makers and overcome the opposition of others
2. Gain the required resources such as people, time and budget
3. Gain commitment of individuals and departments in the company who are involved in front-line implementation
4. Gain the co-operation of other departments needed to implement the plan

Internal marketing can be used to facilitate this process.

Internal Marketing Evaluation

In order to evaluate the success of internal marketing programmes appropriate measures have to be used, such as:

- The extent of support of key players
- Employee satisfaction levels

- Reduced customer complaints
- Higher customer satisfaction scores

Many companies are now conducting regular surveys to monitor levels of staff motivation, acceptance of the marketing concept and perceptions of the organisation. In addition, it could be argued that if internal marketing is being effective then it should be having an impact on external marketing. Measuring levels of customer satisfaction and numbers of customer complaints may give an indication of the success of internal marketing programmes.

ACTIVITY 5.1

Internal marketing

- To what extent do you think your organisation has embraced the concept of internal marketing?
- What impact does this have on their external marketing activities?
- How has your company embraced technology, for example, intranets, in an attempt to improve their internal marketing/communications? How effective is this strategy?

The marketing planning process would not be complete without some form of evaluation of performance and assessment as to whether the marketing objectives have been achieved. There are three main components of control:

1. Setting targets/objectives against which performance can be measured
2. Measurement of performance
3. Corrective action

A key aspect of control is that it should lead to corrective action. Failure to meet targets may be as a result of (a) unrealistic objectives (and therefore targets may have to be reviewed) or (b) poor performance of individuals (and therefore additional training, advice, etc., may have to be offered). If targets are met then individuals should be rewarded and objectives may also have to be reviewed for the future.

Characteristics of Effective Control Systems

In order to develop effective and meaningful control measures it is essential they are flexible and adhere to the following principles (suggested by Drummond and Ensor, 2001):

- *Involvement* – participants in the control process should be involved in the development of the control measures. If not, there is a danger that staff will fail to take ownership of the measures.

- *Target setting* – objectives should be quantifiable and achievable. These targets should be agreed and communicated in advance.

- *Focus* – recognise the difference between the source and the symptoms of the problem.

- *Effectiveness* – ensure that what is being measured is the right thing: 'what gets measured gets done'.

- *Management by exception* – develop tolerance zones and take corrective action if results fall outside this zone.

- *Action* – effective control systems should promote action rather than just identifying problems.

KNOWLEDGE MANAGEMENT AND COMMUNICATIONS

Market orientation represents the implementation of the marketing concept. Interfunctional co-ordination is an important element of market orientation. Technology developments have resulted in an increased interest in trying to implement ideas of knowledge management in the organisation in particular in the area of interfunctional co-ordination, which is principally the concern of knowledge management.

Internal and external communications are about active, possibly even manipulative, knowledge management to further the goals of the organisation. Knowledge management however concerns leveraging knowledge as an 'asset'. In a market-oriented organisation, with a customer focus, knowledge management must centre on sharing and deploying knowledge to satisfy customer needs. This requires the organisation to integrate both internal and external knowledge. Much of the most detailed, and organisational critical, information is held inside the heads of their employees, for example, inside the heads of key account managers. Employees commonly withhold knowledge from others and selectively share their knowledge. Part of the problem can also be that they do not know that some of the knowledge that they possess can be useful to others. Confining this critical knowledge to just one person greatly constrains the extent to which the organisation can serve its customers and be market orientated.

Various tools and techniques exist to facilitate knowledge transfer in both formal and informal systems, for example:

- Organisational intranets including marketing information systems. These include data in customer order profiles and product purchases taken from accounting systems.
  - Various international organisations have taken this concept much further and include a knowledge repository where staff can search

for a wide range of information from product patents, customer product usage, customer profile data to new product idea and customer complaints.

- Regular staff briefings from daily and weekly team meetings to the annual organisational gathering.
- Staff bulletin boards.
- Regular staff social meetings including sports and leisure/arts events.

Through these various devices both tacit and explicit knowledge may be shared for team and organisational benefits in terms of improved performance.

Characteristics of Effective Teamwork/High-Performing Teams

Teams go through stages of development and this is normal. What can we do to achieve or maintain a successful team?

First we must understand the characteristics of high-performing teams. Perhaps ten of the more important include the following:

1. Members are clear about, and agree with, team goals.

2. Members are clear about the role they are asked to play, have the ability and skills necessary to accomplish the assigned or chosen task and agree to accept the role.

3. High degree of interdependence exists, as many team tasks require co-operation.

4. The leader's style changes as necessary to meet group needs as they arise. This may be considered in terms of Tuckman's four stages of group development.

5. A very open communication structure (people as well as systems) facilitates the participation and contribution of all members of the team. In addition, team members provide constructive feedback to each other with the focus on individual performance, productivity and effectiveness, and members actually seek this. In addition, they use this to great effect by translating this into improvements on all aspects of their work – that is, productivity and effectiveness.

6. Time is spent initially on planning how decisions are to be made and problems will be solved. That means that time is spent to ensure that there is consensus as to how decisions are to be made – for example, majority voting prior to the occasion when actual decisions must be made.

7. Team solutions and decisions are implemented and they have in place methods by which implementation of decisions are evaluated. This results in rapid detection of poor decisions or indeed poor implementation.

8. Norms of behaviours encourage creative, innovative performance. Unusual behaviour is accepted if this is considered to help individuals to perform at the highest level for the benefit of the team.

9. Suitable structure – as small as is possible to achieve objectives. Subgroups are encouraged and are not seen as threatening; on the contrary, they are considered to be more efficient, especially if part of the team can effectively resolve a problem leaving the rest of the team to resolve other problems.

10. Highly cohesive with co-operative members. Conflict still occurs; however, effective approaches to handling conflict results in their rapid resolution.

Source: Adapted from Wheelan (1999).

MANAGEMENT THEORIES AND PERFORMANCE

Many studies indicate that teams, and organisations, are successful when people are emotionally engaged and believe in what the team and the organisation is doing. In addition, it is important for them to gain some form of psychological satisfaction for the contribution they make to the organisation, beyond simple monetary benefits.

Herzberg (1965)	Suggested that people are motivated to work in co-operation with others by both extrinsic motivators, such as money, and intrinsic motivators, such as recognition for achievement, responsibility, advancement and personal growth.
Maslow (1948)	Maslow in his hierarchy of needs suggested that when an organisation creates conditions in which people can satisfy their 'self-actualisation' needs (the highest level in his hierarchy of needs) then they are powerfully motivated to work for the good of the team and of the organisation.
Schein (1988)	One of the several authors to consider three categories of relationships. The first two are 'coercive', where individuals only do the bare minimum to evade punishment, and 'utilitarian', where the individual does enough simply to earn the desired level of reward. The final category is a 'normative' form of relationship where individuals value what they are doing for its own sake, as they believe in it. In this situation, the individual's ideology matches that of the organisation and this acts as the highest level of individual motivation for the benefit of the organisation.

Motivation

One of the best-known theories is McClelland's Motivational Theory (McClelland, 1953) which is based on three types of motivational needs that are found to varying degrees in all workers and managers.

1. *Achievement motivation* – The person seeks attainment of realistic but challenging goals, and advancement in the job. There is a strong need for feedback about achievement and progress, and a need for a sense of accomplishment.

2. *Authority/power motivation* – The person needs to be influential and effective to make an impact. There is a strong need to lead and for their ideas to prevail. There is also motivation and need towards increasing personal status and prestige.

3. *Affiliation motivation* – The person has a need for friendly relationships and is motivated towards interaction with other people. The affiliation driver produces motivation, and needs to be liked and held in popular regard. These people are team players. Most people possess and exhibit a combination of these characteristics. Some people exhibit a strong bias to a particular motivational need, and this affects their behaviour and working/managing style. McClelland felt that people with a strong 'achievement motivation' made the best leaders although there was a tendency to demand too much of their staff in the belief that they too are highly achievement focused and results driven.

McClelland suggested that for achievement-motivated people:

- Achievement is more important than material or financial reward.
- Achieving the aim or task gives greater personal satisfaction than receiving praise or recognition.
- Financial reward is regarded as a measurement of success, not an end in itself.
- Security is not the prime motivator, nor is status.
- Feedback is essential, because it enables measurement of success, not for reasons of praise or recognition (the implication here is that feedback must be reliable, quantifiable and factual).
- Achievement-motivated people constantly seek improvements and ways of doing things better.
- Achievement-motivated people will logically favour jobs and responsibilities that naturally satisfy their needs, that is, offer flexibility and opportunity to set and achieve goals, for example, sales and business management, and entrepreneurial roles.

McGregor XY Theory

In 1960, Douglas McGregor advanced the idea that managers had a major part in motivating staff. He divided managers into two categories – Theory X managers who believe that their staff are lazy and will do as little as they can get away with and Theory Y managers who believe that their people really want to do their best in their work. Theory X managers believe that staff will do things if they are given explicit instructions and plenty of stick if they do not do what they are supposed to. Theory Y managers believe their people work their best when empowered to make appropriate decisions.

Achievement-motivated people tend towards X-Theory style, due to their high task focus.

Theory X Assumptions
1. People inherently dislike work.
2. People must be coerced or controlled to do work to achieve objectives.
3. People prefer to be directed.

Theory Y Assumptions
1. People view work as being a natural activity.
2. People will exercise self-direction and control towards achieving objectives to which they are committed.
3. People learn to accept and seek responsibility.

Since McGregor, Theory Z has been advanced by William Ouchi (1982). This states that employees crave responsibility and opportunities for growth all the time. It is strongly influenced by Japanese management styles.

ACTIVITY 5.2

Think about jobs you have had. What do you think the assumptions of your boss were?

What impact did those assumptions have on performance and morale?

Can you generalise about organisations you are familiar with? Can you detect patterns of management that reflect either X or Y assumptions?

Herzberg Motivators and Hygiene Factors

Herzberg et al. (1959) constructed a two-dimensional paradigm of factors affecting people's attitudes about work. He concluded that factors such as company policy, supervision, interpersonal relations, working conditions and salary are hygiene factors rather than motivators. According to the theory, the absence of hygiene factors can create job dissatisfaction, but their presence does not motivate or create satisfaction. In contrast, motivators are elements that enriched a person's job; he found five factors in particular that were strong determinants of job satisfaction: achievement, recognition, the work itself, responsibility and advancement. These motivators (satisfiers) were associated with long-term positive effects in job performance while the hygiene factors (dissatisfiers) consistently produced only short-term changes in job attitudes and performance, which quickly fell back to its previous level.

Satisfiers describe a person's relationship with what he or she does, many related to the tasks being performed. Dissatisfiers, on the other hand, have to do with a person's relationship to the context or environment in which he or she performs the job. The satisfiers relate to what a person does while the dissatisfiers relate to the situation in which the person does what he or she does. A manager may not be able to easily influence all the hygiene factors of a person's job, but he or she can have a big influence on many of the motivators.

Motivator factors that increase job satisfaction:

- Achievement
- Recognition
- Work itself
- Responsibility
- Advancement
- Growth

Hygiene factors – absence of 'good' factors can create job dissatisfaction:

- Company policy
- Working conditions
- Salary
- Peer relationships
- Security

Source: Frederick Herzberg, 1965. *Work and the Nature of Man*.

Equity Theory

Adams' (1965) Equity Theory is based on the principle that individuals want a fair balance between the inputs, or what they give to their job, and the outputs, or what they get from it. Employees develop a view of what is fair by comparing their own situation with other people who they regard as 'referents'. Typical inputs might be effort, loyalty, hard work, commitment and skill. Typical outputs are obvious ones such as pay and expenses and also more intangible ones such as recognition, praise, responsibility, sense of achievement and so on.

If people feel that their inputs outweigh the outputs then they may become demotivated. In this situation, some people switch off and do the minimum that they can, or even become disruptive. Others aim to seek to improve the outputs by making pay claims or looking for other work. The key aspect of the theory is that extrinsic rewards such as level of pay are neither motivating nor demotivating in themselves. Rather it is how fair we perceive them to be when we compare ourselves with significant others, that is, people who we feel should be paid less than or about the same as ourselves, or people whom we expect to be paid more than us.

If we feel that inputs are fairly and adequately rewarded by outputs (the fairness benchmark being subjectively perceived from market norms and other comparable references), then we are happy in our work and motivated to continue inputting at the same level.

JOB ENRICHMENT AND JOB ENLARGEMENT

Motivation Theory has had a large influence in job design and in particular in trying to change work roles. The theory being if you can increase work motivation you will get an increase in satisfaction and ultimately in performance. Two general approaches to this have been popular, namely job enrichment and job enlargement. Job enrichment (getting workers to take on higher level tasks) and job enlargement (greater workers to take part in a greater variety of tasks) have been successful in improving performance and work satisfaction. See the discussion of related issues in Chapter 4, in the section, 'Job analysis and job design' and also 'Competencies and standards that define a good manager'. The case study on Siemens, in the latter section, is particularly relevant. One word of caution, however, is that a 'one approach fits all' has been found not to be successful. Some workers are happy to do a routine job and or do not want more responsibility. They can even find this to be stressful. The mechanism by which these are implemented can also affect worker perception and acceptance. Imposition by senior management can be perceived simply as a cost efficient measure and may even be resented. Where worker co-operation is sought they are more likely to buy into the idea and to benefit personally, which can only be good for organisational performance.

DISCRIMINATION

What the Law Says

There are a number of Acts of Parliament which are relevant to the recruitment of staff. The main provisions are the Sex Discrimination Acts of 1975 and

1986, the Race Relations Act 1976, the Race Relations (Amendment) Act 2000 and the Disability Discrimination Act of 1995. These Acts seek to promote equality of opportunity and to ensure that no person is treated less favourably than another person on the grounds of disability, colour, race, nationality, ethnic or national origins, sex or marital status. The Disability Discrimination Act 1995 gives disabled people the right not to be treated less favourably than others. Special care must be taken in the wording and placing of recruitment advertisements to avoid seeming to prefer one type of person over another. Since 2005, third-party publishers, for example, newspapers, have been liable for publishing discriminatory advertisements. The government has introduced legislation to combat age discrimination in employment and vocational training. It includes every member of the workforce, young and old. Employers will have to adopt age positive practices. This means it will no longer be possible to recruit, train, promote or retire people on the basis of age unless it can be objectively justified.

The 2005 legislation covers young and old alike throughout their working lives.

The Sexual Orientation Regulations apply to discrimination on grounds of orientation towards persons of the same sex (lesbians or gays), the opposite sex (heterosexuals) and the same and opposite sex (bisexuals). They cover discrimination on grounds of perceived as well as actual sexual orientation and the sexual orientation of someone with whom the person associates.

As with other forms of discrimination, the new legislation recognises both direct and indirect discrimination on the grounds of sexual orientation. Since 2005, this definition has been extended to include civil partner employees, i.e. a partner in a same-sex couple who have registered their relationship under the Civil Partnership Act 2004. A person who is in a registered civil partnership of a same-sex couple will be protected from unlawful direct or indirect sexual discrimination on the grounds of being a civil partner.

You should check there are no hidden age barriers in your selection and promotion processes – for example, aim to place advertisements in publications read by a range of age groups. You should also make sure that redundancy procedures are based on business needs rather than age.

In certain circumstances, discrimination may be allowed if it is seen to be a genuine occupational qualification for the job in question.

When interviewing people for a job there are certain questions you should not ask, either directly or indirectly, including whether a candidate is married, in a same-sex civil partnership or plans to have children. You must not attempt to elicit information about a person's sexual orientation or their religion. Read about the actions you should take to give equal treatment to civil partners in your policies, forms and other material on the ACAS website.

Care should also be taken when asking about a disability. Whilst the Disability Discrimination Act does not prohibit an employer from seeking information about a disability, that information must not be used to discriminate against a disabled person. An employer should only ask such questions if they are relevant to the person's ability to do the job, after a reasonable adjustment, if necessary.

Discrimination – Main Forms

The three main forms of discrimination are:

1. *Direct discrimination* – that is where a woman is treated less favourably than a man or vice versa, a married person is treated less favourably than a single person or vice versa, or someone is treated less favourably on grounds that they are intending to undergo, are undergoing or have undergone a gender reassignment. Direct discrimination can occur where someone is treated less favourably on the grounds of their sexual orientation.

2. *Indirect discrimination* – that is applying a requirement or condition which, although applied equally to all groups, is such that a considerably smaller proportion of a particular racial group, sex or married persons can comply with it and which cannot be shown to be justifiable. Possible examples are unjustifiable age limits which could discriminate against women who have taken time out of employment for child rearing and rules about clothing or uniforms which disproportionately disadvantage a particular racial group. Both types of discrimination are unlawful irrespective of whether there has been any intention to discriminate.

3. *Disability discrimination* – While legislation covering discrimination on grounds of race and sex makes discriminatory conduct unlawful, the Disability Discrimination Act 1995 goes further by requiring employers to make 'reasonable adjustments' to the workplace where that would help to overcome the practical effects of disability. Failure to carry out this legal duty amounts to discrimination unless an employer is able to justify it. People with disabilities who feel that they have been unfairly discriminated against can seek redress through Employment tribunals.

Sexual Orientation

The Employment Equality (Sexual Orientation) Regulations 2003 outlawed discrimination in employment and vocational training on grounds of sexual orientation. The law means that it will be unlawful to deny lesbian, gay and bisexual people jobs because of prejudice. The legislation provides protection throughout the employment relationship – during the recruitment process, in the workplace, on dismissal and, in certain circumstances, after the employment has finished. They apply to terms and conditions, pay, promotion, transfers, training and dismissals.

Religion and Belief

The Employment Equality (Religion or Belief) Regulations 2003 outlawed discrimination and harassment on grounds of religion or belief in large and small workplaces in England, Scotland and Wales, both in the private and public sectors. They cover all aspects of the employment relationship and outlaw treating people less favourably than others because of their religion or belief.

Equal Pay

The Equal Pay Act 1970, as amended by the Equal Pay Regulations, covers not only pay but all contractual conditions of service. It gives both sexes the right to an 'equality clause', which means that if any term in their contract is less favourable than that in a contract of the opposite sex, it must be modified to make it equitable. Aspects covered include:

- 'Like work', that is work of the same or a broadly similar nature.
- Work rated as equivalent under a non-discriminatory evaluation scheme.
- Work of equal value in terms of the demands made, for example, under such headings as effort, skill and decision-making.

INTERNATIONAL CULTURE

Culture plays an important role in intra- and interorganisational communication. Large organisations tend to employ staff from a variety of national backgrounds. Naturally, they bring their own national/cultural approach to communication.

Hofstede's Cross-cultural Analysis

Doole and Lowe (2004) present a summary of Hofstede's cross-cultural analysis of the influence of national culture on communication within a single global organisation. People from Northern European cultures (including people from English-speaking advanced industrial economies) communicate in a literal sense; that is, what is said, or written, is what is meant, so-called low-context cultures. In contrast are cultures where the context of the message gives meaning to the message. Who said it, how it was said, the context in which the message was delivered, all in combination must be used to decipher the meaning of a message, whether written or spoken, so-called high-context cultures.

Hofstede further researched the role of national culture within the organisation and identified five dimensions which he argued largely accounted for cross-cultural differences in people's belief systems and values. These he termed as 'uncertainty avoidance', 'masculinity', 'individualism', 'power-distance' and 'Confucian dynamism'.

Individualism Versus Collectivism

(Examples: Individualistic = United States, Great Britain; Collectivistic = Pakistan, Taiwan)

Is the individual the basis of society or does society give meaning to the individual? The United States is the best example of a society in which individualistic traits are most pronounced. For example, differences are admired and the cult of individuals prospers most. Perhaps in direct contrast is the Chinese culture, where society's rights and responsibilities are dominant and individual needs are subservient. Here conformity is generally considered the norm.

Masculinity Versus Femininity

(Examples: Masculine = Japan, Italy; Feminine = Denmark, Sweden)

Masculine cultures emphasise 'assertiveness' compared to 'nurturance' for feminine cultures. High masculine societies, whether individualistic like United States or collectivist like Japan, provide weaker people with, on average, less support whether from within the organisation or from society at large. People learn to admire the strong and to have a relatively negative view of the weak and dependent.

Power-Distance

(Examples: Low = Denmark, Austria; High = France, India)

Measures the extent to which individuals (society) tolerate an unequal distribution of power in organisations and in society as a whole. In high-power-distance organisations, superiors display their power and exercise it. Subordinates expect this behaviour and feel uncomfortable if they do not personally experience their superiors displaying their status and power. In high-power-distance cultures, subordinates feel separated from one another: it is not easy to talk with higher-ranking people and real power tends to be concentrated at the top. In low-power-distance societies, members of organisations, and of society, tend to feel equal and relatively close to each other at work. Power is much more likely to be delegated in low-power-distance cultures.

Uncertainty Avoidance

(Examples: Low = Denmark, Sweden; High = Japan, France)

Measures the extent to which people tend to feel threatened by uncertain, ambiguous, risky or undefined situations. In cultures where uncertainty avoidance is high, organisations promote stable careers and produce rules and procedures which staff must follow (and which staff find comforting to follow). Hofstede argues that uncertainty avoidance is about reducing ambiguity and should not be confused with risk avoidance.

Confucian Dynamism

(Examples: Low = United States, Australia; High = China, Japan)

Measures the extent to which conformity according to 'position' is stable and elicits predictable behaviour between individuals. Behavioural attributes that are valued highly include obedience, deference, maintaining the status quo within organisational and social hierarchies and trouble-free social relations. Where you are in an organisational hierarchy predetermines the way you are expected to treat others and in turn the way you should be treated. Behaviour is much more predictable in Confucian cultures that exhibit high levels of Confucian dynamism.

CASE STUDY

Lessons From Building International Teams with Staff From Contrasting Cultures – Lenovo and IBM

The huge Chinese computer giant Lenovo's acquisition of the personal computer division of IBM for US$1.75 billion in 2004 was intended to generate huge potential benefits. IBM obviously had a global sales reach and tremendous international management expertise. It had become somewhat of a dinosaur with a highly conservative reputation. In contrast, the Chinese-focused Lenovo was, and is, highly innovative. Almost 10, 000 people had to be bound together somehow as a result of this acquisition. For benefits to be realized, a huge team-building management problem had to be overcome. What was this?

The main purpose of the acquisition was for Lenovo to become a world player. To do this, Lenovo managers were required to acquire IBM skills and business culture. However, they first needed to have trust in the IBM staff who were supposed to help them develop.

IBM expats working in China had to operate with an Asian 'relationship' orientation. How could they do this? Spend a lot of informal time with colleagues: for example, outside working hours going 10-pin bowling or eating in restaurants. That would work on trust but to get networks working requires a focus not on the team but on customer needs. This provides a common focus on which co-operative teams are given direction and purpose and a context in which to grow. Collaboration between functional areas allows interfirm networks to develop, including communications networks. Team meetings across the two old organizations, and across areas of functionality, needed to be frequent and this is the context in which problems of managing and coping with change were discussed. This is especially important in Asian countries as such 'collectivistic' orientated societies (in contrast to 'individualistic' cultures) do not cope well with work-role ambiguity.

Contrasting corporate cultures are rooted deeply in the societies in which they are based. People who work in 'western' organizations tend to be highly focused on the job (so called 'task orientation'). This is in contrast to people in 'eastern' organizations, especially Asian organizations, who have the so-called relationship orientation. The focus of the merged organizations needed to develop a 'relationship' orientation for the business to succeed in the long-term, in addition to adopting the international, task orientation.

The problem with using expats from western societies in an Asian context is that they tend to have a task orientation and could ignore the knowledge transfer/training aspects of their work. Senior management must recognize this and ensure that a proportion of expat bonus payments is linked to skills and knowledge transfer to Chinese staff.

According to Fallon (2005), Chinese employees have too much faith in the successful operation of international markets and business systems and all too frequently fail to recognize that they themselves must implement and monitor these systems, as well as refine them. Traditional mini-MBA style approaches to training were adopted but found not to work in the Chinese context, without adjustment to the Chinese consensual, rather than western conflict, approach.

In short, the success of the whole enterprise rested on the building of effective multicultural teams where communication was regarded as crucial, as was building trust through socializing in leisure time and through approaches that included IBM staff adopting Chinese-directed approaches to management. Consequently, implementation of strategy was improved considerably. Fallon (2005) concludes that the approach reported has universal lessons for mergers and acquisitions between 'western' and 'eastern' organizations.

Source: Fallon, M., 2005.

Trompenaars and Hampden-Turner's Seven-Dimensional Model

Trompenaars (1993) and subsequently with Hampden-Turner (1997) follow a functional approach like Hofstede in which the premise is that culture can systematically cause differences in behaviour between people from different countries.

Trompenaars and Hampden-Turner developed the 'Seven Dimensions of Culture Model' to analyse cultural differences and this also provides managers with some insight into the complexity of managing international teams. Readers of Hofstede's work will see connections between his work and the ideas of Trompenaars and Hampden-Turner who share a common general perspective. International experience working for Shell informs the authors' practitioner thinking in which they discuss the implications for managing or being managed, working together, building relationships, team working, negotiating and communicating with people from other cultures. Trompenaars, and subsequently with Hampden-Turner, explains how reconciling cultural differences will lead to competitive advantage.

Trompenaars's basic premise is that an understanding of the underlying values of different cultures leads to greater respect for diverse ways of operating and to the desire and skills for reconciling cultural differences to achieve business performance. Each one of the seven dimensions is presented below along with a summary definition.

Relationships with Other People

1. *Universalism versus particularism* – Cultures with a universalistic tendency emphasis rules and drawing up of detailed contracts, for example, of employment, where particularistic cultures focus on the relationship between people. Here there is consideration of the rules versus relationships. Does the cultural emphasis on living by the rules – respect for law and so on – take precedence over personal relationships or vice versa?

2. *Collectivism (communitarianism) versus individualism* – Consideration of groups versus individuals. Cultures, for a variety of reasons, either tend to value self-orientation or group orientation. This can affect the decision-making process and the extent to which authority resides in an individual to make decisions. This can have a profound effect on working practice with widespread consultation favoured by a common orientation culture. There is a danger, for example, that this might be perceived as procrastination by those from an individualistic background. It is this type of understanding that can help support the development of co-operative relationships inside and between organisations where one or both individuals are inexperienced in working with multi-cultural teams.

3. *Neutral versus emotional (affective)* – This reflects the range of emotions that people are able to express openly. This could have a considerable impact upon the way in which products are promoted, and how relationships are established with customers and the organisations in which they operate.

4. *Specific versus diffuse* – reflects how people will adjust their behaviour in different settings (specific). However, diffuse reflects the consistency of a person's relationships regardless of their situation. This has implications for managing staff, that is 'once the boss, always the boss', as opposed to specific where 'the boss is the boss in work and friend out of work'. This has a number of complexities, particularly for international working relationships.

5. *Achievement versus ascription* – This relates to how status is accorded. Status is achieved via years of experience, service, education and age. In other words the 'respect your elders' scenario.

Orientation in Time and Attitude Towards the Environment

6. *Sequential time versus synchronic time* – This is essentially the difference between a sequence of events or simultaneous events. It is a question of being able to juggle a lot of balls in respect of time or needing to operate in a sequence to differentiate activities. This can indicate a lot about an individual's ability to work individually, within a team, on a self-motivated basis or on a delegated activity basis.

7. *High context and low context* – High-context behaviour will have a form of ritual behaviour in everyday life. Priorities, status and so on will be important. Low context will see little in the way of ritual behaviour and can generally cope with a number of events happening at any one time. Fons Trompenaars and Charles Hampden-Turner (2001) interviewed 15,000 managers in 28 countries to explore the cultural differences between what they called universalist societies and particularist societies. In universalist societies, people follow the rules and assume that the standards they support are the correct ones. Further, they believe that society works better if everyone conforms to them. Particularist societies believe that particular circumstances are more important than general rules, and that people's responses depend on circumstances and on the particular people involved. In universalist countries, written contracts are taken seriously. Teams of lawyers are employed to make sure that a contract is correctly drafted, and once signed it must be policed to ensure it is kept. Particularist countries think that the relationship is more important than the contract and that a written contract is not always necessary – the particular people and the particular situation matter more than the universal rules. Different cultures have different ways of coping with life, a different set of responses to the same underlying dilemmas. In Far Eastern cultures, books start 'at the back' and are read from right to left in vertical columns. To Westerners, this seems a reversal of normal practice. Managers need to display cross-cultural competence and reconcile cultural differences. Successful leaders are those who are flexible, sensitive and skilled enough to be able to ride what they call 'the waves of culture'.

CASE STUDY

The Clash of Two Cultures?

Inevitably when two organizations work more closely together, in whatever form of business relationship, problems can arise. This can be due to differences in culture, sometimes national, sometimes corporate and sometimes a combination of the two. Culture appeared to be an issue with the merger of German car company Daimler-Benz with the US car maker Chrysler. The German car maker was motivated to merge partly to gain access to a broader product base which could be targeted at the emerging markets. Chrysler found the merger to be appealing, driven by concerns about over-capacity in car industry; they needed a partner to survive.

Potential issues emerged at the negotiation stage that are common in many mergers, e.g. the name of the new merged business and the location of headquarters, effectively defining the 'nationality' of the company. These appeared to be more deeply significant to the German business, possibly as a business that is seen by some as a company with a very long history that has been intertwined with the state. Daimler Chrysler became a German entity, and this created major morale issues in the US operations of the merged business, even affecting productivity.

Organizational cultural tensions took a long while to resolve. It has been suggested that the two organizations 'did not simply make cars differently, they lived in different worlds' (Badrtalei and Bates, 2007, p. 310). This was based on a wide variety of differences including executive compensation, provision of first class business travel, formal dress code and decision-making processes. Differences were even as basic as the policy and practice of wine consumption at lunch time and allowance of smoking in the office. The German business offered executives comparably smaller compensation packages, but allowed more levels of management to travel first class and to have larger expense accounts. They operated in a much more formal work environment, including dress code, and routinely worked late rather than confining this to necessity.

Since the 1998 merger these cultural issues have probably been fundamental to the issues that have affected this 'troubled' new business. Operational issues such as closing factories and sacking staff are relatively easier to address compared with more fundamental organisational characteristics that are related to culture.

Source: Badrtalei, J., Bates, D.L., 2007. Effect of organizational cultures on mergers and acquisitions: the case of Daimlerchrysler. *International Journal of Management*, 24(2), June.

This paper is well worth reading for the substantial detail provided on this merger.

An organisation's culture must support it in aligning with the environment if successful strategies are to be pursued. However, as organisations develop and evolve, they tend to progress through a cultural life cycle. Stacey (2003) suggests that cultural evolution goes hand in hand with structural evolution. Initially, a 'power' culture is appropriate when the organisation is in its infancy. It then becomes more appropriate for a 'role' culture to be implemented to operate a functional structure effectively and finally, as the organisation grows and expands, a divisional structure is used and in this context a 'task' culture is most appropriate. What are these cultural types? Handy (1981) cited in Stacey (2003, p. 65) provides a four-category organisational cultural classification:

1. *Power culture* – with the owner manager/entrepreneur acting with complete authority. Such people are risk takers and tend

to see administrative processes and procedures as getting in the way. They are the source of power. They do not emanate from the organisational systems and procedures that legitimise action in larger, long established organisations.

2. *Role culture* – organisations are highly bureaucratic with people specialising on a functional basis. Order, predictability and hierarchy are important. Procedures, rules and regulations for them define the essence of the organisation and adherence to these is the essence of 'good' management.

3. *Task culture* – as the name suggests, these are highly focused on work, whether it is in terms of general work function and/or particular projects with which people are involved.

4. *Person culture* – is where personal goals, satisfaction and interest drive organisational behaviour. This is most commonly manifested in organisations and divisions where technical specialists predominate – for example, engineers, accountants, lawyers and so on. They see their work as a vehicle for personal expression rather than simply getting the job done.

Handy's classification approach is useful when considering most western-style business organisations. However, Burns (1996) suggests that it fails to accommodate Japanese organisations as they contain elements of each extreme. For example, Japanese companies have very tightly defined and highly structured jobs and this is particularly evident at the more junior levels in the organisation. Japanese organisations are very hierarchical and deferential, but in spite of this they exhibit initiative and creativity in problem-solving.

VIRTUAL TEAMS

A virtual team is a group of people who are working together, even though they are not all in the same geographical location. Specifically, teams may be distributed for a variety of reasons:

- Organisation-wide projects or initiatives
- Alliances with different organisations, some of which may be in other countries
- Mergers and acquisitions
- Emerging markets in different geographic locations
- The desire of many people and government organisations for telecommuting

- The continuing need for business travel and information and communications technologies available to support this travel
- A need to reduce costs
- A need to reduce time-to-market

Types of Virtual Team

There are essentially four types of virtual team:

1. *Department Virtual Teams* are made up of people who all work for the same department but based in different locations, for example, a team of sales representatives working for the same manager but who spend most of their time out of the office or working from home. The team members have common objectives, work under the same day-to-day management and have a detailed understanding of each other's responsibilities and working conditions.

2. *Company Virtual Teams* comprising people who all work for the same company but within different departments and, most likely, locations. For example, a product development team formed from research and development, design, manufacturing, marketing and customer care divisions. Although the team members have an overriding shared goal – to produce a successful new product – they do not report to the same line of management and have different day-to-day roles and responsibilities. They are unlikely to know one another personally but will be used to working within the same corporate culture and have shared working conditions and hours.

3. *Organisation Virtual Teams* made up of members who do not all work for the same organisation. For example, a marketing team that works in partnership with an external agency responsible for carrying out creative work on their behalf. The team members will most likely have no existing relationship, work under different management and working conditions, have conflicting ideas about what their objectives should be and have no awareness of their colleagues' other responsibilities or big projects.

4. *Multiple Virtual Teams* made up of a mixture of virtual teams. For example, a cross-department team, all based in different locations, that also works with an external supplier based in another country. In addition to the issues highlighted above there will be more complex communication issues that will make it a difficult challenge for members of this team to co-ordinate their thoughts and ideas collectively.

Team members use communication technologies such as e-mail, videoconferencing and telephone more often than face-to-face meetings to communicate with each other. Common reasons for forming virtual teams are to integrate expertise from different locations, to save on travel time and travel costs, and to build relationships, shared understanding and shared identities across workplaces or organisations. Virtual teams face both the same challenges as traditional teams and some unique ones such as those relating to communication technologies and working at a distance. The dispersion of team members can make it difficult to establish a strong team identity, and it can be more of a challenge for the team members to work towards a common goal. Examples of virtual teams include a team of people working at different geographic sites and a project team whose members telecommute.

It is changes in the nature of teams and not the use of technology that creates new challenges for team managers and members. Most 'virtual' teams operate in multiple modes including having face-to-face meetings when possible. Managing a virtual team means managing the whole gamut of communication strategies and project management techniques as well as human and social processes in ways that support the team. Knowledge of group dynamics can help managers to understand what happens when people interact using new media.

Managers need to help virtual teams identify roles in the same way required of all teams. Virtual teams may need technical and specialists support in using different media. For all roles, virtual teams need to spend more time being explicit about mutual expectations for facilitators, managers and members because the patterns of behaviour and dynamics of interaction are unfamiliar.

Virtual teams form and share knowledge on the basis of information pulled from individual members, not a centralised push. One goal is to find ways that support the transformation of individuals' personal knowledge into organisational knowledge. This means designing environments where all the individuals have incentives to share what they know.

Managers of virtual teams can support their teams by:

- Encouraging members to explore questions that matter including questions about how they are working together.
- Supporting the creation of some kind of shared space (the feeling that there is an infrastructure where people are working together).
- Facilitating the co-ordination of the technology, work processes and the formal organisation.

INSIGHT

Virtual teams are having major problems and managing their progress has been a superlative challenge for most. When it comes down to online collaboration, team coordination and management, there are so many human-based variables at play, so many critical components to effective information exchange, workflow distribution and knowledge sharing, that delegating technology to take the full responsibility of the solution can only do so much to improve our collaboration and co-operation efficiency. Organizations face the need to analyse and comprehend which are the key obstacles to the successful management of effective online collaborative business networks. Virtual collaboration for networked business teams is a complex and challenging activity in which

there are major important components to be accounted for. Virtual business teams DO NOT operate like traditional physical teams, as their requirements reflect a whole new way of communicating, working collaboratively, sharing information and mutually supporting other team members.

The new technologies and approaches required to achieve this are completely alien to most of our present organizational culture. And this is why they fail. Co-operative processes are not the automatic results of implementing collaborative, real-time communication technologies, but the result of a carefully designed and systematically maintained virtual team development plan.

http://www.masternewmedia.org

Seven Things Virtual Teams Can do to Work Better

1. Have face-to-face meetings with all the members as soon as possible after the team is formed.
2. Find ways of building trust between the team members.
3. Clearly define goals, roles and tasks.
4. Ensure all team members are trained in cultural awareness and interpersonal skills.
5. Encourage informal communication between team members.
6. Set standards for time taken to respond to communications and acceptable times to call those in different time zones.
7. Leaders of virtual teams need to be proactive in building the team, and should anticipate and resolve misunderstandings and conflicts before they are allowed to develop.

Difficult areas for dispersed teams include co-ordination and collaboration, and dealing with conflict and performance problems when team members cannot be observed directly.

There is a useful online resource on virtual teams at http://www.startwright.com/virtual.htm

SUMMARY

Teams and individuals implement organisation strategy and marketing plans. Implementation is supported by the classical planning approach through which both the plan, and the individual, is tasked with work activity and finally reviewed, to consider the extent to which objectives have been met. For organisations and teams, the marketing plan may be the subject of review, including staff identified to complete tasks by given dates. The individual's version of this marketing planning review is the annual or more frequent staff appraisal. Internal marketing can be an important device for supporting acceptance of changes in team and individual working practices including changes in terms of job enrichment and/or enlargement.

High-performing teams have, or strive to have, particular characteristics. An important characteristic is that people in these teams are highly motivated. A range of management theories is presented to explain the mechanism by which motivation is understood to work. Based on this thinking the ideas of job enrichment and job enlargement flourished, until people realised that 'one size fits all' did not apply universally, even though frequently, when trying to use motivation theories at the workplace. Another environment in which motivated staff can flourish is where individuals are not subject to intolerance that creates tensions in the workforce, perhaps most commonly in terms of ethnicity and gender. Consequently diversity and discrimination are discussed.

Many teams are now separated geographically. Distance is just one aspect to consider when trying to ensure successful interfunctional co-ordination. Managing virtual teams, as well as their traditional counterparts, to perform is becoming increasingly necessary as well as common. Another major aspect of geographical distance is that team members can often be located in different national cultures, and possibly also be from different organisational cultures, where there has been a takeover or merger. Hofstede and Trompenaars provide helpful theories and dimensions of culture, which may be used to assess problems and issues in managing people from diverse cultures.

BIBLIOGRAPHY

Adams, J.S., 1965. Inequity in social exchange. In: Berkowitz, L. (Ed.), Advances in Experimental Social Psychology. Academic Press, New York.

Burns, B., 1996. Managing Change. Financial Times Management, London 106–120, ISBN 0273611186.

Doole, I., Lowe, R., 2004. International Marketing Strategy: Analysis, Development and Implementation, fourth ed. Thomson, London.

Drummond, G., Ensor, J., 2001. Strategic Marketing Planning and Control, second ed. Butterworth-Heinemann.

Fallon, M., 2005 'What can Lenovo IBM learn from other merged companies? *China Staff, Hong Kong*, February 2005, 11(2): 4–7.

Herzberg, F.Mausner, B.Bloch Snijderman, B., 1959. The Motivation to work. New York.

Herzberg, F., 1965. The Motivation to work among Finnish supervisors. Personnel Psychology 18 (4), 393–402.

Jobber, D., 2001. Principles and Practice of Marketing, third ed. McGraw-Hill.

Lawler, E.E., 1969. Job design and employee motivation. Personnel Psychology 22, 426–435.

Maslow, A.H., 1948. Some theoretical consequences of basic needs gratification. Journal of Personality 16 (4), 402–416.

McClelland, D.C., 1953. The Achievement Motive. Appleton-Century-Crofts, New York.

Ouchi, W.G., 1982. Theory Z: An Elaboration of Methodology and Findings. Journal of Contemporary Business 11 (2), 27.

Schein, E.H., 1985. Organizational Culture and Leadership: A Dynamic View. Jossey-Bass, San Francisco.

Schein, E.H., 1999. The Corporate Culture Survival Guide. Jossey-Bass Inc, San Francisco.

Stacey, R.D., 2003. Strategic Management and Organizational Dynamics. Prentice-Hall, Harlow ISBN 0273658980.

Trompenaars, F., 1993. Riding the Waves of Culture: Understanding Cultural Diversity in Business. Economist Books, London.

Trompenaars, F., Hampden-Turner, C., 1997. Riding the Waves of Culture: Understanding Cultural Diversity in Business, 2nd ed. Nicholas Breazley, London.

Trompenaars, F., Hampden-Turner, C., 2001. Building Cross-cultural Competence: How to Create Wealth from Conflicting Values. Wiley ISBN 0471495271.

Wheelan, S.A., 1999. Creating Effective Teams. Sage Publications, Thousand Oaks ISBN 0761918175.

CHAPTER 6

Improving Team Performance

2.7   Identify potential areas of team conflict, identifying causes and making recommendations for ways in which to overcome it.

2.8   Critically assess levels of performance in order to identify poor performance and reasons for it and recommendations of how to overcome it including consideration of loyalty and motivation programmes.

2.7:

- sources of conflict – interpersonal, change, organisational, external environment
- cultural differences
- assess the impact of conflict both positively and negatively
- conflict resolution and management
- change management strategies.

2.8:

- performance management – measuring performance against objectives and standards and providing feedback
- appraisal and peer review including 360-degree feedback
- internal marketing – employee motivation and satisfaction, customer orientation and satisfaction, interfunctional co-ordination
- competency assessment and achievement.

135

INTRODUCTION

Ultimately, we are interested in how to maximise the performance of teams. There are two dimensions to high performance namely:

1. The absence of problematic issues most commonly manifested in conflict.
2. Development in performance, that is, doing things better, rather than the removal of problems.

These are discussed in this chapter.

CONFLICT IN ORGANISATIONS

Conflict is inevitable but it can be minimized, diverted and/or resolved. Workplace conflict can lower morale and productivity, increase staff turnover and employee burnout, and add greatly to sick pay costs. Some conflicts are good and some not so good. Conflict occurs naturally when people interact, and teams, organizations and even individuals can grow as a result of the new ideas and the new ways of thinking that can emerge through conflict. However, conflict can also be destructive for individuals and for organizations. Organizational change can require members of an organization to work together in new ways and under new rules. Competition can exacerbate personality conflicts and the complexities of communication can make it more difficult for culturally, economically and socially diverse workers to resolve the issues and problems they encounter on the job.

Source: Lankard Brown (1998).

Different people have different ways of dealing with situations but in general, human beings share certain characteristics that are very similar – even across gender, racial and socio-economic lines.

- People tend to like it when people agree with them.
- People tend to not like it when people disagree with them.
- People tend to like other people who agree with them.

- People tend to dislike other people who disagree with them.
- People who are good at resolving conflicts look for some point of agreement and use good people skills to get others to see a different point of view.

Conflict occurs when individuals or groups do not obtain what they need or want and are seeking to look after their own self-interests. Sometimes the individual is not aware of the need and unconsciously starts to act out. Other times, the individual is very aware of what he or she wants and actively works at achieving the goal.

Conflict is destructive when it:

- Takes attention away from other important activities
- Undermines morale or self-concept
- Polarises people and groups, reducing co-operation
- Increases or sharpens difference.

Conflict is constructive when it:

- Results in clarification of important problems and issues
- Results in solutions to problems
- Involves people in resolving issues important to them
- Causes authentic communication
- Helps release emotion, anxiety and stress
- Builds co-operation among people through learning more about each other
- Makes people join in resolving the conflict
- Helps individuals develop understanding and skills.

A FOUR-CATEGORY PERSPECTIVE OF TEAM PROBLEMS

Irwin et al. (1974) suggest that teams encounter problems whether they are project teams or long-standing operational teams. They highlight four particular categories of problems that can result in conflict and poor performance that are interdependent, namely problems with:

1. Goals
2. Roles
3. Processes
4. Relationships

In their discussion of this topic, there is a sense that these four factors form a type of hierarchy of potential problems starting with the broadest directional issues to the detailed specific aspects of relationships between team members. This includes team leader–team member relationships and relationships between team members within the team and between teams.

Goal Problems

Goals may exist; however, they may be unclear or misunderstood by team members. In the worst situations, goals may be poorly specified and/or may be impossible to measure.

Role Problems

Interdependence with the preceding problem is evident on reflection. If there is a lack of clarity about goals, how can there be any clarity about roles for individuals within the team? Once goals, or objectives, have been established, it is possible to clarify individual roles.

This, however, is fraught with many difficulties that are frequently overlooked. To what extent:

- Do individuals understand the boundaries of their roles?

- Do individuals understand the degree of freedom and authority within their roles?

- Does the individual's perception of their role match others' perception? This may lead to, 'Wasn't I supposed to do that' or 'That's my job'. Alternatively, 'I thought you were to do that'.

- Inevitably, roles interact or even overlap. An inability to cope effectively with this source of potential confusion or conflict will inevitably lead to sub-optimal team performance.

Process Problems

There are many potential process issues. One perspective is to consider the more significant as concerned with

   a. decision-making

   b. communications and meetings

   c. leadership style

   a. Progress occurs only when decisions are taken. When more than one person is involved this becomes a process issue. Who has the responsibility and ultimately the authority to make decisions? What rights do team members have, especially in relation to the leader, with regard to decision-making? Do all members of the team need to be consulted? Perhaps people outside of the team must be included in some decisions.

b. How does everyone know that a decision has been made? In other words, how can/will decisions be communicated? It may be that, due to different roles within the team, and certainly as the team size grows, not every member of a team needs to know the outcome of every decision. If consideration is not given to this with larger teams then individuals may suffer from information overload. In the more formal setting of meetings, who attends and how are unavoidable absences accommodated? The team must also have an approach to meeting structure and process.

c. The leader is in a very different category within the team. Leadership styles may tend towards the autocratic or inclusive. Sometimes the fact that inclusive, participative leadership styles have become more common has led some to place less influence on the role of the leader. Group development is fundamentally influenced by the style of the leader and this in particular will affect the efficiency of processes. In a 'performing' team the leader is most likely to seek and accept feedback on two aspects of his/her leadership – fundamental style/ approach and the impact their role is having on the team.

ACTIVITY 6.1

Team process problems

Analyse a team meeting that you have attended recently in which decisions were arrived at. Answer the following questions, which attempt to assess how many process problems you have.

- How were decisions taken? How many participated in making the decisions? How was disagreement resolved? Did only one person make each of the decisions in effect?
- Were you clear as to who had responsibility for each decision?
- Did everyone have the same amount of information to support their contribution to decision-making? Perhaps each team member had specialist information; however, did those bringing most information to the decision have greater influence?
- Was influence purely on the basis of perceived or actual job role or perhaps on the basis of seniority in the team/organisation?
- How was the meeting structured? Was there a clear agenda? How was timekeeping at the meeting?
- Was there a lot of pointless debate? Was there a feeling that the meeting, perhaps only in places, was going nowhere?
- What role did the 'leader' (however defined) take? To what extent did they let participants exert influence or did the leader use an autocratic approach? Obviously, the leader's approach may vary in the course of the meeting.

How many of the answers to these questions indicated the existence of process problems? If there are many, you must hold a team meeting specifically to address process problems, otherwise you can never become, or remain, a high-performing team.

Relationship Problems

Relationship issues may be considered as potentially the lowest level, or most detailed aspect, of potential team problems. They are in fact the most intractable and hardest to resolve as they operate at the most personal level. The other three areas of potential team problems (already discussed) are 'external' to the individual. Individuals are generally not affected fundamentally by changes in any of these. However, relationship problems may be deep-seated. They may arise from a lack of mutual respect or trust in technical competence or judgement.

Unfortunately, 'relationships' may be regarded as an issue when in actual fact the problem is concerned with goals, roles or processes. For example, conflicts between individuals may be due to a failure to clarify goals or roles rather than any personal problem that individuals have with one another.

We understand that teams generally go through various phases, ideally culminating in operating as a 'performing' team. The concept of an evolution of team performance suggests that sub-optimal performance may be different in each phase. The application of the ideas of Irwin et al. (1974) to the different stages of team development is apparent.

Goals and priorities	Vital that goals and priorities are established at the *forming* stage. However, the team leader may not have established his/her authority. In addition, often the team must construct their own goals and priorities. At this stage in development, team members may argue forcibly about these issues and it is vital that this is resolved and members come to an agreement on a shared approach or accommodation that they can work with.
Roles	By the time the team gets to the *norming* stage, roles should be established. Prior to this, especially if a new member joins the team, expectations about the non-specified aspects of the role have to be reconciled – an obvious potential source of conflict.
Processes	Meetings can be a very good indicator of performance problems. At the *performing* stage, team members listen actively to one another and exhibit a high degree of collaboration resulting in rapid decision-making. Process issues, especially with regard to meetings and decision-making, will have been determined and members will be open to continuous modification and improvement. However, prior to this stage, for example at the *storming* stage, team members may be prone to talk and not to listen, time management may be poor with meeting time overruns and decision-making may be fairly crude, simply through majority voting.
Relationships	In a *performing* group, there will be a high level of trust and commitment between team members. Effective team functioning will build shared experience and engaging in co-operative behaviour will reinforce relationships and facilitate their development towards a deeper level.

Extending Knowledge
Taking action to control sub-standard performance is the focus of the section in Brown (2002) on 'Controlling projects – taking action', pp. 74–87. Brown, M., 2002. Project Management in a Week, 3rd ed. Hodder & Stoughton, London.

Some Strategies for Dealing with Conflict

1. Unusual non-verbal behaviour can be an early warning sign of conflict. Ask people to verbalise their feelings wherever possible.

2. *Team development phase* – See the Tuckman forming, storming, norming, performing model. Sometimes conflict is predictable because that is what happens at one particular phase of group development.

3. *Resort to authority* – This means bringing in someone using a legitimate power base (and perhaps other power bases) to lay down the law. This may be necessary if team members are playing destructive roles.

4. *Planning* – Techniques such as task scheduling, timelines and project diaries and meetings may provide an authoritative and neutral way of sequencing tasks to be performed by different individuals or subgroups, thus reducing potential for conflict.

5. *Use communication skills more effectively* – Sometimes it is best to utilise what you know about good communication skills. Try to control destructive role-playing. Acknowledge individuals by praising their input.

6. *Conflict management techniques*:

    ▪ Collaborating: I win, you win
    ▪ Compromising: win some/lose some
    ▪ Accommodating: I lose/you win
    ▪ Competing: I win/you lose
    ▪ Avoiding: no winners/no losers

Collaborating

Fundamental premise – Teamwork and co-operation help everyone achieve their goals while also maintaining relationships.
Strategic philosophy – Working through differences will lead to creative solutions that will satisfy both the parties' concerns.

When to use:

- When there is a high level of trust.
- When you don't want to have full responsibility.
- When you want others to also have 'ownership' of solutions.
- When the people involved are willing to change their thinking as more information is found and new options are suggested.
- When you need to work through animosity and hard feelings.

Drawbacks:

- Takes lots of time and energy.
- Some may take advantage of other people's trust and openness.

Compromising

Fundamental premise – Winning something while losing a little is OK.

Strategic philosophy – Both ends are placed against the middle in an attempt to serve the 'common good' while ensuring each person can maintain something of their original position.

When to use:

- When people of equal status are equally committed to goals.
- When time can be saved by reaching intermediate settlements on individual parts of complex issues.
- When goals are moderately important.

Drawbacks:

- Important values and long-term objectives can be derailed in the process.
- May not work if initial demands are too great.
- Can create cynicism, especially if there is no commitment to honour the compromise solutions.

Accommodating

Fundamental premise – Working towards a common purpose is more important than any of the peripheral issues.
Strategic philosophy – Appease others by downplaying conflict, thus protecting the relationship.

When to use:

- When the issue is not as important to you as it is to the other person.
- When you know you can't win.

- When it's not the right time.
- When harmony is extremely important.
- When what the parties have in common is much more important than their differences.

Drawbacks:

- One's own ideas don't get attention.
- Credibility and influence can be lost.

Competing

> *Fundamental premise* – Associates 'winning' a conflict with competition.
> *Strategic philosophy* – When goals are extremely important, one must sometimes use power to win.

When to use:

- When you know you are right.
- When you need a quick decision.
- When a strong personality is trying to steamroller you.
- When you need to stand up for your rights.

Drawbacks:

- Can escalate conflict.
- Losers may retaliate.

Avoiding

> *Fundamental premise* – This isn't the right time or place to address this issue.
> *Strategic philosophy* – Avoids conflict by withdrawing, sidestepping or postponing.

When to use:

- When the conflict is small and relationships are at stake.
- When more important issues are pressing and you don't have time to deal with this.
- When you see no chance of getting your concerns met.
- When you are too emotionally involved and others around you can solve the conflict more successfully.
- When more information is needed.

Drawbacks:

- Important decisions may be made by default.
- Postponing sometimes makes matters worse.

Source: Culbert (2002).

DEVELOPING THE TEAM

ACTIVITY 6.2

Here is an activity for evaluating your team. Circle the number that is appropriate for your team. What are your priorities for development? – You could also ask a trusted colleague to complete a form like this about you so that you can compare your responses with his or her perceptions. If there were large gaps in perception you might want to pursue this further to understand why your perceptions are different.

Rating team development

How do you feel about your team's progress? (Circle rating).

1.	Team's purpose I am uncertain	1 2 3 4 5	I am clear
2.	Team membership I am out	1 2 3 4 5	I am in
3.	Communications Very guarded	1 2 3 4 5	Very open
4.	Team goals Set from above	1 2 3 4 5	Emerged through team interaction
5.	Use of team member's skills Poor use	1 2 3 4 5	Good use
6.	Support Little help for individuals	1 2 3 4 5	High level of support for individuals
7.	Conflict Difficult issues are avoided	1 2 3 4 5	Problems are discussed openly and directly
8.	Influence on decisions By few members By few members	1 2 3 4 5	By all members
9.	Risk taking Not encouraged	1 2 3 4 5	Encouraged and supported
10.	Working on relationships with others Little effort	1 2 3 4 5	High level of effort
11.	Distribution of leadership Limited	1 2 3 4 5	Shared
12.	Useful feedback Very little	1 2 3 4 5	Considerable

INSIGHT

Learning and Development

Developing our people is one of our most important goals. Essentially, if we do not have the right people, with the right skills and capabilities, at the right time and in the right places, our business will suffer. After all, Serco only has two kinds of product: its processes and its people.

We are committed to developing our people – and we encourage them to learn and grow throughout their careers. In a business as diverse as ours, it is vital that we can share more widely the best practice developed in one market or region. That is why we are using the latest technology to give everyone access to the same information and resources.

We are always being joined by new people as we phase-in new contracts – so we have devised ways of helping them assimilate our values and adopt the Serco culture. Because we have a diverse portfolio of contracts, our training and development processes are designed to produce staff who are versatile, flexible and inventive.

As Serco becomes increasingly global, distance learning is likely to become more important. We are currently investing in solutions that will enable us to deploy and track learning in geographically diverse locations – enabling us to reach all our people, everywhere. Combined with powerful diagnostic tools, including performance appraisal and development centres, this will ensure we deliver learning solutions that meet today's business needs – and help us anticipate future needs.

Source: SERCO: Our World, December 2005.

FURTHER STUDY

Read Boddy, D., 2002. Management: An Introduction. Pearson Education, Harlow (Chapter 13, 'Motivation' and Chapter 15, 'Teams').

PLANNING FOR CHANGE

The major problem with implementation of change management strategies is failure to manage change successfully. Many people are resistant to change because they are familiar with the status quo and fear the consequences of change. Marketing managers need to be aware of the internal barriers that exist, and then need to develop strategies to overcome these barriers. It is essential that in order to facilitate change it is necessary to have an understanding of how change occurs in organisations.

The Three-step Model

Lewin (1958), cited in Burnes (1996), suggested that in many cases change was very shortlived and after a period of time, group behaviour reverted back to its previous pattern. The idea of the three-step model is that change is regarded as permanent. The three steps include:

1. Unfreezing the present level
2. Moving to the new level
3. Refreezing the new level

This model recognises that for new behaviour to be accepted, old behaviour has to be discarded.

The Phases of Planned Change Model

The three-step model provides a general framework for understanding the process of organisational change. However, it still adopts a rather broad approach and therefore a variety of models of planned change have been developed by a number of writers. For example, Bullock and Battern (1958), cited in Burnes (1996), developed a four-phase model of planned change. This model explains change in terms of two major dimensions: change phases and change processes. Change phases relates to the stages through which an organisation moves in planned change. Change processes are the means by which an organisation moves from one state to the next:

1. *Exploration stage* – This is the time during which organisations will decide whether to initiate any changes and, if so, allocate resources to the process. *The change processes* may include becoming aware of the need to change and searching for external assistance.

2. *Planning phase* – This involves understanding the organisations' problem. *The change processes* involved may include: searching for information to make the correct diagnosis of the problem, and establishing objectives and gaining support of key decision-makers.

3. *Action phase* – At this stage the changes are implemented. *The change processes* relate to the establishment of arrangements to manage the change process, gain staff support, evaluation of implementation and taking corrective action if necessary.

4. *Integration phase* – This relates to the development of a new status quo. The change processes include reinforcing new behaviour through reward systems, disseminating relevant information and encouraging improvements in all.

This model is useful because it makes a distinction between the phases of change and the methods of facilitating change.

The Change Process

Burnes (1996) provides a useful framework for analysing the change process. This suggests that the change process consists of three interlinked elements: objectives and outcomes, planning the change and people. This approach acknowledges the multi-dimensional approach to change management that is necessary.

Objectives

It is essential that objectives and outcomes are explicit and open. Burnes (1996) suggests that initially there will be a trigger that prompts the needs for change. From this clarity, agreement must be sought about who has the responsibility and authority to initiate change. It will then be necessary to identify the assessment team who will clarify the problem/opportunity, investigate possible solutions, provide feedback and then present recommendations. If from this the decision is to go ahead, then it becomes necessary to begin the implementation process.

Planning the change

According to Burnes (1996), this involves six interrelated activities:

1. Establishing a change management team.

2. *Management structures* – Special structures may be necessary to facilitate the change process.

3. *Activity planning* – Constructing a schedule to the change programme.

4. *Commitment planning* – This involves identifying key people whose support is necessary for the successful implementation of change.

5. *Audit and post-audits* – It is essential that progress is carefully monitored to identify whether objectives are being met.

6. *Training* – This may be necessary to provide staff with the new skills they will need in the new era or it may involve providing training to help them facilitate change in themselves.

People

This is probably the most overlooked part of the change process. For change programmes to be successful, it is essential that all the people affected are involved and motivated and that their support is gained. This involves creating a willingness to change, involving people and sustaining the momentum:

- *Creating a willingness to change* – Many people will resist change because of the fear of the unknown. It is essential that people are made aware of the need for change and also provided with regular feedback on its progress. In order to create a positive attitude to change, organisations should publicise successful change and the benefits this has brought to employees. It is also essential that the concerns and fears of people should be taken seriously and addressed.

■ *Involving people* – In order for people to 'buy into' the change process, they must be able to take ownership of the process rather than having it imposed upon them. This can be achieved through effective communication (two-way) and getting people involved.

■ *Sustaining the momentum* – It is difficult to sustain the momentum of change particularly when those involved continue to be faced with the day-to-day pressures of meeting customer needs This can be helped by ensuring that sufficient resources are available, support is given to the 'change agents' and desired behaviour is reinforced through rewards. It is likely that change will result in the need for new skills and competences and it is essential that staff are adequately trained, mentored, counselled or coached. It is apparent that the change process is a complex blend of objective setting, planning and people.

ACTIVITY 6.3

The change process

Identify a change that has been recently introduced. Evaluate the extent to which the company considered the three elements identified by Burnes (objectives, planning the change and people) when introducing the change. In particular to what extent did the company acknowledge the importance of 'people'? If people were not involved and motivated, what were the implications of this?

Why Change Fails

As stated previously, up to 80 per cent of change strategies fail. Robbins and Finley (1998) suggest a number of reasons as to why change initiatives fail:

■ *It is the wrong idea* – No matter how well implemented, it is not going to succeed because it is inappropriate.

■ *It is the right idea but the wrong time* – Maybe too soon after a failed change initiative, too few available resources, lack of top management support.

■ *You are doing it for the wrong reasons* – Usually money. For example, companies initiate change as a means of increasing efficiencies and saving money.

■ *It lacks authenticity* – Some companies are led to change not because it is inherently necessary but because it is in vogue: that is, everyone else is doing it.

- *Your reality contradicts your change* – For example, a company may announce a flattening of the organisational structure to encourage a more egalitarian culture. However, the reality is far from that – the old practices such as separate dining rooms for managers and workers send out stronger messages that in fact nothing has changed. This often leads to cynicism and distrust in the organisation.

- *You have the wrong leader* – One cannot underplay the role of a strong leader that inspires and motivates staff. It is essential that the leader is compatible with the culture of the company or else this may result in conflict.

- *Change for change's sake* – Senior management initiate change to alleviate the boredom of everyday life. They thrive on creating turmoil and even gain personal satisfaction from this turmoil.

- *People are not prepared or convinced* – In the short term, this suggests the need for training and communication to encourage people to buy into the new ideas. In the long term, it is probably more of an issue of corporate culture.

- *Bad luck* – Contingencies that are not planned for. For example, terrorist attacks, natural disasters, death of a senior manager.

- *There is nothing you can do* – In some cases, there may be nothing anyone can do to stem the rising tide of failure.

ACTIVITY 6.4

Reasons why change fails

Thinking about your company (or one with which you are familiar), identify the change initiatives that have been unsuccessful, and referring to the list above identify why this was the case. What actions could have been taken, if any, to facilitate the change process?

Beer et al. (1990) suggest that for successful corporate change there are three interrelated factors:

1. *Co-ordination (teamwork)* – within and between departments.
2. *Commitment* – high levels are required to ensure co-operation and co-ordination.
3. *New competencies* – such as analytical, interpersonal skills are essential.

They believe that many company-wide change programmes fail because they do not address all the three factors. Companies can try and avoid the problems associated with pragmatic change by adopting a 'task alignment' perspective, that is, 'by focusing on reorganising employees' roles, responsibilities and relationships to solve specific business problems'. This in turn will shape new attitudes and ideas.

CASE STUDY

Managing Change Successfully – A Finnish Elevator Company in China

The context in which change had to occur was in an international Finnish elevator and escalator company (manufacture, installation and refurbishment) operating in 50 countries worldwide, with a global workforce of approximately 22,000. The particular part of the business where there was a problem was in the service and maintenance (including breakdowns) of existing installations. Success in this business area requires both a technical competence and a customer-focused mindset, often in difficult circumstances. The organization change problem concerned the Chinese workforce in its business operation, especially in the Shenzhen business (not far from Hong Kong).

Before a change management programme could be devised it is necessary to understand the cultural characteristics of the workforce. Managers from outside China perceived the workforce to be over-compliant, operating as if they were working for a dictator. This led them to be totally unresponsive to customer needs. Staff needed to take the initiative themselves, if they have the technical competence, to satisfy the customer and get the job done well and quickly. Taking

account of the consensual Chinese culture and its approach to work, it was concluded that a vital aspect of change management strategy was to create a team-based, self-directed workforce, who could work on improving performance and customer satisfaction. This assessment was informed by the academic work of Hofstede. China is a high power-distance culture in which hierarchy, authority and respect for authority are culturally programmed. However, to work towards organizational learning and continuous improvement requires democracy of the workforce to encourage free exchange of ideas and of approaches to problem-solving, without fear of criticism or of being concerned about being critical and disrespectful of superiors.

The focus of organizational change was therefore on facilitating the development of this approach, while being sensitive to the cultural programming of the local workforce. A more democratic, learning organization was established, however, based on consensual teams, and this resulted in substantial improvements in customer service levels and customer satisfaction.

Source: Based on Elsey, B., Sai-kwong Leung, J., 2004. Changing the work behaviour of Chinese employees using organizational learning. Journal of Workplace Learning 16 (3/4), 167 (12 pages).

ACTIVITY 6.5

Success of change programmes
Consider at least three changes that have been introduced in your company in the last 12–18 months. How successful have they been? Consider the reasons as to why they succeeded or failed.

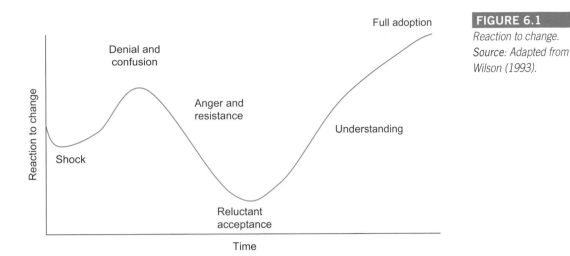

FIGURE 6.1
Reaction to change.
Source: Adapted from Wilson (1993).

Adapting to Change

The development of a culture that embraces change is an essential ingredient of successful implementation. The transition curve can help in understanding how people adapt to change Figure 6.1.

This model is useful because it illustrates that eventually people will internalise the new status quo (or will have left the organisation). Adapting to change can be a very painful process and the expression of anger and frustration is a natural part of this adaptation. The implication for marketers is that the acceptance of major changes in working practices and responsibilities will take time.

ACTIVITY 6.6

Managing change

Select one example of change that has been instigated within your organisation. To what extent did the model in Figure 6.1 fit your experiences of this change? How can managers use this model to their advantage?

Factors Critical for Success

According to Stewart and Kringas (2003), the success of change programmes depends on a number of factors:

- An appropriate change model
- Effective leadership
- Sufficient resources
- Attention to communication

Table 6.1	Factors contributing to successful implementation
Factor	**Comment**
Leadership	A strong and effective leader who is able to motivate and build teams is an essential ingredient for successful implementation.
Culture	Culture refers to the shared values and beliefs. If a plan goes against the dominant culture, it is likely the plan will fail, unless support is gained via internal marketing.
Structure	Organisational structures not only denote levels of responsibility but also facilitates communication. Communication is a key aspect of implementation, and organisations must ensure that the structures do not act as barriers to effective communication.
Resources	Appropriate levels of resources should be available – time, money and staff.
Control	Effective controls should be established to measure the progress and success of plans.
Skills	Skills necessary for successful implementation include technical/marketing skills, HRM skills and project management skills.
Strategy	An appropriate and relevant strategy must be communicated to all participants.
Systems	Effective systems should be in place. For example, marketing information systems that generate relevant and timely information.

Source: Adapted from Drummond and Ensor (2001, p. 150).

Drummond and Ensor (2001) identify a number of factors that will contribute to the successful implementation of plans and can therefore be applied to implementing change programmes. These are illustrated in Table 6.1.

These factors are embodied in the 7-S model developed by McKinsey & Co., as illustrated in Figure 6.2. This model consists of two categories of factors:

1. *Soft or HRM aspects* – style, staff, shared values and skills
2. *Hard or process aspects* – strategy, structure and systems

Implementation strategies focus all too often on the hard or process aspects and ignore the very real 'soft' aspects that must be addressed if implementation strategies are to succeed.

OVERCOMING RESISTANCE THROUGH INTERNAL MARKETING

Internal marketing can be used to facilitate the change process and overcome resistance to change. This section discusses how this happens.

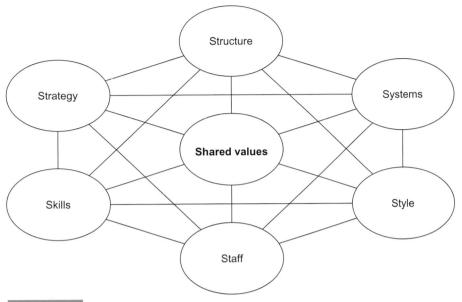

FIGURE 6.2   *The 7-S model developed by McKinsey & Co.*

Internal Marketing (IM)

According to Berry (1981), 'The most important contribution the marketing department can make is to be exceptionally clever in getting everyone else in the organisation to practice marketing.' This is essentially what internal marketing (IM) is concerned with. It is more of a management philosophy and strategy than a marketing function.

Gronroos (1990) identified two separate but integrated elements of internal marketing: attitude management and communications management. Attitude management is associated with motivating employees to buy into the organisation's goals whilst communications management involves providing and managing the information that employees need to perform effectively.

Internal marketing can play a key role in the implementation of plans. It is concerned with adopting the principles and practices of external marketing to the internal market. Figure 6.3 illustrates that in fact there are three types of marketing that occur within an organisation. The success of external marketing lies in the ability of the organisation to satisfy the needs of the customer. Organisations are dependent on their staff to achieve this, particularly in high customer-contact service businesses. Therefore, successful internal marketing is increasingly being seen as a prerequisite for effective external marketing.

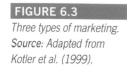

FIGURE 6.3

Three types of marketing.
Source: Adapted from
Kotler et al. (1999).

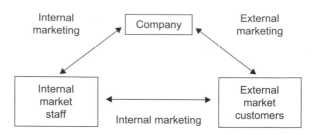

Internal marketing suggests that employees should be treated as internal customers, and marketing plans need to be 'marketed' internally to gain acceptance and to ensure that employees understand the rationale behind the plans, can see how they can contribute to the success of the plan and, importantly, 'buy into' the plan. This is not an easy task. A survey of employees in British companies with 1000 people or more, published by the Marketing & Communications Agency (MCA) and MORI, shows the scope of the challenge. The majority of employees said they feel undervalued, uninvolved and lack confidence in their organisations' leaders and vision (Mazur, 2001). Employees who lack motivation and confidence in their organisations are unlikely to buy into new ideas readily.

Internal marketing can play an important role in managing innovation.

There is no single unified definition of what is meant by internal marketing. However, there is general a agreement that internal marketing involves a planned effort to overcome organisational resistance to change and to align, motivate and integrate employees towards the effective implementation of corporate and functional strategies (Ahmed and Rafiq, 1993). It is likely that any change in strategy will require internal marketing to overcome organisational resistance and to help motivate staff.

Ahmed and Rafiq (2002) have undertaken an extensive review of internal marketing and from this they have identified five main elements of internal marketing:

1. *Employee motivation and satisfaction* – IM acts as a vehicle for staff acquisition, motivation and retention, which in turn leads to increased productivity and external service quality.

2. *Customer orientation and customer satisfaction* – IM can promote customer-orientated behaviour among staff.

3. *Interfunctional co-ordination and integration* – These are key elements of a market orientation as identified by Narver and Slater (1990). IM can be used to co-ordinate the efforts of the different functions in an organisation.

4. *Marketing-like approach to the above* – Other tools can be used to achieve the above. However, IM relies on achieving these through the use of marketing principles and tools.

5. *Implementation of specific corporate or functional strategies* – Piercy (2002) suggests that IM plays a crucial role in the implementation of strategic change by ensuring understanding and support for the strategies and also for removing barriers to change.

Ahmed and Rafiq (2002, p. 11) produced the following definition of IM that encompasses all of the five elements above:

> *Internal marketing is a planned effort using a marketing-like approach directed at motivating employees, for implementing and integrating organizational strategies towards customer orientation.*

Extending Knowledge

See Chapters 1 and 2 of Ahmed and Rafiq (2002) for a more detailed discussion of what internal marketing is and how it works.

CASE STUDY

Internal Marketing – not Just Corporate Mantras

It is more commonly accepted that brands and marketing are no longer the sole preserve of marketers. It makes sense that everyone who represents the brand needs to have a very clear idea of the brand and what it stands for. Many organizations, for example BT, Cadbury Schweppes and Unilever, have developed ever more sophisticated internal marketing programmes to ensure that the message gets through to their own staff. Marketers as experts in communicating with external customers need to be responsible for communicating the message internally in conjunction with HR, who can provide advice on internal communication channels and approaches. However, all too many consider they have discharged their internal marketing duties when staff have completed a fairly dull training session that equips them to quote a few organizational mantras.

Internal marketing needs to operate at a much more sophisticated level, educating staff in the negative perceptions customers have of the sector in which they operate. For example, in the car industry, people frequently like the cars but hate the way they are sold, especially the lack of transparency in pricing. In addition, many in the industry still take a macho perspective in their approach to discussing their products that alienates many customers, especially females. Training needs to address this and ensure that the brand remains relevant to potential and existing customers. It is essential that the brand experience is consistent with the brand message.

Ensuring staff understand brand values and corporate history is an important part of the work of the Honda marketing department. Staff even receive a detailed corporate handbook on joining that has been produced by the company's relationship marketing agency. The thinking is that in providing people with a deeper understanding of the brand and its values they will buy into the brand and in turn become very effective brand ambassadors. If staff are going to be responsible for communicating the brand to customers then the more complete their understanding the better.

Source: Based on, and adapted from, Anonymous [Feature] Case Study – Marketing capability: blend for flexibility, Brand Strategy, London, July 17 2006, p. 30.

The Internal Marketing Plan

The internal marketing plan should take the same format as an external marketing plan with objectives, strategy, market segmentation, marketing mix programmes and evaluation.

- Where are we now?
- Where do we want to be? (objective setting)
- How do we get there?
- How do we ensure/ check we have arrived?

Internal Market Segmentation

Internal markets could be segmented in a number of different ways, such as by job function, role or location. However, these methods may not be the most appropriate. It may be useful to segment according to the extent to which people are likely to accept the proposed change. Jobber (2001) suggests that three different segments can be identified:

1. *Supporters* – likely to gain from the change
2. *Neutrals* – will neither gain nor lose
3. *Opposers* – likely to lose from the change or are traditional opponents

Robbins and Finley (1998) categorise people according to their attitude to change. On one end of the scale, there are those people who not only accept change readily but are also naturally proactive and seek out change. This group of people help to drive organisations forward because they embrace change willingly, as well as initiate it. At the other end of the continuum, there are those people who are largely reactive and resist change. This group of people can be the death of any change initiative. This may be a useful way of segmenting employees. Organisations will have to expend differing amounts of resources and use different strategies for each group.

A separate marketing mix can then be developed for each of these segments. It may also be possible to identify influential individuals that are opinion leaders.

Internal Marketing Execution

Successful execution of the internal plan is reliant on three key skills (Jobber, 2001, p. 658):

1. *Persuasion* – The ability to develop a persuasive argument and to support words with action.

2. *Negotiation* – It is likely that some negotiations will have to take place so that all parties are happy.

3. *Politics* – Organisations are made up of people, all with their own personal agendas. Therefore, it is essential that the sources of power are identified and used to help implement the plan.

Internal Marketing Evaluation

In order to evaluate the success of internal marketing programmes, appropriate measures have to be used, such as:

- The extent of support of key players
- Employee satisfaction levels
- Reduced customer complaints
- Higher customer satisfaction scores.

Many companies are now conducting regular surveys to monitor levels of staff motivation, acceptance of the marketing concept and perceptions of the organisation. In addition, it could be argued that if internal marketing is being effective then it should be having an impact on external marketing. By measuring levels of customer satisfaction and numbers of customer complaints, it may give an indication of the success of internal marketing programmes.

Potential Problems

There are a number of potential problems associated with internal marketing. For example:

- Opposers create convincing counter arguments.

- Insufficient time to implement effective internal plans.

- High staff turnover that causes problems in ensuring all staff is involved.

- Low-paid shop (front-line) staff may result in a 'Why should I bother?' attitude.

- *Cost* – internal marketing programmes can be costly and many organisations are still slow to recognise their importance. Staff training and other solutions can be very expensive and companies have to recognise that there may be diminishing returns on their investment in IM. It is essential that they recognise the optimal level, not necessarily the desired level.

Extending Knowledge
Piercy (2002), Chapter 14, 'Implementing Market Strategies', provides an excellent discussion of internal marketing.

ACTIVITY 6.7

Ahmed and Rafiq (2002) suggest a multi-level model of internal marketing that provides a framework for understanding how implementation of strategy can be created by deploying the internal marketing mix using marketing research, segmentation and positioning. Ahmed and Rafiq (2002) present a case illustration of their multi-level model of internal marketing for Pearl Assurance on pp. 47–54. Read the discussion of this model on pp. 37–44 and then produce your own model for your own organisation similar to that on p. 50.

It is also important to recognise that internal marketing cannot alone solve all employee-related and customer satisfaction problems. In some cases, solutions lie more in ensuring that the right staff are recruited to the right positions in sufficient numbers and that they are adequately trained and motivated.

CASE STUDY

Merger of Lloyds Bank and TSB

The merger of Lloyds Bank and TSB could potentially have caused great problems with staff morale. In order to try and manage this momentous change, an internal marketing campaign was carried out by Jack Morton Worldwide. Their task was to unite the 77,000 staff from the two companies and to rebrand the merged company as Lloyds TSB. The campaign consisted of two stages: first, a trial of the jointly branded bank was established in Norwich; and second, an event to present the rationale behind the merger was held in Birmingham.

Many members of staff visited the pilot branch and feedback from this was used to help refine the messages to be used in the internal campaign. Over 4000 cash machines, 2300 branches and 40,000 uniforms then had to be rebranded.

It was realized that if the new brand values were to be communicated effectively to external customers, the first need was to communicate these to its employees to ensure they were delivering consistent brand images.

Five thousand members of staff, each representing 15 people, were nominated as 'pathfinders' and attended the live event in Birmingham – 'Your Life. Your Bank'. They were tasked with taking the message back to the branches. The presentation focused on explaining the rationale behind the merger, revealing the new blue and green corporate identity and explaining the new brand values with the objective being to gain staff commitment. The presentation culminated in a live concert by the Corrs, who also provided the music for Lloyds TSB's advertising campaign.

Afterwards the information was cascaded down through the entire organization. Extensive research was undertaken by an external consultant to evaluate the process. According to the Managing Director of Jack Morton Worldwide, 'The research concluded that the event was a huge success, that it met its objectives and that there was some change in all areas. The staff felt better informed about the changes, the values of the bank and had greater pride in it.'

Source: Adapted from Benady (2001).

Extending Knowledge

For further discussion of the tools of internal marketing, see Ahmed and Rafiq (2002), Chapter 3. This chapter includes interesting case studies of Sainsbury's and Pearl Assurance.

ACTIVITY 6.8

Internal marketing

To what extent do you think your organisation has embraced the concept of internal marketing?

What impact does this have on its external marketing activities?

How has your company embraced technology (for example, an intranet in an attempt to improve their internal marketing/communications)? How effective is this strategy?

EMPLOYEE BRANDING

Despite many organisations heralding that their employees are their biggest asset, they are often overlooked as a key target audience. Companies have spent millions on building their external brands and developing customer relationship strategies and yet have largely failed to explain to the very people they rely on to deliver the service, the rationale for the strategy and the important role they play. Even in the most customer-focused companies a minority of staff act as 'brand champions'. Others add no value to the brand because they do not engage with it and the worst-case scenario is when staff actually act as brand saboteurs by actually criticising the company publicly (Simms, 2003). There has been an increased popularity in 'employer branding' where marketers 'attempt to adapt the tools and techniques traditionally used to motivate and engage customers, to secure the engagement and commitment of an internal audience' (Simms, 2003).

Increasingly, organisations are recognising that one of their greatest untapped assets is their own employees and that getting staff to act as brand ambassadors is one of the few things competitors cannot directly copy. Internal marketing is therefore important not only to ensure that staff buy into plans but also to transfer employees themselves into a source of competitive advantage. Internal marketing should be seen as complementary to external marketing. An important goal of an employee branding campaign is similar to that of an external campaign, to create an emotional connection with the company.

There is evidence to suggest that many companies are not in a position to deliver their brand experience because of insufficient internal marketing. Intercommunic 8, an internal communications agency, conducted research with more than 1000 people in both the private and the public sectors. They found that there was a gap between what is promised to external customers via external communications and what is delivered by staff. This is particularly of issue as we move further into a service-based economy. The research revealed that 37 per cent of respondents felt that the communication they received was inadequate in helping them to understand what their organisation's values and brand meant. This 'yawning gap' between what is promised and what is delivered has a direct effect on a customer's relationship with that brand. The research revealed that the value of internal communication in improving company performance is best implemented by the retail sector (Anon, 2003).

Unfortunately, in most companies, internal marketing is done badly, if at all. Most managers realise there is a need to keep staff informed of the company's strategy; however, few appreciate the importance of convincing them of the brand's uniqueness. Employees can enhance a brand's reputation with external customers and when employees also believe in the brand, customers are more likely to experience the brand in the way that the company has intended.

Extending Knowledge

For further discussion of how to empower staff, read Chapter 5 of Ahmed and Rafiq (2002).

CASE STUDIES

Employee Branding

B&Q

An employer brand manager has been employed ('great place to work manager') to cut across HR and Marketing divisions. A distinct culture has evolved over the last 30 years that is built on its employees being brand ambassadors. Staff are used in all B&Q advertising and they have a well-known strategy of appointing over-50s. Each morning an 'Energize' session is held to encourage staff to work together and express their opinions about the store. At the centre of its business are five core values; a down-to-earth approach, respect for people, being customer-driven, being positive and striving to do better. These are the values that it wants its employees to work towards. Ensuring brand consistency is a huge challenge due to the size of the business and the geographical distance of its employees – around 22, 000 in 286 stores.

Carlsberg-Tetley

Marketing and corporate communications are responsible for the 'education and engagement of staff in the brands' at Carlsberg-Tetley. Consumers are particularly interested in their product range and it is therefore essential that the 2500 employees are well informed and act as brand ambassadors by communicating the right messages. Staff are regarded as a key target audience and have the opportunity to improve their knowledge and skills through an 'innovative and interactive' marketing-led training programme. 'Brand days' are held prior to the launch of new/revitalized brands, where staff are given the opportunity to sample the products and enter competitions. Staff have the opportunity to see and discuss advertising campaigns and participate in internal promotions linked into key rugby or football sponsorships

Source: Adapted from Simms (2003).

Extending Knowledge
There is an interesting and extremely relevant discussion of internal marketing by Colin Mitchell in the *Harvard Business Review* (January 2002), pp. 99–105. This article outlines key principles of internal marketing and provides many relevant examples.

Ahmed and Rafiq (2002), Chapter 4 provides a comprehensive discussion of the relationship between HRM and internal marketing.

Internal Marketing Communications (IMC)

The boundary between external and internal stakeholders is not as clear as one may first think. For example, there has been an increasing trend towards more flexible working practices, such as part-time workers, temporary staff, consultants and so on, and these people spread themselves across organisational borders. In addition, stakeholders may assume multiple roles in relation to the organisation, such as employee, customer, financial stakeholder and so on. For example, an employee of Bradford & Bingley Building Society may also have a savings account or mortgage with them and in addition may also be a shareholder. This has major implications for the way in which organisations communicate with their various stakeholders. It is therefore essential that internal and external communications are compatible and communicate the same messages, because internal stakeholders will also be exposed to external communications.

Role of Internal Marketing Communications

Internal marketing communications is a key aspect of internal marketing and plays an important role in facilitating change. According to Fill (1999), internal marketing communications has several roles:

- DRIP factors (Differentiate products and services, Remind and reassure customers and potential customers, Inform and Persuade targets to think and act in a particular way):
  1. To provide information
  2. To be persuasive
  3. To reassure/remind
  4. To differentiate employees/groups

- Transactional:
  1. To co-ordinate actions
  2. To promote the efficient use of resources
  3. To direct developments

- Affiliation:
    1. To provide identification
    2. To motivate personnel
    3. To promote and co-ordinate activities of non-members

This demonstrates the important role that internal marketing communications can play in helping to facilitate change management. However, internal communications cannot be viewed in isolation and must be viewed in relation to all external communication.

Performance Appraisal

This is concerned with trying to maximise the performance of staff either individually or in teams. Performance appraisal focuses on the control and development of staff through the setting of objectives and the review of their performance. Areas of strengths and weaknesses may be identified and training needs developed to overcome the weaknesses. Many organisations implement an annual appraisal scheme for staff to review progress and establish objectives for the next year. Effective appraisals call for managers to have good people skills and the process should be seen as a positive and constructive experience. Three key skills are necessary:

- Reviewing performance
- Giving feedback
- Counselling

360-degree Feedback

The focus, and emphasis, here is on teams; however, the preceding discussion reminds us that it will always be necessary to include the role and performance of the individual in planning and evaluation of team performance. An increasingly popular technique, now commonly in use across a wide range of businesses, is 360-degree feedback. This is an approach to performance appraisal that captures a wide range of views on the performance of an individual and in addition requires the completion of a self-assessment. As people work in teams, and with a wide range of colleagues, including people outside the organisation, it makes sense to include all sources of contact. Consequently this process obtains inputs from peers, subordinates, managers, customers, suppliers and support staff.

The intrinsic merits of 360-degree feedback are not in doubt; rather there is an increasing amount of evidence to suggest that the process by which it is implemented has created a barrier to the successful exploitation of this technique. Too often the purpose of the feedback is not identified so that feedback is aimless and not connected to job function, or to organisational goals and strategies. To yield most benefits, participants require training and ideally the allocation of a trained mentor. Trust needs to be developed and it must be made clear whether the feedback is going to be used for personal and professional development or for performance evaluation. Rogers, Rogers and Metlay (2002), cited by Carson (2006), found that organisations using the technique to foster a 'development culture' resulted in higher perform-ance individuals and teams throughout the organisation. This was because individual performance is enhanced and the process fosters the development of a more functionally integrated organisation (Carson, 2006).

Extending Knowledge

McGregor, J., Kripalani, M., 2007. The Employee is Always Right; at India's HCL Technologies, workers get to grade the boss, and everybody can see the ratings, Nov (4059), p. 80.

Carson, M., 2006. Saying it like it isn't: The pros and cons of 360-degree feedback. Business Horizons 49, 395–402.

Rogers, E., Rogers, C.W., Metlay, W., 2002. Improving the payoff from 360-degree feedback. Human Resource Planning 25 (3), 44–55.

Motivation

Understanding motivation and associated attributes of commitment and loyalty is not straightforward when it is recognised that several theories of motivation exist (Stacey, 2003, section 4.7).

One approach is to consider sub-optimal performance in terms of the three-circles model presented by Adair (2002) and use this perspective to question:

1. Do people know where they are going in terms of their common tasks?
2. Are they held together as a team?
3. Are the individual's needs being satisfied?

Davidson (2002, Chapter 4, especially pp. 286–292) expands on the third element, considering the individual in terms of their whole life (employer, family, friends, personal interests and voluntary activities). Ultimately if these are significantly out of balance then the other aspects of life suffer. Working long hours can affect an individual's personal life and ultimately this can have an adverse impact on employee activity.

While teams require people with combinations of attributes, high-performance teams are distinguished by their level of commitment and loyalty to one another. Loyalty and commitment extend beyond simple functionality to complete the job in the highest performing teams, to a strong sense of personal commitment.

Improving the Team's Performance, Including Plans to Improve Motivation, Commitment and Loyalty

Two general approaches to this may be considered. One is continuous, ongoing development of team performance on a daily and weekly basis. The other is to instigate specific team-development events. In addition, this section will be concluded with a discussion of the positive and negative approaches used to incentivise desirable team behaviour, that is, through rewards and discipline (punishment).

Both 'on-going' and 'specific' approaches require some form of review or assessment of the current situation before recommending further action. The general problem-finding approach of goals/roles/processes/relationships provides one suitable approach to improve team performance through team building and development.

The aim of team building is considered by Moxon (1994) to:

help people who work together to function more effectively in teams and to assist the team itself to work more effectively as a whole.

Ongoing Development

Moxon (1994) suggests that team building involves (Figure 6.4):

- Regular meetings to establish and review processes, procedures and objectives. Effectiveness will decline if this is not undertaken.

- Sessions specifically on addressing issues. Strengths and the causes of successes are examine d rather than simply focusing on weaknesses and their causes. The focus is on workable solutions.

- Ongoing emphasis on encouraging open and honest discussion rather than superficial politeness. This requires the creation of a sense of security within the team where team members feel able to take risks and share their deeper and true feelings.

- A commitment to personal change and development and to improve team performance. Change will be detailed in action plans and these will also be subject to review.

- Frequent time away from the job, especially in the early stages of team formation, in support of team development.

- Openness of the leader to receive feedback from the team on leadership style and effectiveness.

- Development of interpersonal skills, especially with regard to processes (e.g. meetings) and relationships. This normally should take place as a team.

Diagnosis	Data collection One-to-one interviews – provides very detailed contextual information, although very time consuming and relies on an open and frank discussion with the manager Questionnaires – quick, less threatening than an interview and allows easy and rapid analysis Provides suitable information in order to arrive at a diagnosis of the problem(s)
Design and planning	Session design can be tailored to the particular problems that must be overcome Define objectives Broad design Exercise selection Administration (of session facilities and equipment) Pre-work (by the team before they attend the session)
Running the sessions	Introduction Discussion Action plans Summary and agreement
Follow-up	Write-up outcomes Review progress Future dates

FIGURE 6.4   *An approach to team development. Source: Adapted from Moxon (1994).*

Team Reward

Team reward aims to reinforce behaviour which leads to effective team-work. It encourages group endeavour rather than individual performance. Most team reward systems emphasise team pay rather than non-financial rewards. However, teams may respond to all types of reward from pay, bonuses and public recognition. An advantage is that team pay can encourage co-operative work and behaviour, and develop self-managed and directed teams.

Team pay works best if teams stand alone with agreed targets and are composed of people whose work is interdependent. For it to work well, everybody must understand and accept the targets and the reward must be linked clearly to effort and achievement.

Teams may be able to plan and implement their own improvement programmes if they receive feedback and meet regularly to discuss performance. Team reward is a way for organisations to demonstrate that they value teams and individuals who perform well, and that high levels of performance are important. The quality of teamwork depends on:

- Culture
- Structure and operating processes
- Values
- Performance management
- Management style
- Employee development programmes.

Discipline

A disciplinary interview can be thought of as having three stages:

1. *Establishing the gap* – Future performance is the main concern, so any discussion about present behaviour should be focused on changes that are needed for the future and how to achieve them. It is important to be specific about concerns and to provide evidence or examples of how there is a gap between present behaviour and what is required.

2. *Exploring the reasons for a gap* – It is important to allow the person subject to a disciplinary interview to explain the circumstances and to put forward their point of view about the gap. This may uncover problems or issues that the manager is unaware of but will need to be dealt with in some way, for example, suggesting that they seek advice and guidance or specialist help.

3. *Eliminating the gap* – There will need to be agreement to a plan of action that may involve training. Arrangements for keeping the situation under review will need to be agreed, and the person should be aware of how and when their performance is going to be monitored. The aim is to help facilitate an improvement in performance.

Assessment of Team Performance and Potential Sources of Conflict

Numerous diagnostic tools exist to establish particular problems and issues. By clarifying these, teams can then construct their own action plans to suggest how they may be addressed. This could, for example, be by the use of a facilitator or by employing an external training organisation. An example of a questionnaire on overall team effectiveness is given below.

ACTIVITY 6.9

Assess your team on each of the criteria presented in Figure 6.5. Read the brief comment supporting the single-word description before assessing your team on the scale of 1 to 9 as shown.

CASE STUDY

Putting it all Together

A highly successful, and growing, air conditioning repair business in the USA achieves its success through teamwork in an industry where many work in isolation. Its success is due to a close and detailed consideration of all aspects of team development and performance. This is a highly thriving business, permanently operating near or at full capacity, obtaining new business based on personal recommendations. It is understandable that customers are highly satisfied when the business sets impressive customer guarantees. This includes refunds of $500 if installation is not achieved on time, $500 refund on property protection and also $500 guaranteeing client respect.

The business obviously expects its people to deliver on these promises and the means by which it achieves this is through operating high-quality teams. How do they do this in a business where many technicians work on customers' sites individually or in pairs? The principle approach is to maintain constant communication and offer high levels of training. Everyone meets up first thing in the morning to foster a team spirit and this encourages a co-operative, supportive working 'mindset' where technicians are comfortable ringing each other for support and advice. Buddy work practices are operated, fostering on-the-job training by more experienced colleagues in the organization, in addition to around three weeks equivalent of off-site, paid training each year for every member of staff. Retention and recruitment

policies attract and keep the best people, while marketing activity is geared towards levelling the peaks and troughs of work inherent in this seasonally influenced industry.

This is not only crucial for work flow but also for staff morale. Employee burnout can be a problem in a service business: someone has to cover the anti-social hours of a 24–7 service guarantee policy, which the business uses as one aspect of its competitive advantage. People do volunteer to support each other when there is a big job that needs more than one or two people to sort out. Such 'goodwill' among employees results from fostering a team mindset of co-operative, supportive behaviour. The company reciprocates by ensuring employees working a long day during the busy season are compensated by a reduced workload on the next day. Performance-linked bonuses, company social get-togethers and daily manager–staff face-to-face contact takes place, especially during peak periods, to see how they are coping.

Recognizing difficulties of obtaining high calibre staff, the business, as it continues to grow, uses word-of-mouth referrals from its own workers to attract new staff. This allows them to be ahead of the competition when it comes to recruitment. High levels of team performance lead to satisfied customers who keep coming back. The individual elements of this success hardly amount to rocket science. However putting it all together is another matter, judging by the numbers of organizations who manage to do it successfully.

Source: based on a trade article: Anon. (2008 Jan 21).

Extending Knowledge
Belbin (2004) Chapter 13: Where are we now, and Stacey (2002) Chapter 4, especially Sections 4.5–4.8 inclusive.

Assess your team on each of these criteria [circle your selection]		
Group objectives Well understood and accepted by all team members. These are reviewed frequently.	1 2 3 4 5 6 7 8 9	We are unclear about our objectives and there is frequent lengthy discussion on our priorities when we have achieved the latest working objective.
Atmosphere Informal and comfortable with everyone at their ease. People are involved and even excited in their work.	1 2 3 4 5 6 7 8 9	There is a high degree of tension. The majority of people are overloaded or have insufficient work to do at times.
Communication We are very good at communicating and highly focused on the task. We are sensitive to the views of one another and listen in a non-judgemental way.	1 2 3 4 5 6 7 8 9	Communication appears to suffer from a few people dominating the conversation. We frequently go off the subject during meetings. It seems that we do not listen attentively to each other.
Conflict resolution We handle conflict, such as exists, very well. People are prepared to disagree and these are debated openly rather than shouted down. The minority who sometimes do not agree with a decision accept the disagreement graciously.	1 2 3 4 5 6 7 8 9	People become highly charged during disagreements or seem not to let conflict arise, either through the role of the chairperson or because there is a concern about being perceived as negative. We tend to use majority voting and it seems the more dominant group members get their way.
Decision-making This is consensual. Team members feel able to raise disagreements. However, we are good at laying bare the basis for disagreement, especially where this is due to subjective weighting of influencing factors.	1 2 3 4 5 6 7 8 9	Decisions seem to be taken far too quickly without sufficient debate or consultation. The leader tends to dominate leaving many uncommitted to the final decision.
Criticism Very open but certainly not personal. We find criticism to be well considered and delivered sensitively. Team members usually take it on board without feeling a loss of status.	1 2 3 4 5 6 7 8 9	It seems that we try and score points off each other. There is a certain pleasure by some in criticising others and this creates a certain degree of tension.
Expression of personal feeling Uninhibited and people do not seem to want to follow a personal agenda.	1 2 3 4 5 6 7 8 9	We are never usually clear about peoples' personal feelings. There is a reluctance to expose our personal feelings to group scrutiny because of the potential risk that this engenders.
Leadership The leader is not overly concerned with exercising and demonstrating authority. In fact, at times, group members appear to take on group leadership. We seem to be more concerned with completing the work rather the display of power.	1 2 3 4 5 6 7 8 9	It is obvious who the team leader is. Frequently, we may discuss an issue and then the leader makes the final decision, even though the case for the decision is not apparent and perhaps many of us have argued against that particular decision.
Achievement of tasks We operate with clear, mutually agreed action plans. We regularly review performance against these plans and indeed, the plans themselves. Team members are highly committed to achieving the action plans.	1 2 3 4 5 6 7 8 9	We don't tend to know who is to do what and by when. We seldom review performance against plans or indeed the plans themselves. When people are given particular tasks, these are often ambiguous. We are not good at following up who has done what
Review of team processes We are in control of our own processes. These are reviewed to see if they can be done better, from decision-making to the way we run meetings and allocate tasks. We assess whether process issues are causing a reduction in the effectiveness of the team.	1 2 3 4 5 6 7 8 9	We do not really discuss team process issues and review these. Some team members like to talk about our failings in private, or outside team meetings when only a few members of the team are present, but for some reason they do not raise these issues in team meetings.

FIGURE 6.5 *Assess the effectiveness of your team. Source: Adapted from Moxon (1994, pp. 102–106).*

SUMMARY

Team conflict is a fairly difficult issue to understand and address. That is because its cause may not simply arise from the participants in the conflict but in the context in which workers find themselves working. For example, the goals, roles and processes with which people must comply may be the original source. Once identified, there are various strategies that may be adopted to resolve conflicts. This involves the individual and the team in change and managers, and the organisation, in the management and implementation of change programmes. An understanding of the change process, and the possible reactions to change, provides a valuable insight into how change may be implemented successfully. Training and development may be part of the solution to successful change. This is perhaps one of the more important outcomes of the ongoing process of performance evaluation and review of individuals and teams, of which 360-degree feedback is an example that is particularly effective in a team context.

A helpful perspective to frame our thinking on improving team and organisational performance is market orientation. By being more market orientated, teams and organisations are likely to be more successful and also, consequently, to suffer from less conflict. Approaches to achieving greater market orientation revolve around better performance focused on the customer in which high levels of interfirm co-ordination exists. An important vehicle in support of this is internal marketing, which aligns individual and team work to organisational requirements. If successful, increased loyalty and emotional involvement with the brand can be achieved. This in turn will result in increased employee satisfaction, loyalty and motivation both for ongoing programmes and 'one off' campaigns.

BIBLIOGRAPHY

Adair, J., 1986. Effective Teambuilding. Gower, Basingstoke.

Adair, J., 2002. Inspiring Leadership: Learning from Great Leaders. Thorogood, London ISBN 1854182072.

Ahmed, P.K., Rafiq, M., 1993. The scope of internal marketing: Defining the boundary between marketing and human resource management. Journal of Marketing Management 9, 219–232.

Ahmed, P.K., Rafiq, M., 2002. Internal Marketing Tools and Concepts for Customer-Focused Management. Butterworth-Heinemann.

Anonymous, S., 2008. Focus – Best Contractor To Work For: Classic Air's One Hour Grows As A Team. Air Conditioning, Heating and Refrigeration News Jan 21, 40–42.

Beer, M., Eisenstat, R., Spector, B. Why change programs don't produce change. Harvard Business Review November–December.

Belbin, R.M., 2000. Beyond the Team. Butterworth-Heinemann, Oxford ISBN 0750646411.

Belbin, R.M., 2004. Management Teams: Why they Succeed or Fail. Butterworth-Heinemann, Oxford ISBN 0750659106.

Benady, D., 2001. The inside story. Marketing Week, 30–31 6 September.

Berry, L.L., 1981. The employee as customer. Journal of Retail Banking, 25–28 3 March.

Burnes, B., 1996. Managing Change. Financial Times Management, London 106–120 ISBN 0273611186.

Carson, M., 2006. Saying it like it isn't: The pros and cons of 360-degree feedback. Business Horizons 49, 395–402.

Culbert, H. 2002. Conflict management strategies and styles: Improving group dynamics, http://home.snu.edu/

Davidson, H., 2002. The Committed Enterprise: How to Make Vision and Values Work. Butterworth-Heinemann, Oxford ISBN 0750655402.

Drummond, G., Ensor, J., 2001. Strategic Marketing Planning and Control, second ed. Butterworth-Heinemann.

Fill, C., 1999. Marketing Communications Contexts, Contents and Strategies. Prentice Hall.

Gronroos, C., 1990. Service Management and Marketing. Lexington Books, Massachusetts.

Irwin, I.M., Plovnick, M.S., Fry, R.C., 1974. Task Orientated Team Development. McGraw-Hill, New York.

Jobber, D., 2001. Principles and Practice of Marketing, third ed. McGraw-Hill.

Lankard Brown, B., 1998. Conflict Management. ERIC Clearinghouse on Adult, Career, and Vocational Education, Center on Education and Training for Employment, College of Education, the Ohio State University, Columbus, OH.

Mazur, L., 2001. Acquisition activity is on a high, but in most cases the deal fails to deliver. Marketing 26 8 February.

Moxon, P., 1994. Building a Better Team: A Handbook for Managers and Facilitators. Gower, Aldershot ISBN 0566074249.

Narver, J.C., Slater, S.F., Oct. 1990. The Effect of a Market Orientation on Business Profitability. Journal of Marketing 54 (4), 20–35.

Piercy, R.M., 2002. Market-led Strategic Change: A Guide to Transforming the Process of Going to Market. Butterworth-Heinemann, Oxford ISBN 075065225X.

Robbins, H., Finley, M., 1998. Why Change Doesn't Work. Orion Business Books, London.

Stacey, R.D., 2003. Strategic Management and Organizational Dynamics. Prentice-Hall, Harlow ISBN 0273658980.

Stewart, J., Kringas, P., 2003. Change management – Strategy and values in six agencies from the Australian public service. Public Administration Review 63 (6) November/December.

Simms, J., 2003. HR or Marketing: Who gets staff on side?. Marketing 23 24 July.

Senior Examiner's Comments – Section Two

The assessment for Section 2 requires you to consider the inputs to team management both from the current team and through the development of a team to enable change and development of marketing activities. A key area in this section is the justification for resources required and consideration of the impact and interdependence of marketing on other areas of the organisation.

In the assessment, you will be required to demonstrate your capability to manage teams of marketers, assessing team and individual performance whilst providing appropriate recommendations to make improvements. Assessments may require you to reflect on your own management style and consider ways in which you can develop yourself, possibly through a personal development plan.

The assignment produced should include plans that illustrate the current situation, justifies proposals for how teams should be managed and the measures that can be used to ensure this happens to produce improvements in all aspects of team and organisational performance. Practical examples of best practice should be used where appropriate and contextually justified. Where priorities for actions are requested, it will be important that you use an appropriate framework for justification of your choice, rather than providing a simple numbered list.

Links between areas of the unit that should be considered include handling conflict and legal considerations of HR activity. Innovative and appropriate solutions to problems associated with team management will be rewarded.

For the assessment tasks related to Section 2, activities for team management should be linked to the infrastructure described for Section 1, building on the recommendations made.

Operational Finances for Marketing

INTRODUCTION

"Perhaps the commonest – and arguably the most critical – question asked by those concerned with planning and controlling marketing programmes is 'how much should we spend?' Certainly this question poses some of the most intractable for the marketing analyst and manager."

Nigel Piercy, 1986, Marketing Budgeting

"I know that half my advertising budget is wasted but I don't know which half."

Attributed to Lord Leverhulme

Central to the concept of management is the ability to control. Control is needed over physical, human, financial and intangible resources, and depends upon information of the right kind being available in the right format and at the right time. It is on the basis of information that managers can take effective, meaningful decisions that are goal-oriented and which serve the strategic purpose of their organisation.

Marketing managers are accountable for the performance of the marketing function and this is linked fundamentally with the process of bidding for, securing and administering financial resources, together with the monitoring, analysing and reporting of activity. This focus on the stewardship of financial resource applies equally to organisations of all kinds. The drive for efficiencies in the public and not-for-profit sectors and the wholesale adoption of private sector practices have lessened the differences that earlier existed between local authorities and limited companies, government departments and charitable bodies. Today, there is a high degree of external scrutiny on all organisations, a heavy emphasis on corporate governance and internal controls, and an ever-rising demand from stakeholders for absolute transparency and accountability.

The marketing function will typically have a set of objectives that may include goals for:

- sales
- income
- growth
- customer/client retention
- market penetration
- customer/client satisfaction
- value for money
- increasing competitive or organisational advantage

It will be expected to achieve these within a pre-set budget. In fact, most managers will be involved in estimating in advance the funds required to deliver the function's targets. Activity and resources must be costed as accurately as possible based on past experiences, economic data, reasonable assumptions and best estimates. This is usually followed by a bidding process through which the manager is required to make a case for their proposed budget, supported by a convincing rationale and relevant background information. The manager will quickly discover that funds are finite, and so it becomes a central concern to seek improvements to marketing effectiveness and performance while operating under financial constraints of some kind.

"I have always found that plans are useless, but planning is indispensable."

Dwight D Eisenhower

A budget is only a plan and is therefore a best guess of what may happen. A vital part of the process is to monitor actual results against planned outcomes. One of the principal benefits of setting a budget is that it allows managers to measure and report on the success of their activity by calculating variances between budgeted and actual performance. Such variances should be analysed and explained so that they can be addressed with corrective action where necessary (or, in the case of positive variances, adopted and repeated in future).

The quote attributed to Lord Leverhulme is well known but most appropriate in the context of budgeting. In allowing a proportion of the scarce resource of finance to be spent on marketing, the board and the various stakeholder groups will want to know what they are getting in return. In fact, it would demonstrate rather poor control to be unable to account for the value gained by 50% of the spend on marketing, and unlikely to endear the marketing manager to the chief financial officer. This highlights, among other things, the need for marketing activity to be set in the wider context of organisational objectives, value for money and financial performance. Managers, perhaps especially those in marketing, cannot afford to work in isolation. Budgeting should be a collective activity with marketing managers developing plans and forecasts in tandem with their colleagues in the finance department as well as in other functional areas.

Therc are many benefits to be gained from the process of budgeting. These include helping an organisation to:

- coordinate functional and cross-functional activity
- clarify objectives
- specify targets
- motivate managers
- manage costs and improve efficiency
- monitor activity
- report financial performance within a structured framework
- reward managers

Marketing managers need to play an active part in this process by equipping themselves with the right information, language and skills to make a really effective bid for funding.

By starting with an examination of the role of marketing managers in administering financial resources, we will identify different ways in which budgets are set and how the leaders of the marketing function can make their unique contribution in the creation and monitoring of plans for targeted spending. Having established budgetary limits, we will also investigate how these can be used to measure effectiveness and determine remedial courses of action.

ACTIVITY

Thinking of the marketing function in an organisation you know, does it have clearly defined goals and targets? If so, what are they? How do they relate to the process of budgeting?

CHAPTER 7

Managing Marketing Finances

3.1 Assess the different requirements of managing the finances of the marketing function and associated marketing activities
3.2 Critically evaluate the different approaches to setting the marketing and communications budget and associated marketing activities
3.3 Evaluate the different information sources required to determine the marketing budget for marketing operations and activities

SYLLABUS REFERENCES

3.1:

The manager's role:

■ Control
■ Managing information
■ Cross functional communication

The purpose of budgeting:

■ Planning
■ Coordination
■ Motivation
■ Control
■ Relationship to management of the marketing team

Budget considerations:

■ Fixed
■ Semi-fixed,
■ Variable and semi-variable costs

3.2:

Creating the budget

- Top-down
- Bottom-up

The financial approach to setting budgets

- The budgeting process
- Percentage of sales/profit
- Competitive parity
- Affordable method

The marketing approach

- Planning and control
- Objective and task
- Share of voice
- Cost-volume-profit

Other considerations

- Forecasting
- Financial analysis
- Balanced scorecard
- Resourcing

3.3:

Types of information

- data, information, intelligence and knowledge

Internal and external data sources

- sales figures
- headcount
- outsourcing costs
- consultant costs
- electronic point of sale (EPOS) system
- MkIS
- exchange rates variances arising from international trading

INTRODUCTION

Increasingly, it is a common practice for the objectives of marketing to be expressed in wider business terms. In addition to the traditional targets of increasing turnover, building loyalty and raising awareness, marketers are being charged with goals that include revenue generation, cash flow and shareholder value. With the emphasis on accountability – to investors, customers and clients, suppliers, staff, the local community, government, the public at large – marketing needs more than ever to be a performance-driven unit.

THE MANAGER'S ROLE

A great deal of research and thinking has been applied to the nature of management. There are many theories used to explain the relationship between a manager and the things that are managed. These in turn depend upon different explanatory models of organisations themselves. One way, for example, of capturing the diverse roles of a manger is through the following mnemonic:

- **C**ommunicating
- **O**rganising
- **M**atching
- **M**onitoring
- **A**cting
- **N**egotiating
- **D**ecision-making
- **E**nergising
- **R**eporting

This list could certainly be expanded, but it illustrates the wide scope of activities that fall within a manager's remit. In this section, we are going to focus on control and managing information, and how these contribute to the budgeting process and managing the finances of the marketing function.

Control

Marketing decisions often depend upon others and must be considered in the context of broader strategy and background information, such as competitor activity, market research, availability of alternative and complementary goods, existing organisational profile, whether the organisation is a price giver or a price taker, whether it is customer led or product led and so on. It is likely that the manager will have to take into account a large volume of information, both qualitative and quantitative, and decide which is relevant to the decision in hand. Effective decision-making also relies on recognising those factors over which it is possible to exercise control – operational finance falls into an area that can be controlled. Decisions are based on past experience with a desire to influence the future. It is important to understand (although obvious) that we cannot influence the past. Energies should be expended on those things that can be changed. At the same time, we must recognise that the future is inherently uncertain, the past being only a guide to what may happen. While this may sometimes result in indecision, we should also regard the lack of decisive action as being a decision in itself.

There is a wide range of decision-making tools (decision trees, the Pareto effect, force field analysis and so on), including cost-benefit analysis that we shall explore in detail later. While useful, these can never make the decision for you. The manager carries the responsibility for exercising due judgement and taking an informed decision. Decision-making goes hand in hand with risk taking. A risk-based approach seeks to identify and measure potential risks as part of the process of deciding upon a suitable course of action. There is nothing wrong with taking a calculated risk. What is inexcusable is taking an uncalculated one, namely one that fails to take into account the relevant information available.

Managing Information

A marketing manager has to exercise control over a range of factors – people, budgets, time and so on. In order to manage any of these components, it is first necessary to manage information.

There is an important sequence to the process of managing information.

- *Objectives* – It is necessary to start with a clear statement of your objectives. What are you trying to achieve? This may include the high-level objectives of the marketing function, such as maximising sales, as well as specific objectives relating to particular issues, such as fixing a problem with the organisation's website.

- *Decisions to be made* – In order to achieve the stated objectives, what decisions must be taken? Typically, these will centre on the marketing mix. If making a decision about price, for example, the marketing manager will want to know what will happen if the price is altered. As decision-making is about trying to influence the future, a lot of the information required may be in the form of forecasting. What would happen if we do this?

- *Type of information* – Having identified the decisions needed to achieve the desired objectives, it becomes a little easier to specify the information required to support the decision. Both qualitative and quantitative data can underpin decisions, and often a combination is required.

- *Format and timing* – The importance of format and timing is often overlooked, resulting in a series of requests for *ad hoc* reports because the original information supplied did not help address the problem in hand. This can be frustrating, time-consuming and expensive as well as derailing the decision-making process. If the volume of sales is required, then this must be decided in advance. If an analysis by geographical region is essential, this must also be agreed. If the value of sales is to be included, this too should be part of the information supplied. However, there is little to be gained from unnecessary detail that may simply complicate the decision-making process. Just because the information can be split by age, gender and any number of other customer characteristics, there is no guarantee that this is relevant to the decision in question.

- *Accuracy/reliability* – Sometimes a close estimate is sufficient and in other situations detailed accuracy may be required. The level of accuracy may relate to the significance of the decision. Where there is a large spend, a long-term impact on the organisation or something as sensitive as potential redundancies then a high degree of accuracy is essential.

- *Application* – Having collected the information, the most important requirement is that it is actually used to inform the decision-making rather than simply stored away.

Information can be drawn from readily available internal sources (such as customer databases, financial records and other reports), from external marketing intelligence (including formal and informal sources of data on competitors and the sector) and from active market research in specific areas of interest.

In Section 3.3 we will see more specifically how the management of information may be used in support of preparing the marketing and communications budget in order to make a persuasive bid for resources. We will also examine the use of marketing intelligence systems (MkIS) as a mechanism for aiding management information.

Cross Functional Communication

Given the imperative for marketing managers to operate in concert with other divisions, cross functional communication is a high priority. It is not just a matter of having good relationships with counterparts in finance, production, human resources, research and development, logistics and so on. It is a way of doing business.

Maintaining effective cross functional communications will help the marketing manager maximise their personal impact as well as the overall impact of the marketing function. It will also help prepare for bids and negotiations around financial resources. Dialogue is always an opportunity for advocacy to promote the needs and interests of the marketing function. At the same time, members of other departments should naturally be regarded as internal customers and so there should be an expectation of delivering excellent customer service. Mutual support and greater organisational effectiveness can be achieved with collaborative (rather than competitive) efforts that are maintained through interdepartmental communication. There is an interdependency that exists between organisational functions. When marketing managers understand the important business drivers that are the primary concerns of their peers as well as the obstacles they face, there is a much better chance that departmental plans will be synchronised and high-level strategy will be effected. It is very useful to develop cross functional communication plans to sit alongside strategies for external communications.

ACTIVITY 7.1

How does your marketing function pro-actively support cross-organisational communication, especially in relation to marketing finances? Is it effective and what more could be done to improve it?

THE PURPOSE OF BUDGETING

Budgeting is so central to the processes of planning, delivery, monitoring and control that it should be considered to belong to the same continuous cycle of management.

Planning

It is often simply the process of joint planning that creates a much higher degree of understanding and coordination. As indicated in the quote from President Eisenhower, the resulting plan may be of less value than the benefits gained of working through the various budgetary stages together. The formal nature of budgeting determines a careful examination of strategies, priorities, assumptions, contingencies, risks, opportunities and so on, and as a joint activity, it should lead to an enhanced appreciation of issues across the organisation.

Coordination

As a marketing budget cannot be properly designed and implemented in isolation from other functional plans, the budgeting process is an effective way of ensuring that organisational activity is appropriately coordinated. Innovations in research and development, production, logistics, routine operations and strategic direction should dovetail neatly into marketing activity – promotional initiatives, product launches, public relations events, internal and external communications, consultation, feedback, advocacy, etc. The timing of such activity is often critical and must coincide with the related activity in other departments. Examples of coordination may include:

- increased production and stockpiling ahead of a new marketing campaign

- changes to inventory and in-store signage to coincide with a price promotion

- staff training and development to disseminate news of a major update of website information

- amendments to invoice handling and processing as new trade and cash discounts are introduced

Budgeting should ensure a higher degree of joined-up thinking and prevent the more selfish indulgences of individual managers pursuing their own objectives. One of the principles of budgeting is that the scarce resource of finance will be applied to the areas where there is the greatest likelihood of maximising the return. Clearly, this is not done to the detriment of essential activity and must be undertaken with a long-term perspective. It will also attempt to sequence cash inflows and outflows as efficiently as possible to minimise liquidity problems and the costs associated with borrowing.

Motivation

The level of coordination achieved across the organisation is also required within functions. For this reason, it is useful to involve staff in the budgeting process, where this is practicable. Greater awareness of thinking behind the numbers is likely to add to a sense of collective responsibility and a desire to hit or exceed targets. Awareness alone may be sufficient to motivate staff and managers. Recognition for higher performance may also act as an incentive and may be given in the form of an announcement and public praise, time off or bonuses. There are always dangers with implementing such schemes and care must be taken not to aggravate or demotivate others, or shift the focus on to targets while ignoring other objectives.

Control

A budget provides a ready set of metrics by which to gauge and evaluate performance. Unless they are produced by simply guessing income or expenditure based on previous years with an allowance for growth or inflation, budgets have to be derived from a series of assumptions about activity. The process of budgeting requires a level of thinking and analysis that naturally leads to a better appreciation of critical areas of performance. Control can be more readily achieved by reacting to warning signs as activity falls short of targets. Variance from planned or expected performance will pinpoint where investigation and possible remedial action are required.

Budgeting and Management

It should be clear from what has already been said that budgeting is very closely integrated with the business of management. Planning, control, decision-making, action, monitoring and motivation may all be linked through the budgeting cycle. Budgets and the budgeting process are also great opportunities for communication. They provide a ready-made message for staff at all levels about priorities, challenges and expectations. The scope for coordination, control and motivation is greatly weakened if the key points are not widely disseminated. Communication, as we have already seen, is one of the components of management responsibility, none more so than for marketing managers.

So as not to overstate the case, it should be remembered that managers may exercise managerial control over people and resources without reference to any budget. Other 'softer' targets are equally appropriate for the purposes of monitoring performance. With reference to a triple bottom line, managers are also rightly concerned with corporate social responsibility, the environment and ethical behaviour. Nevertheless, the budget should form a spine that runs down the middle of operational and strategic plans. An organisation that fails economically is then unable to invest in sustainable resources, reduce its carbon footprint and provide aid to the local and global communities.

BUDGET CONSIDERATIONS

Cost Analysis

There are particular benefits to the marketing department to be gained from the process of budgeting. It requires a focus on measures other than the more traditional but harder to quantify values of customer loyalty, brand profile and corporate image. In order to make a persuasive case to the senior team, and in particular the chief finance officer and CEO, it will be necessary to show how marketing activity contributes to cash flow and earnings per share. It is important to consider marketing's net contribution as a profit centre rather than just a cost centre. Campaigns should be appraised in terms of their return on investment (ROI) and payback.

This focus on costs requires a way of analysing and differentiating between various groups of expenditure items. A common way of doing this is by considering cost behaviour.

- *Fixed costs* are those that remain the same regardless of the level of activity (including no activity at all), at least in the short and medium term. Fixed costs include overheads such as light and heat, salaries, business rates, the lease of vehicles, rent, security and depreciation. Irrespective of the volume of production or the level of sales, such costs remain effectively fixed. In the longer term, they may increase as operations grow or costs rise, or they may be manipulated by altering other aspects of activity through reorganisation, relocation, downsizing and so on (see Figure 7.1).

- *Semi fixed costs* are those that remain fixed up to a given volume of activity and then suddenly step up to another level. An example of this is warehousing costs for holding stock. The cost of maintaining a storage unit – including security and other overheads – remains fixed until that unit becomes full and another is required, causing the costs to rise dramatically and then to remain fixed until the second unit is full, and so on (see Figure 7.2).

- *Variable costs* vary directly with the activity and are zero if the activity is nil. In a production context this would include all the

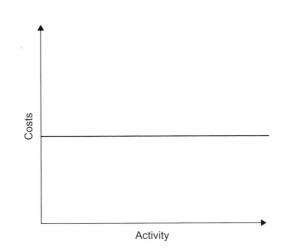

FIGURE 7.1

Fixed cost behaviour.

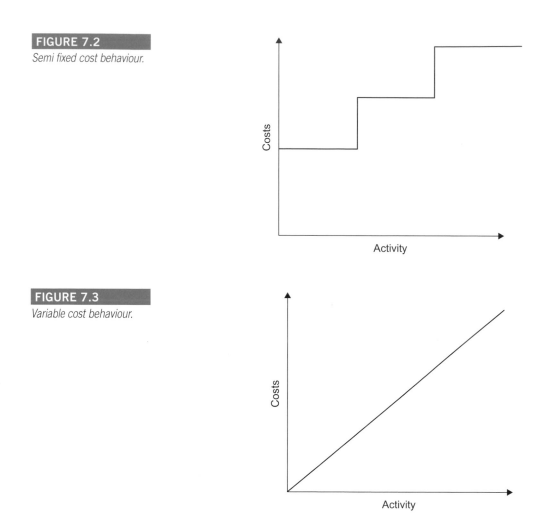

costs of raw materials used in the manufacture of each item as well as wages, assuming this is incurred on a piece rate basis. For a marketing campaign this might include postage costs for mailouts to customers (see Figure 7.3).

■ *Semi-variable costs* vary with activity but do not fall to zero. The cost of sales staff would fit this profile if they enjoy a fixed salary with commission earned on top according to the quantity of items sold (see Figure 7.4).

Knowledge of cost behaviour is important to help identify the impact of costs of a particular strategy. It may help to set the parameters for planned activity as the manager strives to keep costs within budgetary levels. If there

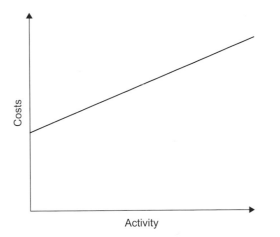

Semi-variable cost behaviour.

is no budget for expanding into larger premises for holding surplus stock, then a different approach to inventory control is required. Understanding cost behaviour also helps the manager to remain focused on those that are the relevant costs to a particular decision. If within the timescale of the proposed decision a given cost remains fixed, then its value is of no relevance to the decision-making process For example, if choosing between two options for stimulating additional sales in the short term, such as a mail out versus a telephone campaign, the fixed costs associated with the salaries of the marketing team are irrelevant since these will be incurred regardless of the option selected.

Having established the importance of budgeting to the role of the marketing manager, we now turn our attention towards the process of setting the budget.

ACTIVITY 7.2

The following costs have all arisen as part of a direct marketing campaign in which customers were contacted by the marketing team through various channels. For each cost decide which type of cost behaviour it is likely to most closely resemble.

- Telephone
- Postage
- Design and printing
- Salaries
- Agency costs
- Consultancy
- Office overheads

SETTING THE MARKETING BUDGET

Introduction

Companies often ask 'how much should we spend on marketing?' Although the average spend in the sector or actual spend by competitors may be useful guides, the answer to 'how much' is that it depends, and ultimately the marketing budget should be determined by the organisational objectives. It is easy to create a mismatch between marketing spend and what is appropriate (either too much or too little) by not building a budget that relates to the organisation's goals.

A number of different approaches are commonly adopted when setting marketing and communications budgets. The choice may depend on historical accident or personal preference, but it is important to be aware of the significance of each method in stressing particular dimensions. A mature organisation may use a combination of different approaches simultaneously to develop a more rounded picture.

Creating the Budget

One simple way of comparing and contrasting different approaches to producing a budget is by considering at what level of detail the process begins. Where the process starts by setting a target or a limit on overall spend first and then breaks this down into discrete tasks, this is a *top-down approach*. Top-down methods include using a percentage of profit or sales as an initial guide for the marketing budget. Similarly, setting parity with competitors' marketing spend as a target for marketing expenditure or starting with an assessment of how much the organisation can afford (usually based on what is left after everything else has been accounted for) are also top-down methods. Consideration of the share of voice may also be used to inform a top-down approach, commencing with a target for gaining a particular share of the available advertising (roughly equivalent to market share) and developing the budget in more detail.

Conversely, when budgets are built up from adding together the detailed planned activity this is known as a *bottom-up approach*. This includes an objective and task method where the goals of marketing are translated into actions and each of these are costed. A planning and control approach is similar, involving working out what it would cost to create and maintain markets that serve the objectives of the organisation. Share of voice considerations may also be used to inform a bottom-up approach, starting with the objective of controlling a minimum percentage of the available media and then identifying and costing the individual tasks needed to achieve it.

Top-down methods include:

- Percentage of sales/profit
- Competitive parity
- Affordable method
- Consideration of share of voice

Bottom-up methods include:

- Objective and task
- Planning and control
- Consideration of cost-volume-profit (CVP)
- Consideration of share of voice

Top-down

Top-down budgeting starts by assessing the costs of higher order tasks first. This is then used to set the parameters for the subsequent evaluation of more detailed activity. For example, the marketing budget may be defined by a number of major headings such as:

- new product launch
- customer website upgrade
- planned PR event
- main catalogue print run

The higher level headings may be individual campaigns or projects as above. Alternatively, the headings may be analysed by types of expenditure such as:

- agency costs
- printing and distribution costs
- staff costs
- broadcast media costs

From these total amounts, the budget is then broken down into more detailed activity, determining how much is to be spent on the sub-components of each of these headings within the overall limits given.

Clearly, a top-down approach relies upon the experience and judgement of the manager who determines the higher level budgetary limits in the first place. There needs to be an appropriate rationale for doing this. Sometimes, it is by *historical budgeting*, that is, by starting with previous budgetary limits or actual spend as a guide. These are reviewed and adjusted accordingly (perhaps by a simple percentage increase but more commonly by an adjustment that takes changed circumstances of the internal and external environment into account).

Bottom-up

Bottom-up budgeting works in the opposite direction from a top-down approach. Typically, the detailed stages of individual projects are identified and costed from which the higher level is then constructed. Costs are estimated based on likely staff hours, materials and other consumables required. Estimates may always be challenged and cheaper sources sought, although usually at the expense of quality or speed. Unlike historical budgeting, *zero-budgeting* may be used whereby the budget must be recreated from scratch. Each figure must be justified rather than simply relying on the past as a reason for repeating the same spend. However, it is also more time-consuming to complete.

In comparison with top-down budgeting, the bottom-up approach has the advantage that it is based on a more detailed, and therefore a more accurate, analysis of the component costs. It is also common to involve more people in the planning process, hence drawing upon their expertise where it counts as well as buying in their commitment. However, there is a danger that these individual items can be over-inflated as the manager (consciously or not) builds in margins for unexpected expenses, wastage or delays, resulting in an overall exaggeration of the resources required. Psychologically, there is a temptation to ask for more than is needed believing you are unlikely to get all of it. This can then lead to inefficiencies as there is no imperative to work within as tight a budget as possible. In comparison, the top-down approach imposes limits at the outset within which the manager must find ways of maximising the benefits of the allocated expenditure. On the other hand, there is no direct relationship between the objectives of the organisation and the limit set on the budget.

ACTIVITY 7.3

Summarise the key arguments for and against top-down budgeting and bottom-up budgeting. What is the preferred approach in an organisation you are familiar with and why do you suppose it is?

The Financial Approach

The financial approach tends to emphasise a top-down model although not exclusively, and it may be on an *historical* or *zero-base*, as referred to above. Total marketing spend is often determined at the outset and then broken down into more discrete activity. However, there are good reasons why this is a popular way of doing things (especially amongst CFOs). As we have seen, budgeting is a process by which the scare resource of finance is apportioned out to different functions and activities with a view to maximising the return. This is why marketing managers need to be able express their intended outcomes in terms that indicate a direct contribution to the bottom line, such as:

- increase to sales
- positive cash inflows
- returns on investment
- growth in customer value

With this kind of analysis, they will have the makings of a very powerful case for the desired resources.

The Budgeting Process

Although there are variations in the relative importance attached to each stage, we can describe a typical budgeting process as being a cycle, normally an annual one that has many if not all of the stages shown in Figure 7.5.

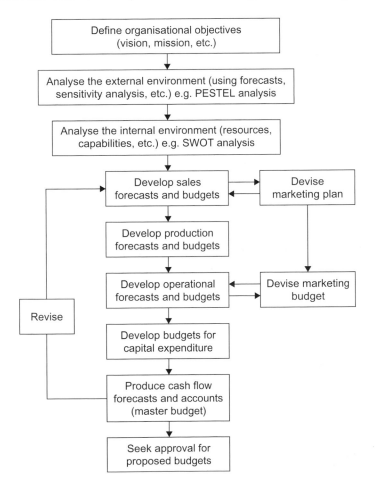

FIGURE 7.5

The budgeting process.

There is a natural sequence to the various portions of the budget. The sales forecasts and budgets should come first, allied very closely to the marketing plan, and everything else is designed to support the achievement of these targets. It is usual that it is an iterative process, such that when the master budget is produced it becomes clear that revisions are required. This may be repeated several times until the total planned income and expenditure is in line with guiding assumptions and expectations.

Percentage of Sales/Profit

One of the most common top-down methods for setting an appropriate limit on marketing spend is by taking a given percentage of sales or profit, either actual or forecast. This allows for comparisons from year to year as well as with other organisations (especially competitors). As a percentage of sales, marketing spend varies quite widely from less than 1% to 10 or 15% and sometimes more. It appears that organisations selling consumer packaged goods are likely to spend the most on marketing. For the launch of new products this may be as high as 50%, falling to between 8–10% thereafter. Retail stores typically spend between 4 and 6%[1].

According to same report, the average spend in advertising as a percentage of gross sales for a selection of different business sectors is given in Table 7.1.

Counsellors to America's Small Business[2] (SCORE) and The United States Small Business Administration[3] (USSBA) indicate the normal range is between 2 and 10% of sales but for B2C, retail and pharmaceuticals it can exceed 20%. The overall average for all sectors is 6%. The scale of marketing spend also varies with the size of organisations, with larger companies spending a smaller percentage of revenue, falling to as low as 2–3% for the very largest, as indicated by Table 7.2.[4]

One of the disadvantages of setting marketing budgets as a percentage of sales or profit is that it indicates a cut in marketing when sales or profits are falling, whereas the received wisdom is that this is precisely when an organisation needs to redouble its efforts to attract attention for itself and its goods and services to protect or gain market share.

---

[1]Source: Schoenfeld & Associates, 2006, quoted in, amongst others, http://www.toolkit.com/small_business_guide/sbg.aspx?nid = P03_7006

[2]http://www.score.org

[3]http://www.sba.gov

[4]Source: http://www.sba.gov quoted in http://www.imageworksstudio.com/client-lounge/articles-tips/setting-a-marketing-advertising-budget.html

Table 7.1	Indicative spend on advertising by sector as a % of gross sales based on US small businesses (Schoenfeld & Associates)
Business sector	**Percentage advertising spend of gross sales**
Grocery stores	1.3
Apparel	2.9
Soft drinks	2.9
Lawn/garden	4.0
Education	5.0
Computers	5.1
TV, radio and electronics	5.3
Catalogue mail order	5.7
Retail stores	5.8
Investment advice	8.6
Cosmetics	10.4
Confectionary	10.6
Memberships	11.0
Toys	14.2
Cleaning supplies	14.5

Table 7.2	Variations in marketing budget in relation to size of organisation, based on US companies
Revenue	**Marketing budget (%)**
<US $5 million	7–8
US $5–10 million	6–7
US $10–50 million	5–6
US $50–100 million	4–5
>US $100 million	2–3

Competitive Parity

Matching competitors' spend on marketing is another approach commonly taken, if the information is available. However, this ignores the fact that organisations have different priorities, means of operating, structures, product portfolios and so on. The comparison may be helpful but it should not be taken too far. Large organisations naturally have large resources at their disposal with which smaller organisations compete at their peril. The ability to focus on distinctive features and the unique selling points is probably more important than absolute spend in a given market.

Affordable Method

Another top-down approach, particularly common for smaller enterprises, is to work out what is needed for the rest of the business for operational costs and planned capital projects and to apportion what is left (or some of it) to marketing. Although financially prudent, it creates an uncertain base for marketing to plan its activities over a period of several years. Marketing budgets must be based on a realistic assessment of what the function can achieve in any given period of time. Promotion is a long-term investment. There are no quick fixes. Translating marketing spend into bottom line performance takes time and care. There needs to be a commitment to marketing that is sustained even in times of less favourable conditions. Maintaining a profile is what will help the organisation survive in the long term. Many marketing initiatives take time to have an impact. Customers need to hear the key messages several times (and maybe in several media) before it creates sufficient interest that can be converted into a sale. Prudently, marketing budgets should not put all their eggs into one basket, favouring a multi-channel, multi-media approach instead. A marketing initiative should commonly include a mix of media relations, promotion and advertising, together with a budget that supports this.

ACTIVITY 7.4

Do you know what your nearest rivals or other similar organisations spend on advertising? How much does this influence the limits set on your own budget?

The Marketing Approach

The marketing approach tends to favour a bottom-up model (although not exclusively) by linking planned spending directly to the function's strategic objectives. Marketing budgets are often supported by an operational plan following the usual kinds of headings (objective, outcomes, milestones, action, by whom, by when and so on) with an additional column for required spending. Each tactical marketing decision can be analysed according to the spend needed for advertising, market research, promotions, PR events, mailout, etc., with a planned date in the business calendar. This may also be analysed to indicate the relevant product, segment, region and channel of distribution the planned tactical initiative aims to address. The following approaches vary in the ways they set and define the objectives in the first place from which the budget is then built. In some cases (such as the share of voice approach), an appreciation of marketing may be used either to inform a top-down or a bottom-up approach.

Planning and Control

When deriving the tactical activities from which the costs are then summarised, a planning and control approach seeks to establish and perpetuate positive contacts with key markets in support of organisational goals. It begins by analysing the intended market and identifying strategies for achieving the level of expansion, penetration, growth or diversification to gain and sustain control over it. Plans are then costed from which the budget is built. The plans must be closely monitored and additional action taken where necessary to keep control of the market. Although similar to other bottom-up approaches such as objective and task (see below), the specific focus on control ensures a very tight grip on what is happening in the market in response to the activity undertaken and the ability to respond to changes in a timely manner.

This may be given in the form of a diagram as shown in Figure 7.6.

It may be necessary to adjust the action plan to deal with adverse variances in performance. As a result, the budget may also need to be flexed. However, it would be impractical to operate a totally flexible budget as it would no longer serve the purpose of controlling spending. Therefore, if actions need to be altered in order to address new circumstances, the marketing manager will either work within the existing total budget or be

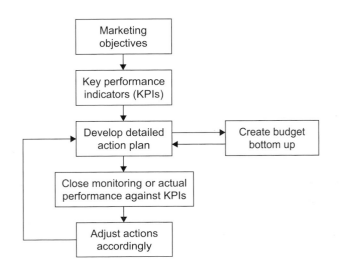

FIGURE 7.6

Planning and control approach to budgeting.

required to seek additional resources through a further process of bidding and negotiation.

The performance indicators or KPIs may reflect different factors, such as:

- total market share or share of market segments
- reported levels of customer satisfaction
- number of direct responses to advertisements
- volume or value of sales
- competitor performance
- distribution of customers
- responsiveness to promotional campaigns
- distributor support
- gross ratings points (i.e. number of impressions or the number of times target audiences receive key messages)

Objective and Task

The objective and task approach is also a bottom-up budgeting model. Expenditure is matched to specific needs insofar as they support marketing and organisational objectives. The objectives are first defined and then the necessary tasks are identified. The tactics are prioritised to enable the marketing manager to highlight those areas of spending that are of the greatest importance. If this process is followed correctly, then the resulting budget is simply a statement of what it costs to achieve the goals of the organisation. If the budget is too high in the context of available resources, then it is the objectives that must be altered, made less ambitious within the targeted timescales.

Share of Voice

Share of voice refers to the share of available advertising for a particular market, or the number of marketing messages in the primary marketing area. Roughly speaking, for established brands (especially fast moving consumer goods) share of voice corresponds to share of market, although this rule of thumb requires very careful application. To maintain your market share, you probably need a slightly larger share of voice – up to 25% more. So, if your product or service enjoys a 10% share of the market, to maintain this position the marketing budget should be sufficient for about 12.5% of the share of voice.

Share of voice is not just about spend and crucially the budget must be focussed to gain the biggest impact for the resources available. Having used this concept to gauge the size of total spend (although for a specific product within a particular market), this can be used as the start of a top-down approach to building the budget. Alternatively, having decided that the ambition is to control a certain share of the available media, the budget could also be built bottom-up by identifying and costing tasks that need to be undertaken to achieve the desired share.

Cost-Volume-Profit

We shall be examining CVP analysis in more detail in Section 3.5 later. At this stage, it is important to note that knowledge of the relationships between volumes of sales, costs and incomes is vital to compiling a budget. CVP can be used to model a range of different scenarios to demonstrate what would happen if:

- unit prices are increased or decreased

- the volume of units sold increases or decreases

- the fixed costs associated with a particular product or service (including marketing and promotion) rise or fall

- the variable costs of producing a product or service (including the cost of bring it to market) rise or fall

This tool can then be used by marketing managers to put together a budget and help set performance indicators. Therefore, it may inform some of the KPIs for a planning and control approach to the budget. It is a very simple model (and can be criticised for being over-simplistic) and perhaps only has applications across a narrow range of activity where costs and revenues conform to approximate straight lines. Nevertheless, it does focus on key factors (costs and incomes) and aids the forecasting, budgeting and decision-making process. It shows very readily the relationship between revenue, costs and profits, and helps inform the decisions about pricing.

ACTIVITY 7.5

It is a common practice to use a number of different approaches to setting the budget. Which of the different approaches described above are part of the way the marketing budget is built in an organisation you are familiar with? Of those that aren't used, are there any that would have a useful application to complement current practice?

Other Considerations

Forecasting

We have already seen that a lot of decision-making is based on information that can be presented in the form of a forecast: what would happen if we did this? CVP is a kind of forecasting. This kind of approach can readily be used to support the budget planning process. What would happen if we spent a further £10,000 here or cut back by £25,000 here?

Forecasting relies on good information and sometimes on detailed computer models. Ultimately, however, it requires experience, judgement and a good dose of gut instinct. The marketing manager will need to make decisions where the timing is critical, such as:

- when to make an investment
- when to launch a new product
- when to retire an old one
- when to hold a PR event
- when to make a major announcement

The budget, as a central component to the plan, will be tied into such deadlines. Knowing the likely pattern of demand for a given product or service is critical for planning other fundamental activities such as:

- coordinating changes to the customer website to ensure the correct sequence of information is available at all times

- managing the availability of staff with the appropriate skills to support promotions, dealing with enquiries, providing after sales service and so on

- engineering the appropriate promotional mix at any period

- scheduling the levels of production required at key points in the year

- working with suppliers and distributors to ease the pressure points on the supply chain

Macro forecasting will provide information of the market as a whole whereas micro forecasting includes a more detailed level by focussing on individual products and services within segments and niches. It is likely that a combination of these will prove useful in compiling evidence to support the proposed budget.

Further comments on forecasting are included in Section 3.3 below.

Financial Analysis

There are many different ways that accountants and finance directors assess the value of a project, either proposed or historical. It is not necessary here to learn the detailed workings of the various models and undertake lengthy calculations, but it is important to recognise the ways in which marketing proposals may be scrutinised and interrogated. We will be looking in more detail at cost-benefit analysis later (see Section 3.5).

Financial analysis of marketing initiatives may focus on their impact on the following aspects of performance:

- increase in sales
- increase in profits
- return on investment
- payback
- discounted cash flow
- break-even analysis

Although the marketing manager may be inclined to focus on the impact certain initiatives will have on brand awareness, customer loyalty, market profile, share of voice and so on, this needs to be supported by an awareness of the financial implications. The first, and perhaps most obvious, hoped-for result will be an *increase in sales*. This could be measured in numbers of units sold but perhaps more usefully in value. As part of a proposal, this can only be estimated and targets can be set for a rise in revenue. To monitor performance, it will be possible to compare actual results with previous years for the same period. Ideally, the marketing manager would like to be able to attribute sales to particular initiatives, and while this may be achieved by asking customers at the point of sale what prompted their purchase or by tracking promotional voucher numbers, the nature of marketing often makes it hard to see any direct and immediate connections between activity and sales (hence Lord Leverhulme's famous quote).

Increased sales revenue is only one part of the intended outcome. If the costs involved in making the sale outstrip the additional cash inflow, it would be necessary to consider whether it was worth it. There is often a good case to be made for securing an initial sale at no profit or even a loss, as a loss leader, to raise awareness, penetrate new markets, gain market share over competitors and encourage repeat purchasing. In the long term, however, it will be an *increase in profits* rather than simply sales that will determine the success of marketing. Even if losses are expected, measurement is still vital to check that they remain within budget.

Sometimes, the return on the outlay is expressed as a percentage of the initial investment. ROI is expressed by the following formula:

$$ROI = earnings/investment \times 100\%$$

The higher the ROI the more attractive the investment. This figure may be compared with the cost of borrowing the capital (from investors, from the bank) or with the return that may be gained from alternative activity. The return would have to exceed these in order to be an appropriate use of scarce funds.

Payback looks at the additional revenues generated by an initiative and calculates how long it will take to recover the initial investment. For example, if a £100,000 spend on a particular marketing initiative this year can be expected to generate an additional £30,000 net income per year, it will not be until the fourth year that the investment has been 'paid back'. *Discounted cash flow* techniques take a more sophisticated approach to payback by also taking into account the decreasing benefit of future incomes. In essence, future cashflows are worth less than present ones since we would rather have the money today than next year or five years hence. This is related to the cost of borrowing and the opportunities for alternative investments that may pay back less quickly but give greater value overall (when discounted to present values).

Finally, *break-even analysis* (much the same as CVP) is another common technique, discussed in Section 3.5 below, that attempts to match incomes, costs and profits. Identifying the level of sales needed at different prices is a useful way of appraising a marketing proposal.

Such models have various strengths and shortcomings. In general, they tend to focus on different features and are best used in combination. No analysis can make the decision for you but they are part of the picture that will help inform such decisions.

Balanced Scorecard

The balanced scorecard is a popular technique for strategic planning and management designed to keep the attention focused on what is important. It was developed by Kaplan and Norton at the Harvard Business School and provides a ready framework within which to monitor high-level goals. As such, it has the potential to be applied to a wide number of areas of management, including the marketing plan and budget.

The scorecard is 'balanced' because rather than providing solely financial measures, it aims to cover and link a broader range of key indicators. Financial measures suffer from being historical and only tell part of the story that managers need to know if they are making decisions about the future direction of their organisation. The process followed to create and monitor the scorecard forces senior manages to clarify their vision and think carefully about their priorities. It includes both internal and external dimensions and drives the organisation towards continuous improvement. It comprises four quadrants:

- *Learning and growth* – this is an internal perspective and focuses on the development of individuals and the organisation as a whole.

- *Business processes* – this is also an internal perspective that considers how well the organisation is running.

■ *Customers* – this provides an outward looking view of the needs and wishes of the organisation's customers, and will be of particular interest to the marketing manager.

■ *Financial performance* – although not the sole focus, profitability and liquidity remain a central concern.

The scorecard contains a range of metrics within each quadrant that are kept under regular review. This approach provides a wealth of understanding and data that can be used to monitor KPIs that form part of the budget as well as provide a focus for setting priorities within future plans. If applied properly, a balanced scorecard should lead to improvements in customer satisfaction, financial performance, operational processes, and employee effectiveness and performance.

We shall be revisiting the balanced scorecard model as part of our considerations of cost-benefit analysis in Chapter 8.

Resourcing

In a general sense, resourcing is concerned with the practicalities of delivery, especially with *who* is going to carry out the planned activities. Consideration of staffing needs to underpin the marketing plan and budget. The marketing manager must consider the level, complexity, volume and required expertise of tasks to assess the staffing needs. Options include:

■ full- and part-time permanent members of the team
■ secondment from other teams
■ fixed-term contracts
■ agency staff
■ outsourcing
■ consultancy

Bidding for extra staff or changes to the composition of the marketing team will be part of the budgetary process requiring analysis and supporting information. There is a balance to be made on the basis of costs, flexibility, expertise, control and risk. Decisions about staffing naturally form part of the budgeting process. Bids for staff costs will form part of the overall proposal.

Resourcing is also used as a term to refer to a particular way of supplementing the marketing budget by enabling the manager to draw upon expertise not readily available within their own team. The process involves engaging staff for a fixed-term as an alternative to permanent additions to the team and thus increasing headcount or undertaking lengthy retraining and upskilling programmes. It is particularly useful where specific specialisms are needed for projects, assignments and campaigns for a limited time period, and can also address seasonal variations in the demand for staffing.

Resourcing is not the same as contracting, which usually implies a commitment for a specified time period, but may be very open-ended. The services of a resourcing agency enable the marketing manager to seek out critical expertise and engage individuals for the duration of a given project. In fact, the individuals used in this way remain employed by the agency throughout the engagement while being based within the marketing manager's team.

Initiatives for which resourcing may be used include:

- market research
- marketing audit
- PR event
- short campaign
- website development
- product launch

There are clear advantages with such an approach. It provides great flexibility and rapidly delivers sought after talents for short or medium term initiatives. This fits the demand within the marketing function to instigate a tight series of events, campaign and particular activities, either as one-offs or as part of a cyclical programme. It also enables the best use to be made of the permanent marketing team members rather than deploying them in contexts to which they are not best suited[5].

ACTIVITY 7.6

Analyse a marketing team in terms of how activity is resourced. What are the costs associated with full-time, part-time, agency, consultancy and other staff costs?

INFORMATION SOURCES NEEDED FOR BUDGETING

Regardless of the approach taken to formulating the marketing budget, it is imperative that it is based upon a broad range of reliable and relevant data. CFOs and CEOs are more likely to be persuaded of the need to increase spend on advertising, for example, if the case is supported convincingly by clearly documented information. It is part of the job of the person preparing and proposing the budget to ensure that the assumptions and predictions stand up to scrutiny. Although there is always the need to exercise a

---

[5]For further details on resourcing see Schweyer, Allan, *Talent Management Systems: Best Practices in Technology Solutions for Recruitment, Retention and Workforce Planning*. Wiley, 2004 as referenced in http://www.bnet.com/2410-13059_23-95566.html

certain amount of professional judgement, this only comes after the available evidence has been duly considered.

Types of Information

Data, Information, Intelligence and Knowledge

Although we tend to use the words interchangeably, we should be careful to distinguish between raw data, information, intelligence and knowledge. *Data* is the simplest form of information such as numbers, words and pictures, but lacking any context. On its own, it does not tell us anything beyond the simple fact that it states. Individual pieces of a jigsaw are not very revealing. When collected together, however, data starts to have meaning and so becomes *information*. The fuller picture emerges as the pieces are assembled. *Intelligence* is a particular way of using this information, of manipulating and applying it. Intelligence can then be seen to provide us with useful *knowledge* that has explanatory power and helps us to understand.

These are not absolute hard and fast definitions, and there are many shades of grey between one term and the next. The important thing to recognise is that data in the form of numbers, pictures, graphs and mere facts needs to be analysed and interpreted, understood in context, connected with other information and applied to a particular issue before we can really begin to say that we have knowledge.

> *Data* might include the volumes of units sold as a series of numbers
>
> *Information* might include other pieces of data about sales, production and profits that fit together into a broader picture about what is happening
>
> *Intelligence* might include the patterns inherent in these figures following analysis, revealing percentage changes
>
> *Knowledge* might include an appreciation of seasonal variations and underlying trends that explains the patterns revealed

A manager relies on information that is accurate, timely, in the appropriate format, comprehensive for the purpose in hand but not unnecessarily detailed. Based on a clear identification of the data required, information systems need to be devised to deliver this in a manner that is not overly time consuming or expensive. Collecting data as a task in addition to ordinary operational procedures can become a significant burden if care is not taken to develop systems efficiently. Good information systems are able to take the required information at the appropriate point as part of routine activity. For example, if it is important to the organisation to count the number of visitors to one of its stores, the best time to do this is at the moment of entry, rather than trying to derive it later from other information. Automated collection of data could be used. Alternatively, customers could be asked to sign in, take a ticket or in some other way register their arrival.

Data mining is a term used to describe the techniques for identifying multiple sources, gathering them and extracting useful and relevant information. The greater the variety of sources used, the more useful data mining is in building up a picture of the internal or external environment in which the organisation is operating. With tremendous advances in information technology used to capture and store data, managers have access to vast arrays. Users can 'drill down' from higher to lower level data to reveal the detail needed. *Data warehousing* refers to the management of collecting, storing and retrieving data from one or more databases, often with the added capability of linking several data sets.

In analysing information either by using software or manually, managers are looking for patterns. In particular, the following may be revealing:

- *Classes* – repeated patterns, such as purchasing habits, that can be used at the basis for predicting similar trends in similar customers in future

- *Clusters* – uneven distribution of data that falls naturally into groupings around events, times, geographical regions and customer characteristics that helps to identify the existence of a recognisable market segment

- *Associations* – relationships that may be uncovered between apparently unrelated data

- *Sequences* – sequential patterns that show the development of customer and/or behaviour and demand enable organisations to provide a changing marketing mix to suit progressive conditions

Such patterns may be exploited to improve efficiency, maximise sales and revenues, and elevate customer satisfaction. Armed with the right data, marketing managers are empowered to take control over the marketing mix, monitoring the effectiveness of decisions made and making adjustments in response to changes in internal and external factors.

Internal and External Data Sources

Technology enables vast amounts of data to be available to marketing managers. This can be liberating and empowering but may also have the opposite effect. Rapidly increasing process speeds and memory space create huge opportunities for analysis and calculation. Advanced data mining techniques may reveal thousands of unexpected correlations between various fields. However, just because the information can be gathered and retrieved does not guarantee that it will be of any use. Managers might find that their time is diverted regarding detailed data that fails to produce any real intelligence pertinent to the issue under consideration.

CASE STUDY

Data Mining

A grocery chain in the United States used data mining software to assess the buying habits of its customers. Quite unexpectedly, they found that when men were buying disposable children's nappies they commonly bought beer at the same time. This was noticeable on Thursdays and even more so on Saturdays. As a result of this discovery, the grocery chain made various changes to its stores, including relocating beer so that it could be found next to the nappies and ensuring that beer was sold at full price on Thursdays.

Quoted by Anderson School of Management, UCLA[6]

Marketing audits are certainly aided by the use of technology and the capability that enables continuous auditing.

Data is routinely collected, very often in electronic form, from transactional processing such as sales, purchasing, wages and salaries and stock keeping. Other forms of data are also held, such as predictive data in the form of forecasts, as well as external data relating to economic trends, competitor performance and market behaviour. It is also possible to hold data about data (meta data) that helps the user find their way around databases and extract what they require.

Sales Figures

The best model we have for predicting the future is the past. There is normally a wealth of data relating to actual performance that can be analysed and used to help support a budgeting proposal. The point was made above that when information systems are designed, it is important to be clear about what is going to be needed. The volume, mix and value of sales figures can be analysed by a wide range of characteristics, including:

■ customer characteristics (gender, age, lifestyle, income, class, occupation, etc)
■ spending per customer

---

[6]http://www.anderson.ucla.edu/faculty/jason.frand/teacher/technologies/palace/data-mining.htm

- geographical location
- timing and date
- buying behaviour (patterns of purchasing)

In order to make sense of this data, it is necessary to understand more clearly what is going on. Statistical tools such as time series analysis help to see the patterns underneath the data and then enable managers to make forecasts. In patterns of data that occur over a period of time, there are three separate causes of variation:

1. random fluctuations
2. cyclical or seasonal variations
3. underlying trends

If we made a simple numerical comparison between one month and the next, we are likely to get a false impression of performance. It is first necessary to identify and separate out the random fluctuations that occur in order to reveal the seasonal patterns that are repeated within the course of a single year or across several years. Seasonal variations arise due to changes in weather, public holidays and culturally determined behaviour. Religious festivals, cold weather, patterns of unemployment and the school calendar all impact on sales to a greater or lesser extent, depending upon the particular sector. Only then is it possible to distinguish the underlying trends. Having done this, firstly one has a much clearer appreciation of the data and secondly forecasts and predictions can be made.

Headcount

Headcount is a measure of the number of employees, and may be broken down by full-time and part-time. It is most likely that staffing costs (including the on-costs of health care, national insurance and pension contributions) are the single largest item in the budget. It is commonly argued that staffs are the most valuable asset (as well as being the most expensive), and so it is important to give headcount a high level of scrutiny when reviewing past performance and preparing future budgets.

We have already examined resourcing options, including more flexible and cost-effective means of securing specialist skills for short periods of time (see Section 3.2). The composition of the permanent membership of the marketing team is critical to the success of any initiative and deserving of special attention.

Some of the data available on staff will relate to their performance. For sales staff, for example, it will be easy to assess the relative effectiveness of each member of the team. For others, it may be more difficult. Such data might be used simply as a means of control and possibly as grounds for dismissal, but it is just as important to learn from the patterns of staff performance as it is from sales data. Careful analysis may reveal a range of highly significant relationships that may be used to reinforce marketing plans, including:

- the relative strengths of individuals
- the importance of timing as a component of high performance
- the impact of training
- cyclical patterns of behaviour related to personal development and motivation
- the effectiveness of feedback and bonus schemes
- the ratio of productivity to salaries and wages

Headcount may also be used to compare the size of the marketing team with other teams within the organisation as well as with competitor and rival firms. It is a very rough measure but may be useful as an indicator of effective power and capability. There are difficulties in counting part-time and fixed-term staff, and practice varies (sometimes within the same organisation). Headcount may simply be the numbers of bodies employed or there may be a more sophisticated attempt to reflect the number of full-time equivalents. As with all data, headcount must be used judiciously.

Outsourcing Costs

Outsourcing (or subcontracting) costs arise when an organisation employs another to undertake some or all of the roles of an entire function, rather than having an in-house facility. This may occur in any number of areas and is fairly common in areas such as:

- internal auditing
- payroll
- information technology support
- human resources
- accounting

It requires a strategic decision to outsource rather than develop or maintain your own capability. The basis for such a decision may be purely economic but there are other advantages to be gained, including greater flexibility, choice, access to expertise and operational effectiveness as well as freeing managers up to focus on areas of greater priority (such as production, selling and marketing communications).

Outsourcing some or all of the marketing function is a consideration that many organisations make. It is likely that portions of it, such as advertising, are already outsourced through the use of agencies. There is great appeal in seeking to benefit from the expertise of specialists in market research,

PR, campaign management, product launches, website development and maintenance, customer engagement, direct mail management and market analysis. When outsourcing, control of the data associated with items outsourced is essential.

Potential benefits of outsourcing are:

- reduction in overall costs
- improved quality of service
- opportunity for better deployment of own staff
- greater predictability of costs
- better access to talent and expertise
- enhanced scope for innovation and change
- greater speed to market
- transfer of operational risk to subcontractor

Outsourcing is not an option that should be entered into lightly. Extensive research and modelling would be needed to support any bid that proposed a move towards moving key functions out of the organisation.

Consultant Costs

Similar points may be made in relation to consultant costs, although it is much easier to enter into short-term arrangements. In preparing marketing plans and budgets, it is important to consider the staffing of each planned activity and identify where consultants may be needed to supplement the skills and expertise of the marketing team. Such costs must be researched and included with an appropriate rationale. The historical costs of consultants used may be an important internal source of information on which to base the prediction for future expenditure.

Electronic Point of Sale (EPOS) System

EPOS data capture through an EPOS system can provide a wealth of useful material with which a marketing manager can develop information to support a budgeting proposal. Used principally to manage inventory and minimise the time taken to move products from warehouse and distribution centres to retail outlets, the system can also be used to gather information about a customer's purchasing habits, which in turn may be applied by targeting future promotions. Supermarket loyalty cards are regarded by customers as rewards for repeat purchasing but for the retailer they provide a substantial bank of serviceable data. Similarly, cookies that record items purchased as well as those previously viewed can be matched to databases of typical customer behaviour and used in e-commerce to make recommendations to the grateful customer. 'Previous buyers of this product also bought the following.'

EPOS data may take many forms and may be used to track any of the following:

- Customer buying habits, including a typical 'basket of goods'
- Impact of promotions on buying patterns
- Stock movements, including time spent on shelves
- Market share of individual products, brands and lines
- Distribution of products

MkIS

Marketing information or intelligence systems (usually abbreviated to MkIS to distinguish it from more general Management Information Systems) is a term used to refer to the processes, equipment and people involved in gathering, analysing and disseminating information to marketing decision makers. It can be a useful tool for supporting a large number of management tasks including information gathering, analysis, evaluation, planning, decision-making, control and budgeting. As with any such system, there is a balance to be had between the amount of data collected, accuracy, cost and speed. It is always possible to gather more data, in more detail and more quickly but this comes at a price (see Figure 7.7).

Marketing intelligence systems vary in terms of the sources and types of information they hold, the complexity of the system and the ways in which users can access the available data. However, despite these differences, marketing research usually plays a central role, providing valuable information about the market and how its responds to various initiatives (see Figure 7.8).

The information works on the basis that raw data is provided from a number of sources, both internal and external. This requires market research

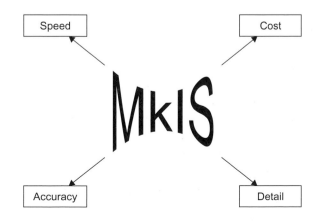

FIGURE 7.7

The competing pressures on information gathering.

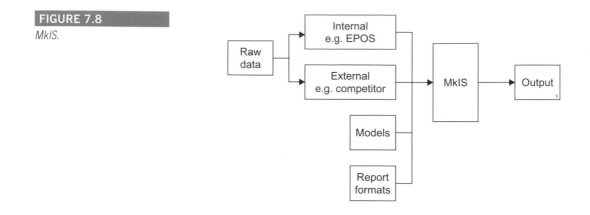

FIGURE 7.8

MkIS.

and market intelligence. The system also needs a number of models. These are prepared programmes that shape the data into useful information on the basis of certain theories and assumptions about the way markets behave. Finally, in order to access the information, there should be a series of defined reports (standard and *ad hoc*) that allows the data to be viewed and presented in a user-friendly format.

ACTIVITY 7.7

How is marketing intelligence assembled within an organisation you are familiar with? If you can, itemise all of the internal and external sources of data that are collected. How much of this is used to inform planning and decision-making?

Exchange Rates Variances Arising from International Trading

If international trade forms a part of current or projected business, then the budget should reflect the costs associated with currency exchange and overseas purchasing and selling. Given the uncertainty of exchange rates, it may be prudent to factor in a number of contingencies should they become less favourable. A combination of historical data analysis and forecasting will be needed. Clearly, the volume of funds subjected to exchange rate variations will affect the scale of the potential impact on the bottom line. The timing of the changes – whether just before or just after a transaction – will also be significant.

CHAPTER 8

Budgeting and Costs

3.4 Negotiate delegated budgets with colleagues and agree provisional budgets.
3.5 Undertake cost benefit analysis of marketing activities establishing priorities and best value approaches to operations.
3.6 Establish effective cost management processes for marketing operations to ensure that costs are managed effectively to achieve viability in the long term.

SYLLABUS REFERENCES

3.4:

- Preparing a budget bid/business case to obtain priority budget for marketing activities
- Negotiation tactics for bidding internally for budget to senior management

3.5:

- The balanced scorecard – learning and growth perspective, business process perspective, customer perspective, financial perspective
- Value chain analysis
- Cost control, cost improvement
- Cost-volume-profit analysis
- Break-even analysis
- Sensitivity analysis

211

3.6:

- Variance analysis – sales variance, cost variance
- Cost control
- Activity-based costing
- Business process re-engineering

NEGOTIATING MARKETING BUDGETS (SYLLABUS REF. 3.4)

There is a difference between simply preparing the budget and making a case for it. There is a skill to organising and presenting information in such a way that it has maximum impact by focusing the attention of the reader on the most important and telling items. The process of bidding for financial resources varies considerably between organisations, and the manager must conform to the specific requirements set.

Preparing A Budget Bid/Business Case

Before preparing a budgeting bid, it is important for the manager to ensure that they are following the criteria set. The formality of such arrangements will depend on the size and nature of the organisation. Sometimes, the submission is purely made in writing, but it is more usual for the manager to make a presentation to a senior panel and be available to explain and justify the proposals.

It is common to have a preset *pro forma* that dictates the layout and composition, with main headings and analysis required. The budget is often divided between:

- operational budget
- capital budget

The operational portion covers all of the routine activities that form part of and support day-to-day trading. This will be further divided between income and expenditure. There may be further subdivisions according to product, service, location, time period or other means of distinguishing different aspects of business appropriate to the organisation. For the marketing budget, there may be a requirement to show each major project and initiative separately. The operational budget is sometimes split between base budget (which is simply a projection of continued activity at present rates with corresponding income and expenditure) and growth (which as the name suggests includes activity additional to previous years).

Ref	Description	Actual 2006/7 £	Actual 2007/8 £	Forecast 2008/9 £	Budget 2009/10 £	Variance £
001	Advertising	11,234	11,488	11,833	12,030	(197)
002	Printing and stationery	802	1,109	1,201	1,458	(257)
003	Postage	209	315	432	587	(155)
004	PR	2,806	1,321	2,571	3,265	(694)
005	Training	5,204	2,836	1,242	3,566	(2,324)

Table 8.1 Sample extract of a proposed budget and the variance with current year's forecast actual outturn

The capital budget covers one-off items of investment that sit outside of normal operations. Such items would include the acquisition or disposal of fixed assets (such as machinery, motor vehicles, computer equipment and office furniture) and the refurbishment of or extensions to premises. Items of expenditure that are deemed to have financial benefit that lasts for more than one year are regarded as capital items, and so it may be decided that a major upgrade to the MkIS or developments to the customer website are to be included in this section of the budget.

It is common that, as next year's budget is being prepared, the current year is still in progress, and so it is necessary to use forecast figures to estimate the most likely outturn for the current year. As the current year is usually incomplete as next year's budget is being prepared, forecast figures will be used instead to estimate the most recent levels of activity. An example of an extract from a budget is given in Table 8.1.

In this case, a marketing budget for the financial year 2009/10 has been prepared. Each cost item has a code number for ease of dialogue and for cross referencing purposes. The historical data for the past two years is available as is the latest estimate for current year. The variance in the final column is a measure of the difference between the forecast outcomes for the current year and the proposed budget for next year. Numbers in brackets indicate adverse variances. In our example this means that the expenditure is set to be greater than the most recent turn out. This kind of budget may be supplemented with a notes column in which explanations can be given as to why training, for example, is set to rise by nearly 200%.

A total proposed figure for the year is useful, but sometimes it is necessary to profile this planned expenditure over the year by quarterly predictions or even monthly. This requires more work in the preparation but once undertaken it provides a very useful set of figures against which to monitor actual performance (we will examine budget variances in more detail in Section 3.7 later).

Table 8.2	Sample extract of a proposed budget with projections per quarter					
Ref	Description	Q1 £	Q2 £	Q3 £	Q4 £	Total £
001	Advertising	2,955	3,020	3,288	2,767	12,030

So, using the same figures as above, the advertising spend has been estimated for each of the four quarters of the budget year in the table Table 8.2.

This could be built up to form a cash-flow projection for the year.

In support of the numerical information, the marketing manager should provide explanatory notes and supplementary data, much of which has already been discussed in previous sections. This may include:

- high level aims and objectives and an explanation of how these support strategic targets
- a review of previous years' activity with an explanation of major variances between planned and actual outcomes
- a marketing audit and an analysis of the internal and external environments (using SWOT, PESTEL, Porter's five forces and so on)
- an operational plan for the coming year detailing activities and events, linked to targeted income and expenditure
- extracts of market research and intelligence in support of key assumptions
- break-even analysis and other diagrams, graphs, charts and illustrations
- sensitivity analysis modelling the effect of positive and negative variations in forecast variables

These elements go beyond the process of budgeting itself and overlap significantly with other matters, most significantly strategic and operational planning and analysis. It should come as no surprise, however, that they are linked so closely.

Negotiation Tactics

If the organisation requires more than a paper-based submission, then it is likely that budget setting will require some form of negotiation. The term 'negotiation' implies a process of dialogue and debate through which two or more parties seek an agreement. It is not confined to the world of work and most people are engaged in a degree of negotiation every day. Of course in an organisational context, the aims of the two parties (here the marketing manager and representatives of the senior management team) ostensibly are the same. However, there may well be disagreement about priorities and the most effective way of achieving goals.

FIGURE 8.1   *The process of negotiation.*

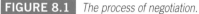

A number of separate stages may be identified in the negotiation process through which the marketing manager hopes to secure a workable budget. These are illustrated by Figure 8.1.

Key to negotiation are the initial stages of anticipation and preparation. The marketing manager should familiarise themselves with the requirements of the process, ensure they meet with the expected deadlines and comply with documentation and so on. It is also vital to attempt to anticipate the possible objections and requests for further information. To be ready with the necessary detail is very impressive and also shortens what might otherwise be a protracted business. The marketing manager should know what the corporate objectives are and have a realistic appreciation of the parameters of what is acceptable and what is not.

In order to make the case as clearly as possible, it may be appropriate to produce a visual presentation. Certainly some kind of summary can be very effective. It is necessary to decide in advance what the key points are that need to be stressed at the outset before you get into the detailed discussions of particular expense headings and various adverse variances. This is about taking control of the situation. Otherwise, the negotiations may quickly become derailed by discussions that prevent you from making your key points.

Supporting the case is all about the preparation you have done previously, having examples, statistics and arguments that you can draw upon if you are challenged. Linked to this is a recognition that you may not be able to win all of your battles. Naturally, managers make more demands on financial resources than can feasibly be met in any given budgetary cycle, and so in creating the master budget, the finance director is required to make some judicious pruning from the initial proposals. Knowing this, it is worth having in mind which of your initiatives you are prepared to concede and which are central to you overall strategy.

The whole process is based on the premise that from a series of proposals, some will be taken up and accepted while others, no matter how good they may seem to the marketing manager, may be shelved or rejected outright. Recognising when the point has been reached beyond which it is not worth arguing is a further key stage in the negotiation process.

The final stage of summing up is often lost and so it remains unclear what has been accepted and what has been rejected. The marketing manager proposing their budget can take the initiative at the end of the process to itemise what they believe has been agreed so that a record is made. Further action may be required at this point and some matters may remain undecided. There may need to be several cycles of negotiation before the budget is finalised.

The style that an individual adopts through the process of negotiation may have real impact on the outcome. Whether someone is combative or more passive in their bidding might depend upon their personal proclivities, but care should be taken to be mindful of the expectations placed upon them in the negotiations. If one is expected to act and talk tough, then it becomes a necessary way of behaving. The same is true if the organisation demands a more gentle and reasoned approach. Above all, a calculated stance that demonstrates political nous will always be advantageous.

ACTIVITY 8.1

What experiences have you had of negotiation? Did you formally prepare for it or did you rely chiefly on gut instinct? In readying yourself for negotiation in the future, what are you likely to do differently? Do you think it is the best way to arrive at the most appropriate budget for your department?

COST BENEFIT ANALYSIS OF MARKETING

Cost benefit analysis is a general approach of adding up the benefits, taking away the costs and seeing whether what is left is worth the original investment in time and resources, including the opportunity cost of doing something else instead. This is not always as easy to do as it sounds. Not all costs and benefits arise in one go and often accrue over time, possibly over many years. Techniques such as payback analysis and discounted cash-flow technique attempt to group all of these costs and benefits together in order to make an overall appraisal. This carries the health warning that future cash inflows and outflows are harder to predict the further ahead in time they are set to occur.

In simple models of cost benefit, only the financial items are included. In more sophisticated models other, less tangible, factors are taken into account, including social and environmental costs and benefits. In this section, we will be examining a range of techniques that help managers understand the relationships between performance, costs and revenues and so evaluate the overall value of marketing initiatives.

The simplest form of cost benefit analysis simply lists all of the costs and all of the benefits. This makes the assumption that is possible to assign a financial value to costs and benefits. Imagine, for example, that an organisation wishes to appraise a proposal for investing in a new customer database. The marketing manager could begin to assess its value by identifying and analysing all the relevant items. Often the costs are easier to quantify than the benefits.

Costs

- Initial purchase of commercial off the shelf software £65,000
- Annual licence £4,000 p.a.
- Customisation of software to meet specific organisational needs £18,000
- Additional annual support licence £1,300 p.a.
- Staff training and development £2,800
- Upgrade of hardware £8,480
- Installation £1,700
- Testing £820
- Data transfer £3,400

Total cost: £105,500 in the first year, £5,300 in each following year.

Benefits

- Shorter processing time of membership applications (calculated as a percentage of data input staff time) £4,500 p.a.
- Savings from reductions in system down time (calculated from emergency call out charges) £800 p.a.
- Improvements to targeted marketing, reductions in mailout costs and increases in sales £31,200 p.a.
- Disposal of old equipment less costs of disposal £22,000

Total benefits: £58,500 in the first year, £36,500 in each following year.

In this case, it would not be until the third year that the project had recovered the initial outlay and ongoing additional costs.

The Balanced Scorecard

We have already considered how budgeting and the balanced scorecard may be connected in setting and monitoring KPIs and feeding back performance into future budgetary limits (see Section 3.2). In this section, we shall examine more specifically how the technique may be applied to appraising activity within marketing.

The first thing to appreciate is that all four quadrants of the balanced scorecard apply as much to marketing as to any other area of the organisation as shown in Table 8.3.

It is common to specify that such targets should conform to the SMART acronym in order to facilitate taking remedial action and make improvements, where SMART stands for:

- Specific, so that it is clear what the expectation is
- Measurable, so that it can be readily monitored
- Achievable, so as to motivate and inspire action rather than describe an unattainable aspiration
- Resourced[1], so that those charged with delivery have the tools to do the job
- Timely, so that there are built in deadlines that prevent constant backsliding and deferral.

One of the principles of the balanced scorecard is that it is designed to drive improvements, so when targets have been achieved new targets should be set as this will facilitate further improvements. Similarly, if it transpires that the unworkable targets have been set (because circumstances have changed or the original analysis was incomplete), these too should be changed since there is no value in chasing impossible goals.

Value Chain Analysis

Value chain analysis is a process first described by Michael Porter. In his model, the value chain consists of a series of activities through which products or services pass and gain value. In fact they gain more value than the sum of all the individual activities put together. The value added is not the

---

[1] Often the R of SMART is given as Realistic, but this is very similar to Achievable, and so Resourced is offered as an important and more helpful alternative

Table 8.3	The balanced scorecard applied to marketing activities
Quadrant of the balanced scorecard	**Application to a marketing context**
Customers	This quadrant is very much core to the marketing function as it attempts to define and measure the effectiveness of the organisation from the customer's perspective. Appropriate measures that may be used include: ■ measures of customer satisfaction ■ rate of new product acceptance ■ the conversion ratio from enquiry to sale ■ market share ■ customer retention rates ■ delivery performance measures (numbers of orders fulfilled correctly and on time) ■ quality performance measures (such as sales returns)
Business processes	There are processes within the marketing function that need to be monitored to ensure that they are both effective and efficient. Measures used to monitor these could include: ■ simple count of tasks completed (phone calls made, letters sent, catalogues dispatched, events held, etc.) ■ percentage of activities carried out within service level guidelines (such as complaints and enquiries responded to within time) ■ efficiency gains in time and cost for key activities (printing costs, stock turnover rate)
Learning and growth	The skills and expertise within the marketing function should be kept under review to ensure it constantly matches the demands being placed upon it. The picture should be broad enough to take into account outsourcing, agency and other resourcing options. Measures used may include: ■ headcount ■ staff turnover rates ■ measures of staff satisfaction ■ compliance with HR requirements for induction and appraisal ■ targets for personal and professional development
Financial performance	Marketing activity should be evaluated on financial indicators. Appropriate financial metrics for monitoring marketing via the balanced scorecard may include: ■ increases in sales and profits ■ net cash flows ■ return on capital employed ■ return on investment ■ average purchase per customer ■ the customer lifetime value ■ the average cost of securing custom

same as the cost of the activity, and in fact a commercial enterprise could not survive if the processes involved in the value chain cost more than the added value for which customers are prepared to pay.

There are five distinct kinds of value-adding or primary activities in the value chain:

1. Inbound logistics, referring to the activities in bringing and preparing materials and resources to production (handling, warehousing, shipping)

2. Operations, referring to production activities (machining, assembly, testing, packaging)

3. Outbound logistics, referring to the activities of taking the goods to market (processing orders, warehousing, transportation, distribution)

4. Marketing and sales, including building brand value, advertising and promotion

5. Service, such as installation and after sales service

There are also capabilities that an organisation requires to carry out the primary activities, which Porter called support activities:

- firm infrastructure
- human resource management
- technology development
- procurement

See Figure 8.2.

The usefulness of the value chain analysis is to enable organisations to focus on and identify those features that create competitive advantage. Each of the five types of primary activities is critical. Being able to compete by offering a better or faster distribution process, or superior after sales service, for example, may prove to be the distinctive benefit that is decisive in gaining market share over competitors.

As part of a cost analysis and control approach, the value chain model provides a generic template for breaking down different kinds of activities and support mechanisms that can then be assessed in isolation. It also provides a means for determining linkages between different parts of the chain, such that the costs of one stage have an impact on later activities. The value chain of any organisation links upstream and downstream into the value chains of others, contributing to a complex value system. All of this analysis can be put into the service of such decisions as outsourcing or resourcing.

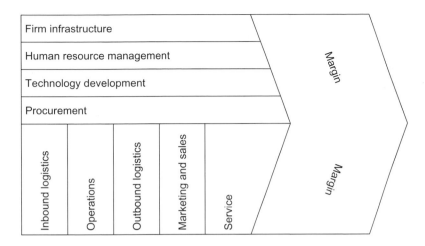

FIGURE 8.2
*Porter's value chain
analysis.*

Cost Control, Cost Improvement

It is worth reminding ourselves that the central purpose of budgeting – indeed one of the core functions of management itself – is to control costs with a view to maximising performance. Marketing should be regarded as an investment in the future of the organisation, but the control of costs is as important here as it is anywhere else. For effective control, it needs to be embedded within normal operating procedures. Cost information should be collected at regular interval and compared with the budget forecast.

Cost control and cost improvement depend largely upon a continual awareness and reappraisal of activity. It is not enough to repeat doing things in a certain because that is how they have always been done. Suppliers should be reassessed regularly and compared with others. The process of tendering and re-tendering may be time-consuming but if handled carefully should be part of a designed approach to improving costs and should ensure that the organisation always gets the best available deal. Similarly, the marketing manager should revisit the question of outsourcing versus doing everything in-house. Joint ventures, sponsorships, alliances and strategic partnerships may provide alternative ways of sharing costs and risks whilst getting a better outcome for the investment.

Cost-Volume-Profit and Break-Even Analysis

We have already seen how cost-volume-profit analysis (CVP) may form part of the process of compiling information in support of a budget (see Section 3.2). As volumes of sales increase so do incomes and costs. Total costs (comprising both fixed and variable costs) will behave like semi-variable costs overall. That is, they will not fall to zero as overheads (rent, rates, light and heat and so on) will be incurred even if sales are zero. They will also rise as sales increase, hopefully at a lower rate than sales income so that at some point the income and total costs lines cross. This point is at the break-even point, where total income is equal to total costs. Any increases in sales above this point means an excess of income over costs so that a profit will be made. Any drop in sales below this point means an excess of expenses over income so that a loss will be made. The steeper the total income line in comparison with the total costs line, the more sensitive the system is to making profits and losses. A small change in sales results in a more rapid increase or decrease in profit or loss (Figure 8.3).

A formula can be derived for the break-even quantity, BEq, as follows:

$$BEq = \text{Fixed costs/Contribution per unit}$$

where Contribution per unit = selling price per unit − variable cost per unit

For example, if a campaign is analysed such that its fixed costs (such as salaries and brochure design) total £15,000, the variable costs per sale (printing and postage) are £12 (based on an assumption of how many brochures need to be sent to different people before one is converted into a sale) and each sale has a net worth of £15, then we would need to make 5,000 sales to break-even (fixed costs £15,000, total variable costs 5,000 × 12 = £60,000, so total costs = £75,000, while total net sales are 5,000 × 15 = £75,000 as well).

We can also calculate profit or loss as being the difference between revenue and costs at any given volume of sales, as follows:

$$
\begin{aligned}
\text{Profit (or loss)} &= \text{total revenue} - \text{total costs} \\
&= \text{volume} \times \text{selling price per unit} - (\text{fixed costs} \\
&\quad + (\text{volume} \times \text{variable cost per unit}))
\end{aligned}
$$

Profit is zero at break-even point as this is where total revenue equals total costs. We can use the model to experiment with changes to price or costs or volumes of units sold. This will yield a sensitivity analysis, revealing how quickly profits will fall in response to changes in one or more of the variables. This strategy is important as we are unable to forecast conditions with perfect precision. Therefore, it is common to take several estimates to define the upper and lower limits of expectations. The margin of safety is the distance between the break-even quantity and the anticipated volume. The larger this margin, the less likelihood that small variations will cause the graph to move into a loss.

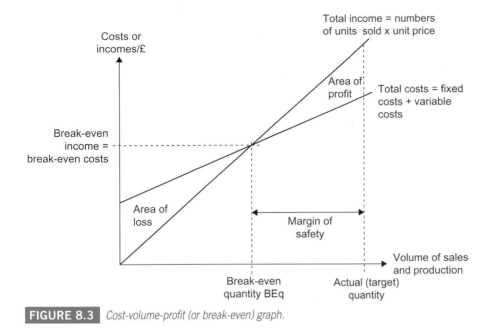

FIGURE 8.3 *Cost-volume-profit (or break-even) graph.*

Sensitivity Analysis

Sensitivity analysis can be applied to any forecast or budget. It involves modelling the effect on other costs and incomes of changes in some of the variables. Price sensitivity analysis, for example, can be used to see what would happen if the price was raised or lowered by any given amount. Costs, volumes and revenues will vary in different proportions, depending upon their particular relationships. The extent to which demand rises or falls (i.e. the price elasticity) will be influenced by

- stochastic influences (random fluctuations)
- availability of substitutes
- variations in the price of complementary goods
- the information available to customers about prices in the market
- the ability of customers to switch between different alternatives
- the strength of brand loyalty

What sensitivity analysis enables marketing managers to do is to consider different scenarios and identify the sources of variability in costs and revenues. Those factors that are the most critical then become subject to closer scrutiny and demand extra levels of control. MkIS is likely to be used to support such analysis. Other bespoke software also provides more sophisticated tools with greater ease of manipulation.

MANAGING COSTS IN MARKETING

As we have already seen, control in general and controlling costs in particular are central to the role of the marketing manager, as for any manager. Planned activity needs to be effectively costed. Budgets and other types of forecasts provide a useful guide for expected results, covering not just predicted revenues and expenditure but also the anticipated volumes on which those predictions were made. Once the actual results begin to emerge (often through monthly management accounts), it is possible to compare these with the budget and so identify and analyse any differences. A detailed understanding of what has caused any variances enables the marketing manager to control costs more effectively and re-engineer processes in a more efficient manner to ensure long-term efficiency gains.

Variance Analysis

A variance is simply a difference. In the context of budgeting and cost control, the term refers to differences between the planned results (from budgets and forecasts) and actual performance. In its most basic form, variance analysis identifies and expresses the absolute difference as shown in Table 8.4).

A favourable variance (F) is one that is better than expected, namely higher income or lower costs. In the earlier example, sales income is higher than the budget and so the variance is favourable, commonly shown as a positive number. An adverse variance (A) is one that is worse than expected, namely lower income or higher costs. In the example, the advertising budget is overspent and hence it is an adverse or negative variance (shown in brackets and sometimes referred to as unfavourable).

Variance is sometimes expressed as a percentage of the planned figure, so using the above figures, sales is showing a 17% favourable (or positive) variance and advertising a 29% adverse (or negative) variance. However, variance analysis really becomes useful when we attempt to break down the difference to understand more clearly what has occurred. This analysis is the first step towards tighter budgetary control.

Rather than making a direct comparison between actual performance and the original budget, variance analysis recognises that actual activity

Table 8.4	Extract of actual results compared with budget and resulting variances			
Budget heading	**Budget for the year to date £**	**Actual for the year to date £**	**Variance £**	**Adverse (A) or Favourable (F) £**
Sales income	11,240	13,182	1,942	F
Advertising costs	2,420	3,111	(691)	A

levels (production and sales volumes) will differ from the master budget, and so naturally you would expect revenues and expenditure to be different also. Before we compare results, we need to do so on a common footing and so the master budget is *flexed*. That is to say, we re-scope the budget on the new assumption of actual activity levels. What would the budget have been if we had expected this level of production or sales? We then compare actual revenues and costs with this flexed budget. This will become clearer by looking at sales and cost variances separately.

Sales Variance

There are two main reasons why the actual sales income may differ from the forecast:

1. differences in sales volume
2. differences in sales price

Sales variance analysis separates out these two components.

In the figures quoted earlier, imagine that the budget had been prepared on the following basis:

Budgeted sales volume: 2,810 units
Budgeted sales price per unit: £4
Hence, budgeted sales income: £11,240

Let us suppose that analysis of the actual results reveals the following:

Actual sales volume: 3,380 units
Actual sales price per unit: £3.90
Hence, actual sales income: £13,182

When we re-scope the budget, we do so on the basis of actual levels of activity. If we had planned to sell 3,380 units (instead of 2,810) what would the budgeted income have been? The answer is 3,380 at the planned selling price of £4, namely £13,520. This is the flexed budget income.

We are now in a position to separate out two variances from the overall variance, namely:

1. sales price variance
2. sales quantity variance

Sales price variance is the variance due to unexpected differences in the selling price and is found by taking the difference between the actual and the planned price and multiplying by the actual number of units sold. In our example:

$$\text{Sales price variance} = (3.90 - 4.00) \times 3{,}380 = £338 \text{ (A)}$$

It is adverse because we sold each item for 10p *less* than budgeted. Overall, the actual income (£13,182) is £338 less than the flexed budget income (£13,520).

Sales quantity variance is the variance due to unexpected differences in the volume of sales and is found by taking the difference between the actual and the planned quantity and multiplying by the planned price. In our example:

$$\text{Sales quantity variance} = (3{,}380 - 2{,}810) \times £4.00 = £2{,}280 \text{ (F)}$$

It is favourable because we sold more items than we planned to.

If we add the variances together (treating adverse variances as negative) we find:

Sales price variance	338 (A)
Sales quantity variance	2,280 (F)
Total sales variance	£1,942 (F)

In other words, the total variance that we calculated originally (£1,942) is shown to be a combination of an adverse variance (because we sold products more cheaply than planned), and a positive variance (because we sold more products than we planned). Overall, the additional sales more than compensated for the drop in price.

There are other important elements to the analysis not covered here. In particular, we are interested not just in sales but in profit, and so a consideration of margins is equally significant. The positive sales variance is only an overall benefit if it results in a positive profit variance.

Cost Variance

As we have seen, it is quite easy to measure the total variance of a cost associated with marketing against the budget. Using the figures quoted above, advertising costs were £691 greater than planned. When considered in conjunction with the favourable sales variance, especially the favourable sales quantity variance, we might be able to identify a causal connection. Certainly, the marketing manager might feel justified in explaining the overspend in such terms.

However, it is harder to carry out the same kind of analysis that we did for sales by attempting to break down the difference between budget and actual into volume and price. There are different approaches that can be made. A common method in the case of production is to *absorb* overheads, such as marketing, into a standard unit cost. This is done on the basis of planned costs for the year being divided in some fashion between the individual units of production, so that we can say the cost of a unit is equal to:

- the direct costs of one unit (materials, labour), *plus*
- a proportion of factory overheads (light, heat, maintenance, depreciation), *plus*
- a proportion of other overheads (administration, accountancy, marketing).

Variance analysis on production costs can then be performed in a similar way to sales variance, namely by flexing the budget to consider what the planned costs would have been had they been based on actual units of production. We can then analyse the variance on the basis of number of units produced and the costs per unit (overheads and variable). Similar analysis can be done for organisations that provide a service rather than produce products.

This analysis can be unsatisfactory for the marketing manager as it is based on the necessarily arbitrary assumption about how much marketing cost goes into producing one unit, when in fact there is no simple correlation that can be made across the organisation to all products. We spend £100,000 on marketing and make 10,000 units in the factory. On a simple absorption costing basis, each unit carries a £10 cost for marketing. When comparing this standard costing with actual results, the variance of most interest to the marketing manager (overhead variance) simply tells us that marketing was more or less than expected. Therefore, a more useful approach is to set standard costs for marketing based on an analysis of the sector and past results.

For example, we may employ telesales staff on a part-time basis and we know how many days we want over the year. We can set standards in terms of how many calls would be expected to be made per day from which a given value of sales would be generated. We can then compare actual performance with the standard model, flex the budget and separate out the different variances. Let us illustrate this with an example.

Suppose the budget was prepared on the assumption that the marketing manager would employ 20 days of telesales staff at a daily charge of £220 (i.e. £4,400). However, the actual costs were £3,900 and this is shown in Table 8.5.

Table 8.5	Extract of a budget variance report			
Budget heading	Budget for the year £	Actual for the year £	Variance £	Adverse (A) or Favourable (F) £
Telesales	4,400	3,900	500	F

In the budget, the following standards for telesales were specified:

Cost per day, £220
Planned number of days over the year, 20
Number of calls per day, 50
Average sales generated per day, £900

Analysis of the results reveals the following:

Actual cost, £3,900
Actual days used, 25
Number of calls per day, 45
Average sales generated per day, £765

The actual daily charge therefore has been £156 (i.e. £3,900/25).

$$\text{The variance in telesales days} = (\text{actual days used} - \text{planned days used})$$
$$\times \text{ planned rate}$$
$$= 5 \times £220$$
$$= £1,100 \text{ A}$$

This is an adverse variance as the marketing team used more days than planned.

$$\text{The variance in telesales costs} = (\text{actual rate} - \text{planned rate})$$
$$\times \text{ actual days used}$$
$$= £64 \times 25$$
$$= £1,600 \text{ F}$$

This is a favourable variance as the cost per day is less than planned.

If we add the variances together (treating adverse variances as negative) we find:

Telesales days variance	1,100 (A)
Telesales costs variance	1,600 (F)
Total telesales variance	£500 (F)

Overall, we have a positive variance of £500. However, when we examine the effectiveness of the telesales we notice that they have made fewer calls per day than planned and have generated fewer sales per day. Even when calculated as average sales generated per call, we find that the plan is £900/50 = £18, while actual performance was £765/45 = £17. So, the telesales staff made fewer calls per day and generated lower sales per call.

This analysis would make clear that although a saving had been made in the overall budget, the results achieved from the spend were disappointing. It seems likely that the telesales staff employed were cheaper because they were less experienced or simply less capable.

This analysis has been carried out to illustrate the importance of revealing a fuller picture than simply the numerical differences between planned and actual spend. Similar analysis could be conducted on variances in advertising, warehousing, mailouts, distribution and so on, depending on the ability to identify a number of different dimensions by which to measure units of input and/or units of output against standard rates. With this kind of analysis, management is in a better position to understand and therefore controls costs and make cost improvements. It may also reveal that there was something wrong with the budgeting process in the first place or that conditions have changed that have undermined the initial assumptions. This is still useful as it deepens the understanding of cost behaviour and helps to separate out the controllable and uncontrollable costs.

Cost Control

The intended result from budget setting and monitoring is to control costs. Control implies something active and dynamic. Any process that requires managers to do more than submit last year's budget proposal creates a need to review and rethink the way things are normally done. We have already reviewed options that may be considered, such as outsourcing, flexible resourcing arrangements, strategic alliances and joint ventures as well as asking suppliers to retender on a regular basis to test their offer against the market. Using monthly management accounts and information systems, it is imperative that costs are monitored as they occur. While it is not possible to control something after the event, the most recent results you can access will provide the best possible guide to what action is needed.

We should note once again the distinction between controllable and uncontrollable costs. The direct costs are more immediately controllable. For marketing, this might include part-time wages, printing and postage. However, where something benefits more than one product or activity, such as advertising costs, it is less controllable in that it would be hard to influence the costs with immediate action. Fixed costs generally are not controllable in the short term. Office overheads, salaries and warehousing fall into this category. Operational decision-making therefore focuses on controllable costs.

Activity-Based Costing

In discussing cost variance, we noted the difficulties of attributing overheads to individual products or services. It is relatively easy to calculate the cost of the labour and raw materials for each unit, but the further away from the process the costs arise, the more difficult it becomes. Machine costs may be apportioned on the basis of the number of hours a product requires of machining, but remote overheads such as administration and marketing seem to have no direct relationship with numbers of units produced. The danger of using an arbitrary basis for absorption is that it does nothing to help with cost control. However, allowing functions within an organisation to operate as cost centres rather than profit centres makes it impossible to determine their contribution to the bottom line.

Activity-based costing (ABC) attempts to draw in as much of the overheads to individual's units or production (or separable items of service provided) in order to improve accountability, manage costs more effectively and produce greater profitability. It reveals more clearly the extent to which one product or service may be subsidising another and hence provides a better basis for decision-making. In essence, ABC seeks to move away from arbitrary percentage-based absorption costing to a closer causal basis on which to attribute costs.

There are several stages to such a process. First of all, the organisation is subdivided into identifiable costs centres appropriate to their activity. For a manufacturer, for example, this may include:

- machining
- assembly
- finishing
- canteen
- administration
- marketing
- logistics

Then, costs that clearly belong to an individual centre are allocated accordingly. Costs that are unique to a cost centre are easily attributable (such as wages of staff). Some costs will need to be apportioned because they are shared between more than one cost centre. A manager, for example, may supervise two departments and so their salary needs to be split.

The difficulties arise in attributing indirect costs (overheads). When apportioning costs, a suitable basis is needed. In the case of salary, the number of hours spent in each division would be appropriate. Relative floor space may be used to split rent, rates, light and heat. ABC uses the principle that whatever activity is the *cost driver* should bear the cost. In traditional manufacturing concerns, this was usually based on the volume of production but such

Table 8.6	Possible bases for apportionment of overheads
Overhead	**Possible basis for apportionment between cost centres**
Light and heat	Floor area
Maintenance	Machine hours
Depreciation	Capital value of equipment held
Telephone	Numbers of staff in administrative roles
HR consultant	Headcount
Business rates	Floor area

an assumption is no longer reflective of many structures and practices. Other more appropriate bases of apportionment need to be used (Table 8.6).

Cost drivers may be distinguished between structural costs drivers (linked to organisational goals and purpose) and executional costs drivers (linked to operational activity). There will inevitably be some costs that are not easily attributable to specific activity and ultimately are regarded as general overheads that apply to the whole organisation (such as the CEO's salary).

Activity-based costing can have direct relevance for the marketing manager. For one thing, some form of ABC is an essential prerequisite for value chain analysis because to identify added value one needs to know the costs associated with each link in the chain. Better knowledge of where costs arise will also facilitate a better marketing mix. ABC analysis can also be applied directly to the question of how much it costs to acquire and retain customers. By identifying services customers receive and the costs associated with each service, it is then possible to work out how much cost is attributable to each user of those services, even to each actual paying customer.

Business Process Re-Engineering

One of the ways of responding to adverse variances or unacceptable increases in costs is to take a fundamental look at business processes in the context of organisational objectives with a view to minimising expenditure. The aim of business process re-engineering (BPR) is to boost efficiency (get things done more cheaply) as well as effectiveness (get things done better).

Business processes often develop organically over long periods of time out of inventiveness born of necessity and soon become embedded through custom and habit. There is no guarantee that they suit the particular requirements of the organisation. BPR seeks a radical reappraisal with the business' strategic objectives in mind. Information technology and advanced network and communication systems provide unprecedented

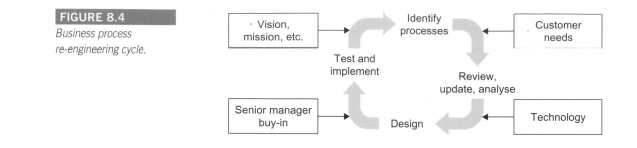

FIGURE 8.4

Business process re-engineering cycle.

opportunities for doing things in a fundamentally different way rather than simply adding IT to support existing processes.

BPR is conceived as a cyclical process, illustrated by Figure 8.4.

The place where BPR begins is with a reconsideration of the strategic vision, mission, tactics and aims of the organisation to ensure that these meet with its aspirations as well as the needs and interests of its customers or clients. Then each process involved in delivering goods and services to its customers is broken down into its constituent parts such as resources, location, activities, costs and information requirements. These are redesigned, sometimes eliminated altogether, to maximise effectiveness (quality, speed, value added) and minimise costs. For example, changing the way that invoices are processed may seem small but can lead to a real impact in overall performance. The process of analysis has to be carried out at the detailed level as well as at the higher order level to ensure that not only are sub-processes operating well, but that a holistic view is taken of each major process and that these too are designed as well as they can be. IT is utilised in its capacity to offer new ways of working and collaboration. Wireless communication, networking, home-working, decision-making tools, shared databases, expert systems and continuous auditing could be applied to shift routines in a profound way.

For BPR to work and to have a lasting impact, recognising the importance of business processes has to remain part of the culture of the organisation. It is one of the quadrants of the balanced scorecard because it is widely regarded as critical to business success. The cyclical diagram highlights the significance of maintaining a process of review, improvement and implementation. Even while implementing new and improved processes, existing ones should be under review for further enhancement.

BPR has been criticised for following the goal of efficiency and effectiveness by implementing new technology while forgetting the impact on individuals. Quite often the process has led to (or perhaps been an excuse for) reorganisation and redundancies. However, while this may be a consequence as an organisation strives for improvements, it would require an imbalanced view to ignore the importance of individuals in delivering processes.

Sometimes, a labour intensive approach is the most appropriate. When implementing change, it is always necessary to anticipate resistance and ensure that hearts and minds are won over. Another criticism is that expectations are often too high that following the PBR philosophy will result in immediate and dramatic improvements to the bottom line.

Given the need to frame business processes within strategic objectives coupled with an ongoing cycle of review, BPR cannot be implemented successfully without support from senior management. However, when entered into sensibly with a long-term commitment, it can provide useful insights into potential improvements and savings and thus add to an organisation's competitiveness.

ACTIVITY 8.3

Are any of the routine operations in the marketing function of an organisation you know well formally set out and recorded (using swim-lane diagrams, for example)? Analyse one such process in detail. Ask yourself whether each stage in the process is as effective and as efficient as it can be. What role could technology play in boosting these? Can you quantify (in time or money saved, errors reduced and so on) the scale of the potential improvements?

CHAPTER 9

Variance and Monitoring

1.7 Assess budget variances, identify causes and recommend corrective actions where appropriate.
1.8 Establish systems to monitor, evaluate and report on the financial performance of marketing operations and associated activities against the delegated budget.

SYLLABUS REFERENCES

3.7:
- Internal variance – organisational, impact of marketing strategy, internal constraints, product portfolio, international exchange rates
- External variance – the macro environment, customers, competitors, partners, suppliers, external stakeholders
- Reconciling variances

3.8:
- Stated standards of performance, KPIs, qualitative and quantitative standards
- Internal sources of data – operating statements, expenditure, profit forecasts, cash-flow statements, MIS, MkIS
- Actual versus forecast
- Plans to improve performance – cost reduction, marketing activities

BUDGET VARIANCE

In practice, there is nearly always a degree of variance between budget and actual results. The budget, after all, is the best-guess forecast, and circumstances are unlikely to run exactly according to plan. We have seen that costs may be controllable or uncontrollable and this applies to variances as well. Variances may arise due to internal or external factors, and it is much more difficult to exercise control over the latter. Nevertheless, controllable or not, variances need to be identified and understood.

Budget variances, whether internal or external, can be grouped under four main headings.

1. Profit variance, where incomes and/or expenses differ from forecast resulting in higher or lower profits.

2. Volume variance, where levels of activity (especially sales or production) are greater or lower than expected.

3. Efficiency (or utilisation) variance, where the usage made of resources to generate activity (staff hours, raw materials, etc.) is more or less efficient than planned.

4. Rate variance, where the unit cost or price differs from plan.

Often, they occur in combination as variances in one area impact on others.

Internal Variance

Internal budget variances normally arise through actions directly under the control of the organisation. These include the decisions it makes about purchasing, staffing, business processes and the promotional mix.

Organisational

Internal variances may be analysed according to variances in profit, volume, efficiency and rate.

Internal profit variances will occur when the value of sales or of costs varies from the original budget. The other internal variances described in the chapter will impact on profit or it may simply be that the budget was based on false assumptions, and items on the operating statement are different from forecast. The result is that incomes and costs vary from the original forecast and so impact on profit. Such variances have nothing to do with changes in the external environment but arise through internal decisions.

Internal volume variances arise when levels of production or levels of sales differ from planned volumes due to organisational factors rather than features of the market or the economy. A manufacturer may produce more units than had been planned due to higher than expected levels of activity, such as more hours worked in the factory or a larger team of sales operatives employed in the field. Alternatively, the organisation may shift a smaller volume of goods to its customers due to changes in its process for warehousing and distribution. The introduction (or failure) of technology may also be a factor. Variances in efficiency often result in volume variances. In addition, one-off events may also arise, causing unexpected shut downs and interruptions to production and sales.

Internal efficiency variances occur when the organisation is able to derive greater or lesser productivity or sales from its units of input. Staff work rate, machine output rate, time taken for goods to move through particular stages of production and the effectiveness of sales operatives may all contribute to such variances.

Internal rate variances will occur when the organisation decides to change its rates of pay or policies on overtime. Alternatively, it may seek new suppliers and accept a different rate on the grounds of the quality or level of service provided. For example, it may be happy to pay more for a superior product or else actively seek a cheaper but inferior alternative.

All these variances are within the control of the organisation and to some extent should not be unexpected as they spring from actions taken or from an internal change of circumstance. Nevertheless, they may indicate the need for remedial action. For example, if work rates have fallen there may be a need to review aspects of training, performance management or employee reward schemes. If changes to systems have had an unexpected impact on the efficiency or effectiveness of processes, it may be necessary to think again (as would be the case with a cyclical approach to business process re-engineering (BPR) – see Section 3.6). With the decision to pay less for raw materials and accept a reduction in quality should come the readiness to accept adverse variances in other areas, as more material may be wasted or more finished products rejected as faulty.

Impact of Marketing Strategy

Analysts sometimes refer to the net marketing contribution, that is, the impact that marketing has on the organisation, as measured by a combination of sales volume, price and product mix. In other words, it is the difference between net profits as a result of marketing. It is hard to measure unless we are able to attribute sales and income streams to particular marketing activity, and that is the challenge to the marketing director. The change in net marketing contribution is sometimes expressed as the sum of the volume variance, price variance and product mix variance.

The marketing plan should contain an element of flexibility to enable the marketing manager to respond to variances as they emerge. Within the advertising budget, for example, there could be an amount set aside as a contingency for disappointing sales. Variances require careful interpretation and it is unlikely that there will be any quick fixes. However, all aspects of the marketing mix may be adjusted if adverse internal budget variances indicate that it is not working as expected.

The KPIs set by the marketing function are a showcase of the intended impact of the marketing strategy. Performance against anticipated financial targets for sales, profit, share premium, return on investment and others will be indicated by the monthly management accounts, and internal budget variances are likely to have a direct effect on them. Additional spend on advertising to alleviate shortfalls in sales will impact on costs and create a variance with the budget unless the amount had been set aside as part of the original plan.

Internal Constraints

Although, in general, it is easier to exert control over internal variances than external ones, a number of internal constraints may also impede action. These may include:

- *Authorisation levels and internal controls:* Additional spend or the ability to vire amounts from one budget heading to another may require approval from a more senior manager and may in some cases be prevented altogether. This is a necessary part of budgetary control, but to enable a marketing manager to respond rapidly to adverse variances a degree of flexibility and trust is required.

- *Resistance to change*: There is always a natural tendency to resist innovation as it can be disruptive and unsettling, even if budget variances indicate that change is necessary. Keeping others informed and involved in the process are useful strategies for countering this resistance.

- *Time*: In responding to budget variances, the marketing manager is already at a disadvantage as the information is based on past activity. Even if a decision is taken rapidly, there will be some delay before it has an impact on performance. This is why it is vital to monitor actual performance against targets very closely on a regular basis. An unfavourable trend over six months may be very hard to redress over the remainder of the year.

- *Resources*: Resources (money, staff hours, equipment and other resources) are usually in limited supply. Taking action to address adverse variances means diverting resources away from planned activity. Care should be taken not to simply create a problem somewhere else.

■ *Indecision*: In the midst of an emerging problem, it is not always clear what to do. Adverse variances may be interpreted as the start of a worrying trend or just a blip that will somehow go away. Not knowing what is going to happen next may result in indecisiveness. In our earlier discussions of the role of the manager (Section 3.1), we noted the importance of decision-making. Not taking a decision is a kind of action but of the worst kind, undermining the effectiveness of management. Managers need to take control over controllable variances.

Product Portfolio

The product portfolio, if properly managed, will have a built-in resistance to adverse budget variances. Knowing that the future is inherently uncertain, there is good sense in spreading the risk. The greater the uncertainty the greater the need to invest in a mixed portfolio, selling, as it were, a mix of ice creams and umbrellas to survive in any environment. Market intelligence plays a vital role in this. The following strategies may be used to offset the impact of possible adverse variances:

■ monitoring the market and competitor activity closely

■ applying marketing intelligence in strategic planning

■ understanding the market and customers or clients

■ soliciting continuous customer feedback

■ segmenting the market on the basis of appropriate characteristics and targeting products or services accordingly

■ staying mindful of product life cycles and the need to vary the promotional mix at different stages

■ maintaining an active research and development function to keep the product portfolio refreshed and exciting

International Exchange Rates

It is quite easy for fluctuations in international exchange rates to cause cost (and profit) variances. Goods and services purchased from international divisions of the organisation may become effectively cheaper or more expensive if the exchange rate varies. Similarly, the price of goods sold to other international divisions is impacted on by exchange rates changes. At the time of initial budgeting, the costs and sales prices would be determined based on a forecast exchange rate for the budget period and this may well change during the period considered. The marketing manager may need to respond to these by considering other changes to the marketing mix to compensate for the cost or sales price variances. At the time of preparing the budget, an estimate has to be made based on available information about how the rate of exchange will vary over the next 12 months. A contingency might be set aside in the budget to be used to offset any unexpected unfavourable shifts.

External Variance

External budget variances arise through actions outside the direct control of the organisation. These include changes in the external environment, the economic climate, demographic changes, new legislation and competitor behaviour.

The Macro Environment

Budgets and forecasts are framed on the basis of assumptions and guesswork. These will include attempts to anticipate levels of demand, interest rates, inflation, competitor activity, economic viability of suppliers, the price of fuel and international exchange rates. The organisation has little direct control over such factors and yet its performance could be significantly affected by them. A risk-based approach takes account of the likelihood and impact of things not going as expected, so that suitable contingencies can be put in place. Even though the costs may be inherently uncontrollable, the variances still need to be investigated and understood to determine whether the planned (or unplanned) remedial actions need to be implemented.

One could formulate potential variances arising in the macro environment following a PESTEL assessment, as illustrated in the Table 9.1.

Clearly, individual organisations would need to decide for themselves the relevant sources of external variances that could impact on them. The potential external budget variances arising from activity by a range of stakeholders and the possible contingencies that may be used by the marketing manager to offset them is illustrated in Table 9.2.

ACTIVITY 9.1

Itemise all of the internal and external causes of variance that impact on your own marketing budget. Do you have metrics to measure them? How do you control these causes of variances?

Table 9.1	Potential source of budget variances from the external variance
Aspect of the external environment	**Potential source of budget variance**
Political	■ Strikes in protest of the government action cause delays in production and distribution
Economic	■ New import and export tariffs add to the costs of materials and reduce the competitiveness of sales overseas ■ The collapse of key organisations results in a supply failure ■ Increases in fuel prices add to the costs of distribution ■ Falls in unemployment make specialist staff harder to find and more expensive to engage
Social	■ Changes in fashion renders product or service less desirable and so demand drops ■ Customer demands for environmentally friendly policies add to the cost of operations ■ A flu epidemic results in a fall in productivity due to absence of staff
Technological	■ Advances in technology makes it easier for competitors to copy product, eroding its perceived added value and reducing demand ■ A new computer virus has the potential to destroy customer databases and requires an expensive solution
Environmental	■ Shortages of raw materials such as timber add to production cost ■ Severe weather causes disruptions to operations and an inability to fulfil client orders on time
Legal	■ New health and safety requirements add to the costs of production ■ New employment legislation adds to the cost of labour

Reconciling Variances

To reconcile is to bring into agreement. In the case of budget variances, it is not possible to amend actual results so that they agree with the budget for individual items (unless there has been an accounting error), but it may be possible to make changes elsewhere. What is required is to explain them financially and to seek ways of recovering the position, where possible. We have already described the processes for identifying the cause of variances. It should be possible to *account* for the difference by detailing what has occurred in comparison with the assumptions in the budget.

Table 9.2	Possible budget variances arising from activities by stakeholders and possible contingencies for mitigating their impact	
Stakeholder group	**Possible source of external budget variance**	**Possible contingencies**
Customers	Demand for the organisation's product or service changes due to changes in ▪ lifestyle ▪ disposable income ▪ fashion/taste ▪ availability of complementary goods ▪ availability of substitutes	▪ continually refresh the product portfolio ▪ anticipate changes in market conditions (using MkIS) and adjust promotional mix ▪ launch new products as old ones reach end of product life cycle ▪ find new and innovative ways to communicate brand value
Competitors	Demand for competitors' products or services increase due to changes in their ▪ price ▪ distribution ▪ promotion ▪ features ▪ perceived brand value	▪ change own promotional mix ▪ increase share of voice ▪ appeal to customer loyalty through direct marketing
Partners	Partners may ▪ withdraw from or reduce commitment to joint initiatives ▪ enter partnerships with competitors ▪ have their reputation damaged through scandal or corporate failure and so damage the reputation of the organisation by association	▪ draw upon reserves or other sources of funding or credit from pre-prepared sources ▪ use PR to promote own good reputation
Suppliers	Suppliers may fail to fulfill contracts due to financial failure or may raise prices, causing volume and rate variances	▪ maintain a database of alternative suppliers that are able to satisfy resourcing requirements
External stakeholders	▪ Investors may seek higher returns or withdraw funding altogether, causing liquidity problems and possible fall in share value	▪ communicate strength of financial position to market to bolster confidence and draw upon reserves or alternative sources of finance

(Continued)

Table 9.2	(Continued)
■ Trade unions may encourage industrial action, causing disruption to activity and volume variances ■ Members of the public may take legal action, causing increased costs and profitability variances ■ Government may pass new legislation requiring expensive compliance, causing profitability variances	■ maintain a contingency fund in the budget for industrial action, legal claims and compliance issues

For example, suppose that the budgeted spend on telesales for the year to date was £2,100 and the accounts reveal an adverse variance of £300. A possible attempt at reconciliation might be produced as follows:

Budgeted telesales = 14 days @ £150 = £2,100

Actual spend = 16 days @ £150 = £2,300

Reason for additional spend: response rates for telesales campaign were lower than expected requiring additional activity to generate target level of sales.

Plans to recover budgetary position: £300 of planned expenditure in PR event has been saved by scaling back the guest list.

In this case, the adverse profit variance of £300 has now been addressed by reducing expenditure in another area.

EVALUATING PERFORMANCE OF MARKETING OPERATIONS

There is a much quoted saying in management circles: if you can't measure it, you can't manage it. This probably overstates the case for having metrics, but it serves to highlight the need for defining your expectations and gauging your successes accordingly and is the direct counter to the much quoted words of Lord Leverhulme.

Stated Standards of Performance, KPIs, Qualitative and Quantitative Standards

In discussing the use of the balanced scorecard as part of the model for monitoring and control (see Section 3.5), we identified a series of potential SMART targets that could be used for marketing. These are quantitative measures, in that they can be expressed in numerical form. Some of these may be formally expressed and promoted to internal or external customers in the form of a service level agreement. It is common, for example, to have standards relating to the speed with which queries and complaints will be addressed. Customers know that if they send an email or a letter they can expect a reply within so many working days. Some organisations report to their customers the actual performance against such standards. These standards can be added to other key performance indicators (KPIs) for gauging the effectiveness of the marketing function. Actual performance can be compared with budget or KPIs as well as with previous years and benchmarks for the sector.

The CMO Council – an US-based peer group of Chief Marketing Officers – has produced a classification of marketing metrics, arranging them under four headings:

1. Business acquisition and demand generation (such as market share)

2. Product innovation and acceptance (such as product adoption rates and customer churn)

3. Corporate image and brand identity (including brand value and customer retention)

4. Corporate vision and leadership (e.g. share of voice)[1]

The following table takes a series of measures of performance and suggests possible quantitative measures that a marketing manager may use (Table 9.3).

In setting targets, it is vital to be sensitive to the needs of the organisation, the product, the market, the suppliers and the customers. For example, it may be inappropriate to set an across-the-board target that sales of all products will grow by 5%. We know about product life cycles and problem children. A certain amount of sensitivity and good sense are required. This is illustrated with examples in the table Table 9.4.

Qualitative standards are harder to specify and monitor as they are by definition not readily quantifiable. Nevertheless, they can provide valuable insights into the effectiveness of the marketing function. Customer

---

[1]See http://www.cmocouncil.org

Table 9.3	Possible metrics for marketing
Measure	**Possible standard or KPI**
Customer satisfaction	85% of customers who respond to a quarterly online survey report that they are pleased or very pleased with the service they received
Rate of new product acceptance	New product is amongst the top ten best sellers by volume in the market within two years of launch
Conversion ratio from enquiry to sale	15% of logged enquiries are converted into a sale within six months
Market share	Market share of product x increases by 5% within six months from a baseline of 32%
Customer retention	88% of customers make a repeat purchase within 12 months
Delivery performance	97% of orders received are fulfilled correctly (no errors) and on time (within 14 days of order being received)
Quality performance	No more than 5% of sales by value are returned by the customer as unsatisfactory
Customer liaison	New catalogue to be dispatched to 100% of customers on the database within three months of publication
Customer complaints	98% of customer complaints are responded to within 5 working days or fewer
Increases in sales	Sales volumes of product x increase to 1,550 per month within the year from a baseline of 1,230 per month
Sponsorships	Income from sponsorships to exceed £150,000 over the year
Return on investment	Growth in profit on sales of product x to exceed 12.5% of the product launch costs
Average purchase per customer	Average annual purchase per customer to increase by 4% from £328
Retention cost per customer	Average retention cost (customer service, invoicing, promotion and so on) per customer falls to below £80 by end of July

feedback, for example, will reveal important first hand experiences of dealing with the organisation and using the product or service. It is not possible (or appropriate) to respond to every criticism or suggestion but customers are often the best source of innovative ideas. That is why it is common to maintain consumer panels of one kind or another. It is also worth trying to spot unsolicited feedback, either made directly to the organisation or else appearing elsewhere in blogs, newsletters, articles, reports and so on. Being

Table 9.4	Marketing metrics arranged by strategic priorities
Priority for organisation and/or particular product	**Appropriate metrics may include:**
Penetrating new markets	Speed to market Share of voice The number of value of strategic alliances Rate of new product acceptance Conversion ratio from enquiry to sale
Growing market share	Number of customers Number of new leads generated Share of voice Share of distribution Increase in sales volume Conversion ratio from enquiry to sale
Retaining existing customers	Customer loyalty measured by retention or churn rates Customer satisfaction rate Customer lifetime value
Growing market value	Price/share premium Increase in profits Increase in share value

able to employ someone to scan the media looking for stories may seem like a luxury but it is surprising what this may turn up.

Being qualitative does not mean that you cannot have targets or metrics. Marketing managers should leave room in their KPIs that reflect the wow factor of their products, the personal impact felt by customers of their advertising and the level of desirability attached to the brand.

ACTIVITY 9.2

Review the range of metrics used in your marketing function. Are they appropriate for the strategic priorities you are trying to achieve? What changes could be made to provide you with a better dashboard of measures?

Internal Sources of Data

In all cases, care must be taken to ensure that the data required to support the KPI can be readily found. Collecting statistics can be time consuming and expensive and may get in the way of routine operations. It is better to think of innovative ways to exploit the data that is routinely collected and stored. From previous discussions earlier, we have already noted that most organisations have at their disposal a wealth of internal sources of data, none more so the general Management Information System (MIS) and the Marketing Intelligence System (MkIS).

The *operating statement* fulfils the same role as the Trading and Profit and Loss Account. It provides details of all incomes earned and expenditure incurred for a given period of time. It is produced annually for the purpose of reporting the results of the year's trading, but more usefully for managers it is common to have internal reports on a quarterly or monthly basis. It is important to distinguish the operating statement from the cash flow. The operating statement is based on the so-called accruals principle that aims to match incomes and expenses to the period in which they arise, regardless of when money changes hands. Many sales are made on a credit basis, and for the purpose of the operating statement they are recorded at the point of sale rather than at the moment of payment. The same is true of purchases and other costs. Operating statements often contain details of previous years' performance and budgeted figures at the same point in time (year to date) for comparison.

Expenditure forms part of the operating statement. The ways in which the items are analysed and grouped together will depend entirely upon the needs of the organisation.

Profit forecasts go beyond the actual performance to date and extrapolate figures to the end of the year on the basis that current levels of activity will be sustained. They provide a useful guide about likely outturns and may provide early indication of whether it is going to be a good year or not.

Cash-flow statements show the movement of funds in and out of the business (or segments of it). While the operating statement measures profitability, the cash-flow statement shows liquidity (the availability of funds). Organisations generally need both, at least in the long term.

Management information systems refer to any structured collection, storage and reporting system of operational data specific to the organisation. This may included related or stand alone databases for details on personnel, customers and finances. *MkIS*, as discussed in Section 3.3, take raw data from a range of sources and combine it with some means of analysis based on various models and assumptions. Output is provided in the form of standard or *ad hoc* reports.

A summary of the usefulness of data available from internal sources is shown in the Table 9.5.

Actual versus Forecast

Forecasts, budgets, metrics, targets and KPIs are devised to help control performance through timely decision-making. It is essential that actual results are monitored in comparison with these, and, as we have seen, this is the basis of variance analysis. The outcome of this scrutiny will lead to developing plans for improvements, which is the final section of this chapter.

Table 9.5	Internal information sources to support potential KPIs	
Information source	**Available data**	**May be used to support the following KPIs**
Operating statement	Actual sales, expenditure and profits for the year to date (may also include historic and budget figures for comparison)	Growth in sales (year to date) Growth in profitability (year to date) Share premium Return on investment (year to date) Average purchase per customer
Expenditure	Actual expenditure for the year to date (may also include historic and budget figures for comparison)	Retention cost per customer
Profit forecasts	Projected figures for income and expenditure to the year end	Return on investment (year end) Growth in profitability (year end)
Cash flow statements	Cash inflows and outflows and net position, usually on a monthly basis	Debtor payment period Creditor payment period Net cash flows
MIS	Personnel records Financial records Customer records	Headcount Customer retention Customer complaints Customer profile
MkIS	Internal data plus market intelligence and competitor analysis	Share of voice Share of wallet Market share Market penetration

Plans to Improve Performance

Cost Reduction and Marketing Activities

The purpose of control and of setting performance targets is to make improvements. Let us suppose that the marketing manager has followed the steps described elsewhere in this chapter, has produced a budget and supported it with a detailed operational plan and a series of bespoke performance indicators which are routinely monitored. What are the processes needed to respond to variances and prepare a plan for corrective action? This is summarised in the Figure 9.1.

First of all one should always check the data, especially when the variance is unexpected or significant. It is possible that the method of collecting and reporting the figures has failed somehow and something has ended up in the wrong box.

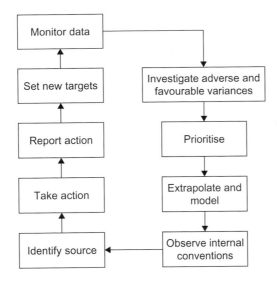

FIGURE 9.1

Using variances to improve performance.

Assuming the data proves to be correct, the marketing manager should be interested in investigating both favourable and adverse variances. It is a common fault to miss the good news and thereby fail to repeat successes.

Depending on the pressures of time and the number of variances under review, it is helpful to prioritise them in some fashion. Uncontrollable items relating to the external environment are still worthy of consideration, even though they cannot be addressed directly, as other mitigating actions may be needed elsewhere to minimise the impact. At the very least, they need to be understood for what they are, rather than making the assumption that it is outside of direct control.

Things to watch out for that may affect the urgency with which a variance is addressed include:

- Unexpected variances – before seeing the variance report, the manager will have a feel for actual performance, and so unexpected variances are more startling and potentially the cause of greatest concern

- Large variances

- Variances that have been occurring for a period of time, especially those that may be increasing over time (it is getting worse more quickly)

- Costs that impact on the value chain

- Completely unbudgeted items – something that is not just different in value from what was expected but not anticipated in the first place

We have seen that internal financial reports may include a column for variance which may be expressed in absolute terms or as a percentage. It is also useful to extrapolate year to date figures to show what will happen if the trend continues (as is shown in profit forecasts, for example). Organisations have their own internal rules for responding to performance reports. They may have preset limits for allowable variances, particularly for budgetary overspends, before formal action is required, in the form of a resubmission for further funds or at least an account of what has occurred and what remedial action is being taken.

Identifying the source of the variance may be difficult. Variance analysis (splitting the total difference between different dimensions such as efficiency, rate and volume) will help isolate the problem, although further detective work is likely. Sometimes, an apparent overspend is simply a timing issue, as the agency invoice was received earlier than expected, say, and will rectify itself over the rest of the year. Here the marketing relies upon their knowledge and expertise in being able to drill down into the problem.

Once it is identified and explained, it is time to consider what action is appropriate. This is where it useful to understand whether it is a controllable item. It may also be necessary to query the original budget assumptions – perhaps we simply got it wrong, forgot to include the annual renewal fee or something similar.

To make improvements, as with much good management behaviour, it is advisable to involve the members of the team. The closer the owner of the cost is to the cost driver activity, the more chance is that they will be able to exercise control over it in a timely fashion. This is not always true, of course, because sometimes the problem only becomes apparent when information is amalgamated and the overall pattern emerges.

Senior Examiner's Comments – Section Three

For Section 3, the assessment will require you to make and justify financially sound activities. You are not expected to produce financial accountancy figures, although you may need to use these to produce appropriate management accounting data to include in budgets and variance analysis.

Overall, the assessment for this section requires you to consider the financial implications of the structural and team issues proposed and recommended for Sections 1 and 2. The approaches to budget setting and sources of information available will need to be considered along with appropriate models for measuring the approaches currently used and proposed.

The process by which the operational finances for marketing are determined, justified, negotiated and measured are more appropriate than the actual figures provided, although figures should be appropriate for the context of the organisation considered. A thorough consideration of the costs involved in marketing activities should enable appropriate budgets to be set and justified through cost benefit analysis.

Marketing managers need to be comfortable dealing with quantitative data, financial or otherwise, in addition to qualitative data. The elements of the integrative assessment for this section will require this to be demonstrated through the evaluation and use of appropriate financial concepts.

Within tasks for Section 3, you should be discussing budgets and other financial considerations of the infrastructure and team developments proposed for Sections 1 and 2.

Feedback on Activities

ACTIVITY 4.3 FEEDBACK

There are various aspects of work and team roles covered by this site. In particular two areas of the site:

http://www.belbin.com/interplace-indsamples.html#Rank

This provides an individual sample report generated on an individual's team role. http://www.belbin.com/belbin-faq.html

Another highly informative part of this site is in the category FAQs on Belbin Team Roles and Reports.

ACTIVITY 4.4 FEEDBACK

Belbin uses a 'self-perception inventory' to determine the role of individuals in the team. The original inventory (i.e. self-assessment based on a variety of questions) is available in the original text. This has, however, been amended and superseded due to several limitations, which have now been discovered. These include, for example:

- Lack of account taken of specialist knowledge, which is particularly critical for people who are in fact specialists.

- No account is taken of false self-perceptions. The latest version now includes a peer/colleague observation/assessment dimension.

Students purchasing their own copy of the second edition of Belbin's text have the opportunity to complete the most up-to-date version of the self-perception inventory, free of charge. You can do this online by visiting the Belbin Associates website at http://www.belbin.com. However, you must first mail the original card inside the textbook (photocopies not accepted) to register for the free test.

253

ACTIVITY 6.6 FEEDBACK

This model provides a representation of the stages people move through when faced with change. Different individuals will progress through the stages at different paces and some may not pass through all the stages in a linear manner. This model will highlight the need for managers to help staff to accept as rapidly as possible, for example, by promoting the benefits of the change and offering incentives to adapt. It is inevitable that some people will continue to resist change and may in fact choose to leave the organisation, rather than accept changes.

ACTIVITY 6.8 FEEDBACK

Many organisations continue to overlook the fact that happy, motivated and committed staff can improve profitability. For example, motivated staff may provide a greater level of customer service, and therefore customer retention may improve. Committed staff who are happy with their work will be less likely to leave the organisation, and therefore staff training will be worthwhile. Highly motivated staff may be more inclined to suggest new ideas because they feel valued. These examples show that there is a link between internal and external marketing.

The intranet is an ideal tool for communicating with all staff and also other external parties. It ensures that all staff can access relevant information. This is particularly useful for organisations that operate on a number of sites or even in a number of countries. The one problem with intranets is that organisations have to avoid overloading users with information. This can result in users being bombarded with messages and choosing not to use the intranet in the intended way.

ACTIVITY 6.9 FEEDBACK

Add up your score.

Less than 30	You really are in a good team.
30–59	Could do better. Concentrate on improving the scores in areas with a rating of five or more.
Over 60	You don't want to work there. Call in the team doctor. An urgent meeting is necessary to put together an improvement plan.

Index

7-S McKinsey & Co. model 152–3
360 degree feedback 69, 162–3

A

ABC *see* activity-based costing
abilities, recruitment issues 99–106
absorbed overhead costs 227–9,
    230–3
accommodating conflict-resolution
    strategies 141–5
account management 11, 80–6
accountabilities
    innovation audits 59–60
    operational finances for
        marketing 174–5, 177
accounting measures
    see also budgets
    balance sheets 29–30, 31, 35–7
    cash-flow statements 29–30, 31,
        37–9, 183, 185, 247–8
    concepts 29–30, 31–9
    profit and loss accounts 29–30,
        31–5, 56–7, 247–8
accuracy levels, information
    management 181, 238–9
achievement motivation 116–17
achievement/ascription dimensions,
    cultural issues 127
ACSI *see* American Customer
    Satisfaction Index
act stage, PDCA (plan, do, check,
    act) cycle 17, 24–6
action
    action-centred leadership model
        71–4
    four-phase model of planned
        change 146–8
    mindset of management 70–4
active management by exception
    76–7, 113
activity-based costing (ABC)

concepts 230–3
    definition 230
ad hoc reports 181
Adair, J. 71–4, 85–6, 163
Adam's equity theory 118–19
adjourning stage of team
    development 83–6
administration resources/structures
    3–4
adverse variances, concepts 224–9,
    248–50
advertised job vacancies 94–5,
    99–100
advertising 6–8, 32–5, 94–5,
    99–100, 173–5, 192–3, 238
affiliation motivation 116–17
affordable method, budgets 188–9,
    194
age discrimination 120–1
agencies 32–5, 94–5, 189–90,
    201–2, 229
    recruitment issues 94–5
    resourcing 201–2, 229
agreeableness personality trait 75
air conditioning repair business 167
ambiguity 124
American Customer Satisfaction
    Index (ACSI) 46–8
analogies/metaphors, idea
    generation methods 59–60
analytical mindset of management
    69–71
Ansoff matrix 34–5
Apple 76–7, 105
application uses, information
    management 181, 238–9
applications-handling
    considerations, recruitment
    issues 97
aptitudes, recruitment issues
    99–106
Armstrong, G. 17

assets
    balance sheets 29–30, 31, 35–7
    definition 36
attitudes
    leadership 74–7
    management aspect of internal
        marketing 153–9
    measures 30, 50–2
audits, change process 147–8
authority/power motivation 116–17
autocratic leadership styles 72–4
avoiding conflict-resolution
    strategies 141–5

B

B&Q 160
B2B *see* business-to-business
B2C *see* business-to-consumer
Badrtalei, J. 128
balance sheets
    concepts 29–30, 31, 35–7
    definition 35–6
    ratios 36–7
balanced scorecard 50–2, 58–60,
    200–2, 218–19, 244–6
    see also innovation and
        learning...
    budgets 200–2, 218–19
Bates, D.L. 128
behavioural interviews 101–6
Belbin's team roles 60, 78–9, 81–6,
    88–90, 167
benchmarking 4, 17–18, 23–4, 30,
    54–6, 60–1, 193–4
    competitor comparisons 60–1
    concepts 17–18, 23–4, 30, 54–6,
        60–1, 193–4
    employees 23–4
benefits, cost-benefit analysis 180,
    198–200, 216–18
bidding processes, budgets 174–5,
    212–16

biographical interviews 101–6
blogs 46–8, 95–6, 245–6
   see also Internet
Boddy, D. 145
bottom-down approaches, budgets
   188–202
boundary spanning activities 30
BPR *see* business process re-
   engineering
brainstorming 59–60
brand awareness 7, 43–5
brand champions 159–60
brand equity 3–4, 9–11, 43–5
   concepts 9
   customer equity 9–11
brand organisational structure
   benefits 9
   concepts 3, 9–11, 15–16
   critique 9
   Nestlé 9–10
brand saboteurs 159–60
brand value cycle 37, 43–5, 155,
   244–6
Branson, Richard 76
break-even analysis 199–200, 214,
   221–3
Brown, Lankard 136, 141
BSI Standards Solutions, PAS2050
   22–3
BT 155
budgets 3–4, 7–8, 9–11, 16, 29–31,
   39, 68–70, 174–5, 177–8,
   182–210, 211–33, 235–43,
   248–50
   see also marketing performance;
   variances
   advantages 175, 184–8
   affordable method 188–9, 194
   approaches 178, 188–202
   balanced scorecard 200–2,
   218–19
   bidding processes 174–5, 212–16
   bottom-down approaches
   188–202
   business case preparations
   212–16
   capital budgets 212–16
   co-ordination purpose 182–4
   competitive parity method 188–9,
   193–4
   concepts 174–5, 177–8, 182–210,
   211–33, 235–43, 248–50
   consideration of CVP method
   188–9, 197–8, 200, 221–3

consideration of share of voice
   method 188–9, 196–7
controls 29–30, 31, 39, 68–70,
   174–5, 184–5, 221, 248–50
cost analysis considerations
   184–8, 221
creation procedures 174–5, 178,
   187–202, 249–50
decision-making constraints 239
definition 174
expenditure 212–16
external budget variances 236,
   240–3
financial analysis 198–200
financial approach 190–4,
   198–200
flexed budgets 225–9
historical budgeting 189–90
income 212–16
information sources needed
   202–10, 246–8
internal budget variances 236–43
internal constraints 238–9
management 68–70, 174–5,
   184–5, 212–50
marketing approach 194–202
motivational purposes 183–4
negotiations 212–16
objective and task method 188–9,
   196
operational budgets 212–16
percentage of sales/profit method
   188–9, 192–3
planning and control method
   188–9, 195–6
planning purpose 182–4
presentations 212–16
principles 183
pro forma guidelines 212–16
process overview 191–2
purposes 174–5, 177–8, 182–4,
   221, 229
resourcing 201–2, 229, 238–9
scarce resources 183
selfish managers 183
sensitivity analysis 214, 223–4
setting considerations 174–5,
   178, 187–202, 249–50
stages 191–2
timing factors 238–9, 249–50
top-down approaches 188–202
zero-budgeting 190
bulletin boards 114
bureaucracy, formalisation

dimension of organisations
   5–16, 58–60
business case preparations, budgets
   212–16
business process re-engineering
   (BPR)
   concepts 80–6, 231–3, 237
   critique 232–3
   cycle 232
   definition 231–2
business processes, balanced
   scorecard 50–2, 58–60, 200–2,
   218–19, 244–6
business-to-business (B2B) 8, 43–5
business-to-consumer (B2C) 8,
   43–5

C

Cadbury Schweppes 155
campaigns, financial appraisals 185,
   198–200
capital
   balance sheets 36–7
   balanced scorecard 51–2, 200–2,
   218–19, 244–6
capital budgets 212–16
   see also budgets
careers fairs 94
Carlsberg-Tetley 160
Carson, M. 163
cash-flow statements
   concepts 29–30, 31, 37–9, 183,
   185, 247–8
   definition 37, 247
centralisation/decentralisation
   dimension of organisations
   5–16
change processes, models
   146–8
changes
   7-S McKinsey & Co. model
   152–3
   audits 147–8
   barriers 145–59
   BPR 80–6, 231–3, 237
   co-ordination needs 149–52,
   154–9
   commitment needs 149–52,
   163–4
   communications 151–9
   continuous improvements 20,
   26, 150
   controls 151–2
   cultural issues 150–2

Deming's 14 quality
  improvement steps 26–7
factors critical for success 151–2
failed change programmes 145,
  148–52
four-phase model 146–8
internal marketing 111–31,
  152–9
leadership roles 68–71, 75–7,
  149–52, 177–84
management 68–71, 75–7,
  145–52, 238–9
models 145–52
new competencies 149–52
organisational structures 151–2
planning 145–52
resistance to change 145, 147–59,
  238–9
skills 151–2
success factors 149–59
systems 151–2
transaction curves 151
transformational leadership
  perspective 71, 75–7
unfreezing–change–refreezing
  model 145–6
channel management 11
charismatic leaders 76–7
  see also leadership;
    transformational…
Charter Mark 21
check stage, PDCA (plan, do, check,
  act) cycle 17, 24–6
China
  cultural issues 123–5
  Finnish elevator company in
    China 150
Chrysler 128
Cilliers, F. 75–7
The CMO Council 244
co-ordination needs
  budgets 182–4
  change enablers 149–52, 154–9
  internal marketing 154–9
  matrix organisational structures 13
coercive relationships 115
cognitive styles
  concepts 30, 58–60
  innovation audits 58–60
collaboration
  conflict-resolution strategies
    141–5
  mindset of management 69–71,
    80–6

collectivism, cultural issues 123–5,
  126–9
college/university recruitment 94
COMMANDER mnemonic of
  management 177–80
commitment needs, change enablers
  149–52, 163–4
communications
  change success factors 151–9
  conflict-resolution strategies 141–5
  cultural issues 122–5
  Hofstede's cross-cultural analysis
    122–5, 133, 150
  innovation audits 59–60
  internal marketing aspect 153–69
  knowledge management 113–15,
    131–3
  management roles 177–84
  measures 29–30, 46–8, 50,
    113–15
  methods 46–8
  resources/structures 3–4
  self-assessments 43
  technological innovations 46–8,
    55–6, 75–7, 232, 240–1
  virtual teams 129–33
company virtual teams 130–1
comparative analysis, concepts 30,
  53–6
competencies
  change enablers 149–52
  good managers 86–8
competing conflict-resolution
  strategies 141–5
competitive advantages 174
competitive parity method, budgets
  188–9, 193–4
competitor comparisons
  see also benchmarking
  budget variance contingencies
    242–3
  concepts 30, 60–1
complaints, customers 46–8, 112,
  157–9, 244–6
complexity issues, management
  68–70
compromising conflict-resolution
  strategies 141–5
conflicts
  accommodating conflict-
    resolution strategies 141–5
  authority solutions 141
  avoiding conflict-resolution
    strategies 141–5

collaborating conflict-resolution
  strategies 141–5
communications 141–5
competing conflict-resolution
  strategies 141–5
compromising conflict-resolution
  strategies 141–5
concepts 135–69
constructive/destructive aspects
  137
disagreements 136–7
employees 13, 81, 82–5, 114–15,
  131–3, 135–69
evaluation questionnaires 144–5,
  168
four-category perspective of team
  problems 137–41
planning solutions 141
reasons 136–7, 166–9
resolution strategies 141–5,
  166–9
teams 81, 82–5, 114–15, 131–3,
  135–69
Confucian dynamism, cultural
  issues 123, 124–5
conscientiousness personality trait
  75
consideration of CVP method,
  budgets 188–9, 197–8, 200,
  221–3
consideration of share of voice
  method, budgets 188–9, 196–7
consultants 201–2, 208
consultative leadership styles 72–4
continuous improvements 20, 26,
  150
controllable/uncontrollable costs
  229–33, 249–50
controls 17, 24–6, 66–70, 72–4,
  112–14, 151–2, 173–5,
  177–210, 221, 229–50
  see also monitoring…;
    operational finances…
  budgets 29–30, 31, 39, 68–70,
    174–5, 184–5, 221, 248–50
  change success factors 151–2
  cost controls 229–50
  disciplinary interviews 166–9
  effective control systems
    112–14
  management roles 66–70,
    177–84, 221, 229–33
  PDCA (plan, do, check, act) cycle
    17, 24–6

conversion rates 33, 43, 244–6
core message, self-assessments 44
corporate governance 174
corporate identity, standards 244–6
corporate image 7, 244–6
corporate social responsibility
    20, 184
cost accounting techniques 52–6
cost drivers 230–1, 250
cost variances, concepts 226–9,
    236–43
cost-benefit analysis 180, 198–200,
    216–18
cost-volume-profit (CVP) 32, 189,
    197–8, 200, 221–3
    break-even analysis 221–3
    budgets 197–8, 200, 221–3
costs 29–30, 31–5, 52–3, 56–7,
    184–8, 189, 197–8, 199–200,
    210, 212–16, 221–3, 224–33,
    235–50
    see also variances
    ABC 230–3
    analysis considerations 184–8,
        221
    break-even analysis 199–200,
        214, 221–3
    budget considerations 184–8,
        211–33
    controllable/uncontrollable costs
        229–33, 249–50
    controls 229–50
    direct costs 52–3, 227–33
    improvement exercises 221
    internal marketing 157–9
    management 224–33, 243–50
    overhead costs 185–8, 221–3,
        227–33, 236–43
    profit and loss accounts 29–30,
        31–5, 56–7, 247–8
    quality systems/processes 26
    reduction plans 248–50
    types 52–3, 184–8, 221–3
creativity, organisational structures
    3–16
cross-functional teams
    see also matrix organisational
        structure
    concepts 12–13, 15–16, 26, 80–6,
        181–2
    management roles 181–2
cultural issues 4, 6, 11, 14–16,
    58–60, 75–7, 106, 122–9, 150
    achievement/ascription
        dimensions 127

change success factors 150–2
collectivism 123–5, 126–9
communications 122–5
concepts 122–9, 150
Confucian dynamism 123, 124–5
evolutionary developments 128–9
femininity 123–5
Handy's classification approach
    128–9
high/low context dimensions
    127–9
Hofstede's cross-cultural analysis
    122–5, 133, 150
individualism 123–5, 126–9
masculinity 123–5
neutral/emotional (affective)
    dimensions 126–9
power-distance dimensions
    123–5, 128–9
sequential/synchronic time
    dimensions 127–9
specific/diffuse dimensions 126–9
teams 122–9
Trompenaars and Hampden-
    Turner's seven-dimensional
    model 125–9, 133
uncertainty avoidance dimensions
    123, 124–5
universalism/particularism
    dimensions 126–9
current assets 36–7
current liabilities 36–7
current performance, concepts 30,
    58–60
customer equity, brand equity 9–11
customer relations 6–8, 43–8
customer services 9–11
customer-focused/centred
    approaches 19–20, 111–15,
    150, 154–9
customers 3–4, 19–20, 29–30, 32–5,
    41–8, 49–52, 53–6, 58–60,
    111–13, 157–9, 161–2, 174,
    200–2, 218–19, 223, 244–8
    see also relationship marketing and
        customer-related measures
    balanced scorecard 50–2, 58–60,
        200–2, 218–19, 244–6
    budget variance contingencies
        242–3
    complaints 46–8, 112, 157–9,
        244–6
    conversion rates 33, 43, 244–6
    DRIP factors 161–2
    engagement metrics 46–8

expectations 46–8
lifetime values 50
loyalties 3–4, 32–5, 43–8, 223
perceptions 46–8, 50
recruitment measures 30, 49–50,
    53–6
retention measures 29–30, 43–8,
    49–50, 53–6, 174, 219, 244–8
satisfaction levels 19–27, 43–8,
    50–2, 112–13, 154–9, 219,
    244–6
segmental analysis 30, 42–4, 54,
    56–7
word-of-mouth recommendations
    46–7
CVP see cost-volume-profit
cycles, PDCA (plan, do, check, act)
    cycle 17, 24–6

D

Daimler-Benz 128
data 49, 178, 180–1, 202–10, 244–8
    see also information...
    definition 203
    meta data 205
    mining 204–5
    sources 178, 180–1, 202–10,
        244–8
    warehousing 204
data-collection methods 49,
    203–10, 246–8
databases 55–6, 113–15, 203–10,
    242–3
    see also knowledge...
debriefings, interviews for jobs
    104–5
decentralisation/centralisation
    dimension of organisations
    5–16
decision trees 180
decision-making
    cost-benefit analysis 180,
        198–200, 216–18
    force field analysis 180
    high-performance teams 114–15,
        133, 140–1
    management roles 66–70, 138–
        41, 177–84, 198–200, 216–18,
        239, 247–50
    Pareto effect 180
    risks 180
    styles 4, 13, 58–60, 114–15
    teams 114–15, 133, 138–41, 250
    tools 180–2
    variances 239

Deming, W.E. 17, 24–7
Deming's 14 quality improvement
    steps, concepts 17, 26–7
democratic leadership styles 72–4
department virtual teams 130–1
development of teams 79–86,
    114–15, 140–1, 145
differentiated product/services,
    DRIP factors 161–2
differentiation dimension of
    organisations 5–16
diminishing returns, productivity
    measures 41
direct costs 52–3, 227–33
direct discrimination 121–2
direct mail campaigns, marketing
    performance 33–4
Disability Discrimination Act 103,
    120–1
disagreements 136–7
    see also conflicts
disciplinary interviews 166–9
discounted cash flows 199–200,
    217–18
discrimination
    concepts 103, 119–22
    forms 121–2
    legislation 103, 119–21
discussion forums 46–8
disseminator role of management
    66–70, 177–84
distribution and logistics 6–8, 9–11,
    245–6
disturbance-handler role of
    management 66–70, 177–84
diversification growth method of
    multinational organisational
    structures 14–15
diversification strategies, Ansoff
    matrix 34–5
diversity issues
    interviews for jobs 103, 106
    teams 80–1, 103, 106, 119–22
do stage, PDCA (plan, do, check,
    act) cycle 17, 24–6
DRIP factors 161–2
dynamics
    quality systems/processes 18–19
    teams 60, 82–5, 114–15, 131–3,
    140–1

E
e-commerce 46–8
e-recruitment 95–7

earnings per share 185
EBITDA 57
effective control systems 112–14
    see also controls
effective performance, planning
    teams 88–9, 106, 114–15
efficiency (utilisation) variances
    236–43
EFQM see European Foundation of
    Quality Management
Eisenhower, Dwight D. 174, 182
elasticity of demand 223–4
electronic point of sale systems
    (EPOS) 178, 208–9
Elsey, B. 150
elusiveness issues, quality systems/
    processes 18–19
emails 46–8
employees 3–16, 26, 50–2, 68–71,
    76–7, 81–2, 89–106, 110–33
    see also motivations;
    recruitment…; teams
    action-centred leadership model
    71–4
    balanced scorecard 50–2, 58–60,
    200–2, 218–19, 244–6
    benchmarking 23–4
    brand champions 159–60
    brand saboteurs 159–60
    branding concepts 159–69
    commitment needs 149–52,
    163–4
    conflicts 13, 81, 82–5, 114–15,
    131–3, 135–69
    Deming's 14 quality
    improvement steps 17, 26–7
    disciplinary interviews 166–9
    discrimination 103, 119–22
    diversity issues 80–1, 103, 106,
    119–22
    EFQM 19–20
    empowerment issues 8–9, 13, 71,
    76–7, 88–90, 114–19
    external recruiting 94–106
    headcount data sources 201–2,
    206–7, 246–8
    induction programmes 90–3
    informal organisational
    structures 6
    information sources 206–7
    internal marketing 110–33,
    152–9
    internal recruiting 93–4
    job analysis/design 86, 119
    job descriptions 94, 97–101, 102–6

knowledge workers 76–7
loyalties 6, 13, 163–9
management theories
    115–19
outsourcing 201–2, 207–8, 221,
    229
performance appraisals 50–2, 97,
    162–9
person specifications 98–106
personal/professional
    development 50–2, 55
remuneration benchmarks 23–4,
    115–19, 146–8, 186–8, 201–2,
    206–7, 236–43
resistance to change 145, 147–59,
    238–9
reward schemes 11, 23–4,
    115–19, 146–8, 165–9, 186–8,
    201–2, 206–7, 236–43
satisfaction benchmarks 6, 13,
    23–4, 50–2, 91–2, 111–13,
    115–19, 154–9, 163–9, 219
self-improvement programmes 27
silo mentalities 7, 12
skills 4, 7–16, 23–4, 50–2,
    99–106, 114–15
training 20, 23–4, 26, 50–2, 55,
    60, 90–4, 157–9, 183, 206–7
turnover rates 23–4, 91–3, 157–9,
    219
work–life balance 163–9
empowerment issues 8–9, 13, 71,
    76–7, 88–90, 114–19
engagement metrics, concepts 46–8
entrepreneur role of management
    66–70, 177–84
environment
    PESTEL analysis 191–2, 214,
    240–1
    variance impacts 240–1
environmental management
    standards
    ISO 14001 17, 22
    PAS2050 17, 22–3
EPOS see electronic point of sale
    systems
Equal Pay Act 1970 122
equity theory of motivation
    118–19
ethics, leadership traits 76–7
European Foundation of Quality
    Management (EFQM), concepts
    17, 19–20
evolutionary developments, cultural
    issues 128–9

exchange rate factors, variances 210, 239–40
expectations, customers 46–8
expenditure
    budgets 212–16
    profit and loss accounts 29–30, 31–5, 56–7, 247–8
experience requirements, recruitment issues 99–106
explicit knowledge 113–15
    see also knowledge…
exploration stage, four-phase model of planned change 146–8
exporting 15
external budget variances 236, 240–3
    see also variances
external data sources 204–10
    see also data
external marketing, internal marketing 153–9, 161–2
extraversion personality trait 75

F
FA *see* Football Association
Fallon, M. 125
FAQs 47–8
favourable variances, concepts 224–9, 248–50
feedback loops 3–4, 17, 24–6, 69, 72–4, 114–15, 116–17, 162–9, 245–6
    see also controls
    360 degree feedback 69, 162–3
    PDCA (plan, do, check, act) cycle 17, 24–6
femininity, cultural issues 123–5
figurehead role of management 66–70, 177–84
finance division 6–8, 11, 12
financial analysis, concepts 198–200
financial approach, budgets 190–4, 198–200
financial performance, balanced scorecard 50–2, 58–60, 200–2, 218–19, 244–6
Finnish elevator company in China, successful change 150
fixed assets 36–7
fixed costs 185–8, 221–3, 229–33
flexed budgets 225–9
flexible teams 81–4
Football Association (FA) 11

force field analysis 180
forecasts 191–202, 214, 223–4, 247–50
    concepts 197–8, 247–8
    macro/micro forecasts 198
    sensitivity analysis 214, 223–4
    variances 8, 174–5, 210, 212–16, 224–9, 247–50
formalisation dimension of organisations 5–16, 58–60
formats, information management 181
forming stage of team development 83–6, 140–1
four-phase model of planned change 146–8
Friedman, L. 86
functional organisational structure
    benefits 7
    concepts 3, 6–8, 12, 15–16, 80–6
    critique 7–8, 12

G
Germany, cultural issues 128
Gerstner, Lou 77
global organisational structures 14–16, 69–70
goodwill 36
Gosling, J. 68–70
groups, teams 79
growth issues, profit and loss account measures 34–5, 247–8

H
Hampden-Turner, C. 125–9
Handy, Charles 128–9
Harvey, R.J. 86
headcount data sources 201–2, 206–7, 246–8
'headhunters' 94
Hennessey, D. 14
Herzberg's motivation model 115, 117–18
high/low context dimensions, cultural issues 127–9
historical budgeting 189–90
historical data, quality systems/ processes 18–27
Hofstede's cross-cultural analysis 122–5, 133, 150
holistic approaches 18–19, 50–2, 62

innovation and learning performance measures 50–2
quality systems/processes 18–19
Hollensen, S. 15
Honda 155
horizon scanning, idea generation methods 59–60
horizontal differentiation dimension of organisations 5–16
horizontal integration dimension of organisations 5–16
HR *see* human resources division
human capital, balanced scorecard 51–2, 200–2, 218–19, 244–6
human resources division (HR) 6–8, 12, 90
    see also employees
hygiene factors, motivations 117–18

I
IBM 77, 124–5
ideas
    see also innovation…
    generation methods 59, 70–4
    innovation audits 59–60
IM *see* internal marketing
IMC *see* internal marketing communications
implementation concepts 110–33
improvement opportunities/ problems, marketing performance 4, 29–30, 52–61, 135–69, 237–43, 247–50
inbound logistics, value chain analysis 220–1
inclusive leadership styles 72–4
income
    break-even analysis 199–200, 214, 221–3
    budgets 212–16
    profit and loss accounts 29–30, 31–5, 56–7, 192–3, 247–8
indirect costs 52–3, 227–33
indirect discrimination 121–2
individualism, cultural issues 123–5, 126–9
induction programmes, employees 90–3
influence metrics, customer engagement 47–8
informal organisational structures 6
information
    budgets 202–10

definition 203
EPOS sources 178, 208–9
external sources 204–10
internal sources 204–10, 246–8
MkIS 3–4, 55–6, 113–15, 178,
    209–10, 223–4, 246–50
patterns 204, 250
qualities 180–1
sources 178, 180–1, 202–10,
    246–8
types 178, 180–1, 203–10
information capital, balanced
    scorecard 51–2, 200–2,
    218–19, 244–6
information management 16,
    66–70, 113–15, 178, 177–84,
    202–10, 238–9, 246–50
    see also data; intelligence;
        knowledge…
    accuracy levels 181, 238–9
    application uses 181, 238–9
    concepts 177–84, 202–10, 238–9,
        246–8
    formats 181
    roles of management 66–70,
        177–84
    timing factors 181, 238–9,
        246–50
innovation audits
    accountabilities 59–60
    concepts 30, 57–60
    definition 58
    focus areas 58–60
    self-assessments 58
innovation and learning
    performance measures,
        concepts 50–2, 58–60, 200–2,
        218–19, 244–6
innovations 4, 20, 30, 50–2, 57–60,
    115, 244–6
    see also ideas; product
        development
    concepts 50–2, 57–60, 115,
        244–6
    opportunities 57–8
inputs versus outputs
    see also productivity…
    concepts 29–30, 39–41, 52–3
    critique 41
    metric types 40–1
intangible assets 36–7
integration dimension of
    organisations 5–16
integration phase, four-phase model
    of planned change 146–8

intelligence 3–4, 6–8, 9–11, 55–6,
    113–15, 178, 203–10, 214,
    223–4, 246–8
    see also information…
    definition 203
    MkIS 3–4, 55–6, 113–15, 178,
        209–10, 223–4, 246–8
interaction metrics, customer
    engagement 47–8
internal budget variances 236–43
    see also variances
internal controls 174
internal data sources 204–10, 246–8
    see also cash-flow statements;
        data; profit and loss accounts
    MISs 246–8
    MkIS 3–4, 55–6, 113–15, 178,
        209–10, 223–4, 246–8
internal marketing
    attitude management 153–9
    changes 111–31, 152–9
    communications management
        aspect 153–69
    concepts 110–33, 152–69
    costs 157–9
    definitions 153–5, 161–2
    DRIP factors 161–2
    employee branding 159–69
    evaluation measures 111–13,
        157–9
    execution success factors 156–9
    external marketing 153–9, 161–2
    five main elements 154–6
    multi-level model 158
    planning 111–13, 153–9
    problems 157–60
    roles 111–13, 153–5, 161–2
    segmental analysis 111–13,
        156–9
internal marketing communications
    (IMC)
    affiliation roles 161–2
    concepts 161–9
    definition 161–2
    DRIP factors 161–2
    transactional roles 161–2
internal marketing plans, concepts
    156–9
internal measures of performance
    attitude measures 30, 50–2
    concepts 30, 48–50, 166–9,
        246–8
    recruitment measures 30, 49–50
    retention measures 30, 49–50,
        53–6, 154–5

international cultures 122–9
    see also cultural issues
International Organisation for
    Standardisation (ISO) 20–1
    critique 21
    ISO 9000 91
    ISO 9001 17, 20–1
    ISO 14001 17, 22
international/multinational
    organisational structures
    concepts 3, 14–16, 69–70
    evolutionary stages 15–16
    growth methods 14–15
    local/global forces 14, 15–16
    matrix organisational structure
        15–16
    statistics 4
    types 14–15
Internet 6–8, 32–5, 46–8, 91, 95–6,
    245–6
    see also technological innovation
interpersonal roles, management
    66–70, 177–84
interviews for jobs
    see also recruitment…
    assessments 104–5
    concepts 101–6, 120–1
    conducting the interview 103–4
    debriefings 104–5
    Disability Discrimination Act
        103, 120–1
    discrimination 103, 119–22
    diversity issues 103, 106
    do's and don'ts 104–6, 120–1
    drawbacks 105–6
    finishing the interview 104
    interview rooms 102
    methods 101–2
    numerical critical reasoning 105–6
    objectives 103
    open questions 104
    panel interviews 101–2
    planning 102–4
    results 104–6
    shortlists 104–6
    tests 105–6
    written records 104–5
intimacy metrics, customer
    engagement 47–8
intranets 112, 113–15, 159
Investors in People 21, 91
involvement metrics, customer
    engagement 47–8
Irwin's four-category perspective of
    team problems 137–41

ISO 9000 91
ISO 9001, concepts 17, 20–1
ISO 14001, concepts 17, 22
ISO *see* International Organisation for Standardisation

J
Jack Morton Worldwide 158
Japan
    cultural issues 123–9
    influences of Deming 26
Jeannet, J.-P. 14
job analysis/design 86, 119
job centres 94
job descriptions 94, 97–101, 102–6
job enlargement, concepts 110, 119
job enrichment, concepts 110, 119
Jobber 111–12, 156
Jobs, Steve 76–7
John, O.P. 71, 75–7
Johnson, W.C. 22
joint ventures 221, 229

K
Kaplan, R. 51
KCOM 56–7
key account management 11, 80–6
key performance indicators (KPIs) 4, 9, 11, 195–202, 218–19, 238, 244–8
Knight, K. 13
knowledge management
    see also information…
    concepts 113–15, 131–3, 203–10
knowledge specifications, recruitment issues 99–106
knowledge workers 76–7
Kolb's learning cycle 24
Kotler, P. 17
Kotter, J.P. 67–8
KPIs *see* key performance indicators
Kripalani, M. 163

L
lateral thinking, idea generation methods 59–60
leadership
    see also management; strategies; vision
    action-centred leadership model 71–4
    attitudes 74–7
    challenges 77

change-management roles 68–71, 75–7, 149–52, 177–84
characteristics 68–71, 74–7
COMMANDER mnemonic 177–80
concepts 65–107, 116–19, 138–69, 244–50
definition 68–71
Deming's 14 quality improvement steps 17, 26–7
EFQM 19–20
five big traits 71, 74–7
good leaders 74–7, 86–8
McGregor's XY theory 117
management contrasts 68–70
management role 66–70
personality traits 71, 74–7, 116
roles 67–74, 87–8, 138–69, 177–210, 250
situational perspectives (contingent models) 71–4
skills 74–7, 87–8, 116–19
styles 71–7
Tannenbaum's management styles continuum 71, 72–4
traits 71, 74–7, 116
transactional leadership perspective 71, 75–7
transformational leadership perspective 71, 75–7
war analogies 68–70
learning
    see also organisational learning
    innovation and learning performance measures 50–2, 58–60, 200–2, 218–19, 244–6
    reflective mindset of management 69–71
learning organisations 50–2, 80–6, 150
legal issues 11, 16, 103, 119–21, 191–2, 214, 240–3
legislation 16, 103, 119–21, 240–3
Lenovo 124–5
Leverhulme, Lord 173, 174, 243
liabilities
    balance sheets 29–30, 31, 35–7
    definition 36
liaison role of management 66–70, 177–84
lifetime values, customers 50
Likert scale 41
Lloyds TSB 158

local/global forces, international/multinational organisational structures 14, 15–16
logistics
    distribution and logistics 6–8, 9–11, 245–6
    value chain analysis 220–1
long term liabilities 36–7
loss leaders 34–5
loyalties
    customers 3–4, 32–5, 43–8, 223
    employees 6, 13, 163–9

M
McClelland's motivational theory 116–17
McCrae, R.R. 71, 75–7
McDonald's 94
McGregor's XY theory 117
macro environment impacts, variances 240–1
macro/micro forecasts 198
management 16, 23–4, 65–107, 109–33, 138–69, 173–5, 177–210, 212–50
    see also operational finances…
    ABC 231
    budgets 68–70, 174–5, 184–5, 212–50
    changes 68–71, 75–7, 145–52, 238–9
    classical roles 67–8, 177–210
    COMMANDER mnemonic 177–80
    communication roles 177–84
    competencies and standards 86–8
    concepts 65–107, 109–33, 138–69, 173–5, 177–210, 243–50
    costs in marketing 224–33, 243–50
    cross-functional communications role 181–2
    decision-making roles 66–70, 138–41, 177–84, 198–200, 216–18, 239, 247–50
    definitions 66–70, 177–84
    good managers 74–7, 86–8
    incompatible objectives 68–70
    information management 16, 66–70, 113–15, 178, 177–84, 202–10, 238–9, 246–50
    interpersonal roles 66–70, 177–84
    leadership contrasts 68–70

McGregor's XY theory 117
marketing finances 177–210
mindsets 69–70
multinational organisational
    structures 16
planning roles 67–70, 177–84
rewards 175
roles 66–70, 87–8, 138–69,
    177–210, 250
skills 16, 23–4, 74–7, 87–8
styles 71–7
teams 68–74, 80–6, 87–9,
    109–33, 138–69
Theory X/Y/Z management
    assumptions 117
virtual teams 131–3
war analogies 68–70
management accounting techniques
    54–6
management by exception 76–7,
    113
management information systems
    (MISs) 246–8
management theories, concepts
    115–19
managing marketing finances
    177–210
    see also operational finances…
managing marketing teams
    see also leadership; management;
        teams
    concepts 63–170
market development strategies
    34–5, 244–6
market penetration strategies 34–5,
    174, 246–8
market research and intelligence
    6–8, 9–11, 214
market segment/niche
    concepts 30, 42–4, 54, 56–7
    self-assessments 42–4
market shares 40–1, 219, 244–6
marketing
    see also internal…
    ABC 231
    cost analysis budget benefits
        184–8, 221
    cost-benefit analysis 180,
        198–200, 216–18
    roles 30, 153–4, 174–5, 178–7
    strategy impacts on variances
        237–43
    types 153–4
    value chain analysis 218–21,
        231–3, 249–50

marketing administration 6–8
marketing approach, budgets
    194–202
marketing communications 9–11,
    113–15
    see also communications
marketing and communications
    division 6–8, 12
marketing costs as a percentage
    of turnover, profit and loss
    accounts 32–5
marketing finances
    see also operational finances…
    concepts 177–210
marketing implementation,
    concepts 110–33
marketing infrastructure
    see also marketing performance;
        organisational structures;
        quality systems/processes
    concepts 3–62
    definition 3–4
marketing intelligence systems
    (MkIS) 3–4, 55–6, 113–15,
    178, 209–10, 223–4, 246–8
marketing mix 111–13, 231
marketing performance 4, 29–61,
    109–33, 135–69, 184–8,
    195–202, 221, 237–43, 247–50
    see also accounting…; controls;
        innovation and learning…;
        internal…; productivity…;
        quality systems/processes;
        relationship marketing…;
        variances
    balanced scorecard 50–2, 58–60,
        200–2, 218–19, 244–6
    benchmarking 4, 17–18, 23–4,
        30, 54–6, 60–1
    budgets 29–30, 31, 39, 68–70,
        174–5, 195–202, 235–43
    comparative analysis 30, 53–6
    competitor comparisons 30, 60–1
    concepts 29–61, 109–33, 184–8,
        195–202, 235–50
    cost analysis budget benefits
        184–8, 221
    effective control systems 112–14
    financial analysis 198–200
    improvement opportunities/
        problems 4, 29–30, 52–61,
        135–69, 221, 237–43, 247–50
    innovation audits 30, 57–60
    KPIs 4, 9, 11, 195–202, 218–19,
    238, 244–8

management theories 115–19
managing teams 110–33
measuring and monitoring 4,
    29–61, 110–33, 166–9, 200–2,
    218–19, 235–50
operations evaluations 243–50
qualitative standards 244–6
quantitative standards 218–19,
    244–6
self-assessments 41–5, 58
teams 109–33, 135–69
time series 53–6
marketing plans
    see also planning
    concepts 110–33, 153–9,
        191–202, 238–43
marketing productivity analysis
    see also productivity…
    concepts 30, 39–41, 52–6, 206–7
marketing productivity measures
    see also productivity…
    concepts 29–30, 39–41, 52–3,
        154–9, 206–7
    trends 52–4
marketing strategies 16, 34–5,
    68–70, 76–8, 110, 145–52,
    155–9, 174, 237–43
marketing teams
    see also teams
    types/contexts 80–6
marketing value, organisational
    structures 3–16
masculinity, cultural issues 123–5
Maslow's hierarchy of needs 115
mass marketing 54
matrix organisational structure
    see also cross-functional teams
    benefits 12–13
    concepts 3, 12–13, 15–16
    critique 13
    multinational organisational
        structures 15–16
    types 13
Mayo, Elton 6
measuring and monitoring
    marketing performance 4,
    29–61, 110–33, 166–9, 200–2,
    218–19, 235–50
mentors 92
mergers and acquisitions 4–5,
    14–15, 129–30, 158, 229
meta data 205
Metlay, W. 163
metrics considerations, quality
    systems/processes 18–19, 244–6

mind mapping 59–60
mindsets, management 69–70
Mintzberg, H. 66–70
MISs see management information systems
mission 49, 191–202, 232
Mitchell, Colin 161
MkIS see marketing intelligence systems
monitoring role of management 66–70, 177–84, 235–50
   see also controls
Montgomery, C.A. 77
morals, leadership traits 76–7
motivations 6, 13, 26, 50–2, 68–71, 76–7, 81–2, 91–3, 100–1, 110–33, 153–9, 163–9, 184–5
   Adair's three-circles model 163
   Adam's equity theory 118–19
   budgets 183–4
   concepts 110–33, 153–9, 163–9, 184–5
   Herzberg's motivation model 115, 117–18
   hygiene factors 117–18
   job enlargement/enrichment 110, 119
   McClelland's motivational theory 116–17
   McGregor's XY theory 117
   management theories 115–19
   Maslow's hierarchy of needs 115
   Schein's motivation model 115
Motorola 21–2
Moxon, P. 164–8
multi-level model of internal marketing 158
multinational organisational structures
   see also global...; international...; transnational...
   concepts 14–16, 69–70
   evolutionary stages 15–16
   growth methods 14–15
   matrix organisational structure 15–16
multiple virtual teams 130–1
Munroe Fraser 5-point plan, recruitment issues 100–1

N

Nasa 12
negotiations
   budgets 212–16

internal marketing execution 156–9
   role of management 66–70, 156–9, 177–84, 212–16
Nestlé 9–10
neuroticism personality trait 75
neutral/emotional (affective) dimensions, cultural issues 126–9
NHS 86–7, 91
Nolan, D. 51
normative relationships 115
norming stage of team development 83–6, 140–1
numerical critical reasoning, interviews for jobs 105–6

O

objective and task method, budgets 188–9, 196
on-the-job training 94
online accounts 46–8
online user panels 46–8
open questions, interviews for jobs 104
openness personality trait 75
operating statements see profit and loss accounts
operational budgets 212–16
   see also budgets
operational finances for marketing
   see also budget...; costs; variances
   accountabilities 174–5, 177
   concepts 173–5, 177–210, 243–50
   managing marketing finances 177–210
operations
   concepts 12, 220–1, 249–50
   value chain analysis 220–1, 249–50
organic growth of multinational organisational structures 14–15
organisation virtual teams 130–1
organisational aspects, variances 236–40
organisational capital, balanced scorecard 51–2, 200–2, 218–19, 244–6
organisational climate
   concepts 30, 58–60
   innovation audits 58–60
organisational learning 50–2, 80–6, 150, 200–2, 218–19
   see also learning

innovation and learning performance measures 50–2, 200–2, 218–19
organisational structures
   change success factors 151–2
   concepts 3–16, 58–60, 79–86
   definitions 3–5
   dimensions 5–6, 58–60
   importance 4–16
   informal organisational structures 6
   restructuring considerations 4–5
   teams 79–86
   types 4–16, 79–86
Ouchi, William 117
Out of the Crisis (Deming) 26–7
outbound logistics, value chain analysis 220–1
outputs, inputs versus outputs 29–30, 39–41, 52–3
outsourcing 201–2, 207–8, 221, 229
overhead costs
   ABC 230–3
   concepts 185–8, 221–3, 227–33, 236–43
overlay kind of matrix organisational structure 13, 16

P

panel interviews 101–2
Pareto effect 180
partnerships 20, 242–3
PAS2050 concepts 17, 22–3
passive management by exception 76–7, 113
payback appraisals, campaigns 185, 198–200, 217–18
payments, cash-flow statements 37–9, 183, 185, 247–8
PDCA (plan, do, check, act) cycle
   concepts 17, 24–6
   six sigma 24
penetration pricing 34–5
percentage of sales/profit method, budgets 188–9, 192–3
performance appraisals, employees 50–2, 97, 162–9
performance issues
   see also controls; marketing performance; variances
   360 degree feedback 69, 162–3
   balanced scorecard 50–2, 58–60, 200–2, 218–19, 244–6
   high-performing teams 114–15, 133, 140–1

improvement opportunities/
problems 4, 29–30, 52–61,
135–69, 221, 237–43, 247–50
KPIs 4, 9, 11, 195–202, 218–19,
238, 244–8
management theories 115–19
marketing operations evaluations
243–50
measuring and monitoring 4,
29–61, 110–33, 166–9, 200–2,
218–19, 235–50
qualitative standards 244–6
quantitative standards 218–19,
244–6
ROA 36–7, 219, 238, 245–8
ROI/ROMI 32–5, 185, 198–200,
219, 238, 245–8
SMART objectives 218–19, 244–6
teams 59–60, 88–9, 106, 109–33,
135–69
variance uses to improve
performance 248–50
performing stage of team
development 83–6, 140–1
person cultures, Handy's
classification approach 129
person specifications, recruitment
issues 98–106
personal greetings 46–8
personality traits 71, 74–7, 116
PESTEL analysis 191–2, 214, 240–1
Piercy, N.F. 80–1, 155, 157, 173
planning 3–4, 16, 17, 24–6, 42–4,
59–61, 67–71, 72–4, 110–33,
156–9
see also marketing plans
budgets 182–4
changes 145–52
conflict-resolution strategies 141
four-phase model of planned
change 146–8
innovation audits 59–60
internal marketing 111–13,
153–9
internal marketing plans 156–9
interviews for jobs 102–4
management/leadership roles
67–71, 72–4, 177–84
PDCA (plan, do, check, act) cycle
17, 24–6
plans 174
teams 88–9, 110–33
planning and control method,
budgets 188–9, 195–6
plans

marketing plans 110–33, 153–9,
191–202, 238–43
planning 174
Polestar Group 93
policies
concepts 30, 58–60, 75–7
innovation audits 58–60
politics 16, 157–9, 191–2, 214,
240–1
Porter, Michael 214, 218–21
Porter's five forces 214
power-distance dimensions, cultural
issues 123–5, 128–9
PR 32–5, 243
practices
concepts 30, 58–60
innovation audits 58–60
presentations, budgets 212–16
prices
elasticity of demand 223–4
price wars 34–5
sales price variances 226–9,
236–43
pro forma guidelines, budgets
212–16
problem children 244
process re-engineering 80–6, 231–3,
237
processes 3–4, 17–27, 54–6, 70–1,
80–6, 137–41, 146–8, 231–3,
237
see also quality...
balanced scorecard 50–2, 58–60,
200–2, 218–19, 244–6
BPR 80–6, 231–3, 237
change process models 146–8
Irwin's four-category perspective
of team problems 137–41
product development 9–11, 12,
34–5, 55–60, 244–6
see also innovations
Ansoff matrix 34–5
product mix 3–4, 239
product portfolios, variances 239
product/market organisational
structure
benefits 8
concepts 3, 8–9, 12, 15–16
critique 8–9
production concepts 6–8, 9–11, 12,
24–7
productivity analysis, concepts 30,
39–41, 52–6
productivity measures
see also marketing performance

concepts 29–30, 39–41, 52–3,
154–9, 206–7
critique 41
definition 39–40
inputs versus outputs 29–30,
39–41, 52–3
metric types 40–1
products 3–4, 8–11, 12, 15–16,
17–18, 34–5, 55–60, 239,
244–6
see also quality...
profit and loss accounts
see also return...
concepts 29–30, 31–5, 56–7,
192–3, 236, 247–8
definition 31, 247
growth issues 34–5, 247–8
marketing metrics 32–5, 247–8
ratios 32–4
profit variances 236–43
see also variances
promotions 32–5, 47–8
psychometric tests 89
public relations 6–8

Q

qualifications, recruitment issues
99–106
qualitative standards 244–6
quality assurance 3–4, 24–7
quality management systems,
marketing performance
improvement 4, 54
quality models individual models
benchmarking 4, 17–18, 23–4,
54–6, 60–1
concepts 17, 19–24
EFQM 17, 19–20
ISO 9001 17, 20–1
ISO 14001 17, 22
PAS2050 17, 22–3
six sigma 17, 21–2
TQM 17, 19
quality systems/processes 3–4,
17–27, 54–6, 244–6
see also marketing performance
areas of application 18
benchmarking 4, 17–18, 23–4,
54–6, 60–1
concepts 17–27, 54–6, 244–6
costs 26
definitions 17–18
Deming's 14 improvement steps
17, 26–7

quality systems/processes
  (*Continued*)
  dynamic aspects 18–19
  elusiveness issues 18–19
  historical data 18–27
  holistic approaches 18–19
  importance 18–19
  metrics considerations 18–19,
    244–6
  PDCA (plan, do, check, act) cycle
    17, 24–6
  quality models 17, 19–24
quantitative standards 218–19,
  244–6

R
R&D *see* research and development
Race Relations Acts 120
random variations, comparative
  analysis 53–6
rate variances 236–43
receipts, cash-flow statements 37–9,
  183, 185, 247–8
reconciliation efforts, variances
  241–3
recruitment issues 30, 49–50, 53–6,
  89–91, 93–106, 154–5, 167–9
  see also employees; interviews
  agencies 94–5
  applications-handling
    considerations 97
  aptitudes 99–106
  e-recruitment 95–7
  employees 89–91, 93–106,
    154–5, 167–9
  experience requirements 99–106
  external recruiting 94–106
  internal recruiting 93–4
  job descriptions 94, 97–101,
    102–6
  knowledge specifications 99–106
  measures 30, 49–50, 53–6
  Munroe Fraser 5-point plan
    100–1
  person specifications 98–106
  qualifications 99–106
  skills and abilities 99–106
  special requirements 99–100
  teams 89–91, 93–106
  training history 99–106
reflective mindset of management
  69–71
  see also learning
relationship marketing and

customer-related measures
  communication measures 29–30,
    46–8
  concepts 29–30, 41–8, 49–50,
    111–13, 154–9
  retention measures 29–30, 43–8,
    49–50, 53–6, 174, 219, 244–8
  satisfaction measures 29–30,
    45–8, 111–13, 154–9
  self-assessments 41–5
relationships
  Irwin's four-category perspective
    of team problems 137–41
  Trompenaars and Hampden-
    Turner's seven-dimensional
    model 125–9, 133
religious discrimination
  120, 122
reminders 46–8
remuneration benchmarks,
  employees 23–4, 115–19,
  146–8, 186–8, 201–2, 206–7,
  236–43
repeat business 43–4, 46–8
research and development (R&D)
  6–8, 11, 12, 55–6
resource-allocator role of
  management 66–70, 177–84
resourcing, concepts 201–2, 229,
  238–9
response rates 33
restructuring considerations 4–5
retention measures 29–30, 43–8,
  49–50, 53–6, 154–5, 174, 219,
  244–6
return on assets (ROA) 36–7, 219,
  238, 245–8
return on (marketing) investment
  (ROI/ROMI) 32–5, 185,
  198–200, 219, 238, 245–8
revenue, profit and loss accounts
  29–30, 31–5, 56–7, 192–3,
  247–8
reward schemes 11, 23–4, 115–19,
  146–8, 165–9, 175, 186–8,
  201–2, 206–7, 236–43
risks
  decision-making 180
  productivity measures 41
ROA *see* return on assets
Rogers, C.W. 163
Rogers, E. 163
ROI/ROMI *see* return on
  (marketing) investment

role cultures, Handy's classification
  approach 129
role plays 59–60

S
Sai-kwong Leung, J. 150
sales 6–8, 29–30, 31–5, 39–41, 56–
  7, 191–202, 218–21, 226–9,
  236–43, 247–8, 249–50
  CVP 32, 189, 197–8, 200, 221–3
  data sources 205–6
  forecasts 191–202, 247–8
  price variances 226–9, 236–43
  productivity measures 39–41
  profit and loss accounts 29–30,
    31–5, 56–7, 192–3, 247–8
  quantity variances 226–9, 236–43
  self-assessments 44
  value chain analysis 218–21,
    249–50
  variances 225–9, 236–43
satisfaction measures
  customers 29–30, 43–8, 50,
    112–13, 154–9, 219, 244–6
  employees 6, 13, 23–4, 50–2,
    91–2, 111–13, 115–19, 154–9,
    163–9, 219
scarce resources, budgets 183
Schein's motivation model 115
Schmidt, W.H. 72–4
seasonal variations, comparative
  analysis 53–6
secondment kind of matrix
  organisational structure 13
segmental analysis
  concepts 30, 42–4, 54, 56–7,
    111–13, 156–9
  internal marketing 111–13,
    156–9
self-actualisation 115
self-assessments
  innovation audits 58
  marketing performance
    41–5, 58
self-improvement programmes 27
self-managed teams 70, 80
selfish managers, budgets 183
semi fixed costs 185–8, 221–3
senior examiner comments
  Section One 62
  Section Three 251
  Section Two 170
sensitivity analysis 214, 223–4

sequential/synchronic time dimensions, cultural issues 127–9

Serco 145

service level agreements 244

service providers 7–8, 220–1

service-based economies 159–60

Sevin, C. 39

Sex Discrimination Acts 119–20

sexual orientation discrimination 120, 121–2

share capital 36–7, 242–3

share of voice
budgets 188–9, 196–7
standards 244–6

shareholder value 177, 242–6

Shell 125

Siemens 87–8

silo mentalities 7, 12

situational interviews 101–6

situational perspectives (contingent models) leadership styles 71–4
action-centred leadership model 71–4
Tannenbaum's management styles continuum 71, 72–4

six questions technique, idea generation methods 59–60

six sigma
concepts 17, 21–2
PDCA (plan, do, check, act) cycle 24

six thinking hats, idea generation methods 59–60

size dimension of organisations 5–16

skills 4, 7–16, 23–4, 50–2, 74–7, 87–8, 99–106, 114–15, 116–19
change success factors 151–2
employees 4, 7–16, 23–4, 50–2, 99–106, 114–15
leadership 74–7, 87–8, 116–19
recruitment issues 99–106
teams 81–4, 114–15

SMART objectives 218–19, 244–6

SMS texts 46–8

social factors
PESTEL 191–2, 214, 240–1
Web 2.0 technologies 95

social networking, recruitment 95–6

'soft' information 66–7

sourcing issues
resourcing 201–2, 229, 238–9
teams 89–93

spans of control, dimensions of organisations 5–16

special requirements, recruitment issues 99–100

specialisation dimension of organisations 5–16

specific/diffuse dimensions, cultural issues 126–9

spokesperson role of management 66–70, 177–84

sponsors 245–6

Stacey, R.D. 163, 167

staff *see* employees

standard costing 227–9
see also variances

standard deviations 21–2
see also six sigma

standards 17, 18–27, 218–19, 227–9, 244–6
see also quality models
qualitative standards 244–6
quantitative standards 218–19, 244–6
SMART objectives 218–19, 244–6

storming stage of team development 83–6, 140–1

strategies 16, 34–5, 68–70, 76–8, 110, 145–52, 155–9, 174, 237–43
see also leadership

structures of organisations *see* organisational structures

supply chain management 9–11, 14–15, 218–21, 242–3

SWOT analysis 191–2, 214

synergies, teams 79

systems 3–4, 17–27, 151–2
see also quality…
change success factors 151–2
definition 17–18

T

tacit knowledge 113–15
see also knowledge…

Tannenbaum's management styles continuum 71, 72–4

task cultures, Handy's classification approach 129

tasks, action-centred leadership model 71–4

teams
see also employees

action-centred leadership model 71–4

Belbin's team roles 60, 78–9, 81–6, 88–90, 167
characteristics 81–4, 114–15
concepts 65–6, 68–107, 109–33, 135–69, 250
conflicts 81, 82–5, 114–15, 131–3, 135–69
contexts 80–6
creation/development of teams 79–86, 114–15, 140–1, 145
cross-functional teams 12–13, 15–16, 26, 80–6, 181–2
cultural issues 122–9
decision-making 114–15, 133, 138–41, 250
definitions 77–9
disciplinary interviews 166–9
diversity issues 80–1, 103, 106, 119–22
dynamics 60, 82–5, 114–15, 131–3, 140–1
effective performance planning 88–9, 106, 114–15
evaluation questionnaires 144–5, 168
flexible teams 81–4
four-category perspective of team problems 137–41
goal problems 137–41
groups 79
high-performing teams 114–15, 133, 140–1
Hofstede's cross-cultural analysis 122–5, 133, 150
improving performance 164–9, 250
induction programmes 90–3
innovation audits 59–60
internal marketing 110–33, 152–9
management 68–74, 80–6, 87–9, 109–33, 138–69
management theories 115–19
marketing performance 109–33, 135–69
marketing teams 80–6
matrix organisational structure 12–13, 15–16
Moxon's team-building techniques 164–6
organisational structures 79–86

teams (*Continued*)
  performance issues 59–60, 88–9,
    106, 109–33, 135–69
  planning for effective performance
    88–9, 106, 114–15
  process problems 137–41
  recruitment issues 89–91,
    93–106
  relationship problems 136–41
  rewards 165–9
  roles 77–9, 81–6, 88–9, 114–33,
    137–41, 250
  self-managed teams 70, 80
  skills 81–4, 114–15
  sourcing issues 89–93
  stages of development 82–5,
    114–15, 140–1
  successful teams 80–1, 106,
    114–15, 140–1
  synergies 79
  team-building techniques
    164–9
  transactional–transformational
    leadership perspective 77
  Trompenaars and Hampden-
    Turner's seven-dimensional
    model 125–9, 133
  Tuckman's model of team
    development 82–5, 114–15,
    140–1
  types 80–6
  virtual teams 129–33
technological innovation 4, 46–8,
  55–6, 75–7, 191–2, 214, 232,
  240–1
  see also Internet
telesales budgets 243
territory organisational structure,
  concepts 3, 9–11, 15–16
Tesco 91
tests, interviews for jobs 105–6
*The Theory of Social and Economic
  Organisation* (Weber) 5
Theory X/Y/Z management
  assumptions 117
three-circles model of motivation 163
time series, comparative analysis
  53–6
timing factors
  budgets 238–9, 249–50
  cash flow statements 37–9
  information management 181,
    238–9, 246–50
  variances 238–9, 249–50

top-down approaches, budgets
  188–202
total net assets, definition 36–7
total quality management (TQM),
  concepts 17, 19
trading and profit and loss accounts
  see profit and loss accounts
training
  employees 20, 23–4, 26, 50–2,
    55, 60, 90–4, 157–9, 183,
    206–7
  innovation and learning
    performance measures 50–2,
    200–2, 218–19
  recruitment issues 99–106
transaction curves, changes 151
transactional–transformational
  leadership perspective 71, 75–7
transformational leadership
  perspective 71, 75–7
transnational organisational
  structures 14–16, 80–6
transparency 174
transportation resources/structures
  3–4
trends, variances 250
Trompenaars and Hampden-
  Turner's seven-dimensional
  model 125–9, 133
trust 26–7, 76–7, 80–6
TSB 158
Tuckman's model of team
  development 82–5, 114–15,
  140–1
turnover rates, employees 23–4,
  91–3, 157–9, 219

U
UK Customer Satisfaction Index
  (UKCSI) 46–8
uncertainty avoidance dimensions,
  cultural issues 123, 124–5
uncontrollable costs 229–33,
  249–50
underlying trends, comparative
  analysis 53–6
unfreezing–change–refreezing model
  145–6
Unilever 155
United States (US)
  air conditioning repair business
    167
  cultural issues 123–5, 128

universalism/particularism
  dimensions, cultural issues
  126–9
US *see* United States
utilitarian relationships 115

V
value chain analysis, concepts
  218–21, 231–3, 249–50
value for money (VFM) 62, 174–5
Van Eeden, R. 75–7
variable costs 185–8, 221–3
variances 8, 174–5, 210, 212–16,
  224–9, 235–43, 247–50
  see also budgets
  concepts 174–5, 210, 224–9,
    235–43
  corrective actions 235–43,
    248–50
  cost variances 226–9, 236–43
  decision-making constraints 239
  exchange rate factors 210, 239–40
  external variances 236, 240–3
  forecasts 8, 174–5, 210, 212–16,
    224–9, 247–50
  internal constraints 238–9
  internal variances 236–43
  macro environment impacts
    240–1
  marketing strategy impacts
    237–43
  organisational aspects 236–40
  performance-improvement uses
    248–50
  product portfolios 239
  reconciliation efforts 241–3
  sales variances 225–9, 236–43
  timing factors 238–9, 249–50
  trends 250
  types 224–9, 236–43, 250
  urgent-action indicators
    249–50
vertical differentiation dimension of
  organisations 5–16
vertical integration dimension of
  organisations 5–16
VFM *see* value for money
Virgin 76
virtual teams
  concepts 129–33
  definition 129–30
  management 131–3
  problems 132–3

reasons 129, 131
roles 129–31
types 130–1
vision 42–4, 49, 68–71, 76–7, 154, 191–202, 232, 244–6
see also leadership
volumes
see also sales...
CVP 32, 189, 197–8, 200, 221–3

sales quantity variances 226–9, 236–43

W
Wal-Mart 14
war analogies, management and leadership 68–70
Web 2.0 technologies 95
Weber, Max 5
website management 6–8, 32–5, 46–8

what-if analysis (synectics) 59–60
word-of-mouth recommendations 46–7
work–life balance 163–9
worldly mindset of management 69–71

Z
zero-budgeting 190